THE NEXT WORLD WAR:
TRIBES, CITIES, NATIONS, AND ECOLOGICAL DECLINE

Preoccupied with the war on terrorism, we have lost sight of a more dangerous enemy of social peace and progress – the inability of the world's people to access the ecological goods and services they need to maintain and build their societies. By 2025, the combined demands of continued economic growth and the reduction of global poverty will require, annually, the ecological equivalent of three or four Earths. If history is our guide, the options for meeting these enormous 'provisioning' needs are extremely limited. Like the tribes, cities, and nations of earlier times, we may end up fighting our neighbours for privileged access to declining ecosystem goods and services. This confrontation will inevitably pit the wealthy beneficiaries of the global economy against the billions of excluded, and lead to accelerated ecological collapse, the derailment of growth, and social chaos. The only alternative to this dismal prospect is to mobilize on a scale as if for war in order to meet this provisioning challenge on the battlefields of directed technological innovation.

In *The Next World War*, Roy Woodbridge argues that the international community must redirect present sustainable development and poverty reduction efforts in ways that place the provisioning of societies at the heart of political decision-making. To move this highly focused agenda forward, he calls on the United Nations to convene a World Forum on Global Provisioning to declare war on ecological decline and set the battle plans for the next world war – the war to equitably provision continued growth.

ROY WOODBRIDGE is the president of Woodbridge & Associates, an environmental policy consulting firm in Vancouver.

The Next World War

Tribes, Cities, Nations, and Ecological Decline

ROY WOODBRIDGE

UNIVERSITY OF TORONTO PRESS
Toronto Buffalo London

© University of Toronto Press Incorporated 2004
Toronto Buffalo London
Printed in Canada

ISBN 0-8020-8830-9 (cloth)
ISBN 0-8020-8603-9 (paper)

∞

Printed on acid-free paper

National Library of Canada Cataloguing in Publication

Woodbridge, Roy M.
Next world war : tribes, cities, nations and ecological decline /
Roy Woodbridge.

Includes bibliographical references and index.
ISBN 0-8020-8830-9 (bound).
ISBN 0-8020-8603-9 (pbk.)

1. Environmental degradation. 2. Globalization – Environmental
aspects. 3. Sustainable development. 4. Human ecology.
5. Economic development – Environmental aspects – History. I. Title.

GE140.W66 2004   363.7   C2003-907504-4

University of Toronto Press acknowledges the financial assistance to its
publishing program of the Canada Council for the Arts and the Ontario Arts
Council.

University of Toronto Press acknowledges the financial support for its
publishing activities of the Government of Canada through the Book Publishing Industry Development Program (BPIDP).

Contents

Preface   vii

Part I The Enemy Is Ecological Decline   1

1 A Shift in the Angle of Vision   3

2 Provisioning Societies   23

Part II From Common Genes to the Global Economy   37

3 Round One: The Spread of Hunter-Gatherer Societies   39

4 Round Two: The Rise and Spread of Agricultural Societies   49

5 Round Three: Urbanization   59

6 Round Four: From City-States to Nations   80

7 Round Five: Reliance on Global Business Networks   100

8 The Organization and Potential of Round Five   117

Part III The Twenty-Five-Year Challenge to Growth and Social Stability   137

9 From Egalitarian Tribes to Global Inequity   139

10 Ecological Roadblocks to Growth and Poverty Reduction   165

11 The Catalysts of Calamity   205

Part IV The War to Provision the World 219

12 Our Common Enemy 221

13 Mobilizing Nations for War 230

14 Mobilizing the International Community 250

15 Round Six: The Age of Global Provisioning 261

Notes 279

Bibliography 297

Index 319

Preface

This book focuses on the actions the peoples of the world must take to avoid the economic and social devastation that is going to result from the massive increase in human pressures on natural systems – pressures that will come to a head by 2025. To sustain global economic growth and to reduce global poverty, the international community must mobilize as if for war in order to place the provisioning of human societies with adequate access to essential natural capital at the centre of political decision making in every country of the world.

The book is motivated by a profound sense of frustration at the global community's continuing inability to slow the pace at which human actions are eroding the viability of the ecosystems on which all human welfare depends. In the late 1960s and throughout the 1970s, I had been intensely involved in the international development effort and the beginnings in Canada of the debate over growth and the environment. When I re-entered the world of international discussion surrounding these issues in the early 1990s, I was overwhelmed with a sense of déjá vu. This was not a reaction to the tedious processes of debate that are a necessary part of international diplomacy in our complex world of economically linked nation-states and cultures. Nor was it a reflection of the ennui I felt when again I found myself having to wade through the mounds of unwieldy documents laboriously assembled by expert wordsmiths among the legions of professional, international meeting attendees who haunt United Nations venues. Rather, it was a gut reaction to the fact that little real progress had been made in combating the core issue of ecological decline.

The discussion still focused on the same 'population, growth, resources, environment' paradigm that had triggered earlier environmental protection efforts; however, the challenges had broadened and grown more severe. Major new environmental issues had been added to the agenda – notably, climate change, the erosion of the ozone layer, the consequences of rapid urbanization, growing stress on ocean and forest resources, and the accelerating pace of biodiversity loss. The context of the debate over ecological decline was also more complex, with new social and political issues competing for attention. In little over a decade, another billion people had been added to the global population. The end of the Cold War and rapid technological advance had dramatically accelerated the processes of global economic integration, and attention was again focused on the widening gulf between the world's leading economies and those still mired in poverty. As a result, discussions of the old paradigm were taking place under the new, integrating umbrella and language of the concept of sustainable development – the concept that formed the basis for Agenda 21, the action plan that came out of the Rio Conference on Environment and Development in 1992. Yet all the while, perhaps hidden to some extent by other dramatic changes taking place and by the clamour of competing agendas, human demands were continuing to erode global ecological systems faster than solutions were being found and implemented.

This situation continues today. The outer edges of the environmental envelopes that sustain human populations are beginning to collapse as human societies push more and more relentlessly to exploit essential sources of ecological goods and services. And this process continues even after more than a decade of remarkable international dialogue over how to achieve sustainable development – a dialogue that culminated, as this book was being completed, in the World Summit on Sustainable Development (WSSD) held in Johannesburg between 26 August and 4 September 2002.

The WSSD's agenda was a bit of a mishmash of issues. As the solution to poverty and environmental degradation, it baldly promoted growth as well as mechanisms for integrating all nations into the global economy. The 2002 summit also addressed a broad range of social policy issues and made specific (albeit confusing) calls for greater commitment to the accelerated development of lagging African nations; in addition, it offered some tepid proposals for tinkering with the international institutional arrangements for promoting sustainable development. As a whole, the WSSD added to an already serious imbalance in the international 'sustainable development' agenda between the push for global economic growth and the enormous challenge of halting ecological decline. Although environmental issues received heavy media coverage, it was continued growth – growth that was already rumbling along quite nicely – that got another boost.

The portions of the WSSD agenda dealing specifically with ecological sustainability were pretty much defined by the WEHAB papers – the five framework documents prepared by the UN regarding the big issues: Water, Energy, Health, Agriculture, and Biodiversity.[1] The grounds for pessimism about the pace of progress in these critical areas is that most of the summit's 'achievements' were rehashed recommendations from earlier international meetings. For example, in the case of the recommendations regarding the global water crisis, there is little in the summit's final report that was not called for in the report of a water conference held in Mar del Plata, Argentina, in 1977 – a conference that led, through several other international meetings, to the recommendations coming out of the Rio Conference and, more recently, the global water conference held in The Hague in 2000. Indeed, the WEHAB framework paper on water and sanitation issues lists fifty-three 'major agreements' coming out of earlier international gatherings. In a similar fashion, the framework paper for action on agriculture lists twenty-two agreements, the paper on energy lists eighteen, the paper on health and the environment twenty-three, and the paper on biodiversity twenty.

The papers themselves are well written and replete with expert analysis and opinion. They define the issues very well and provide comprehensive recommendations for possible actions to address these diverse challenges. The international meetings may also be necessary to help inch the global community toward a common understanding of these big issues. However, in the progression from meeting to meeting, new data are factored in, new dimensions to the specific challenges are added, and the eventual 'action plans' become calls to do everything. The individual papers and sets of recommendations cover such a broad diversity of subjects that they lose coherence along with any sense that they can ever be converted into practical, on-the-ground initiatives. Based on past experience, there is little reason to think that the implementation of this high-principled rhetoric will be adequate to forestall the impending acceleration in the demands made by human societies on already faltering ecological systems. In the end, the

WSSD is likely to become merely the prelude to the next international meeting, which will have to be called because implementation targets are not being met.

Clearly, the global response to ecological decline is inadequate, given the scale of the challenge and the all too short time frame for taking decisive action. At some point we will have to stop stepping back to look at the big picture in order to make it even bigger and, instead, define with clear focus the essential things we must do to make a difference within time frames that matter. The intricacies of the problems are already well documented. Taking more time to polish the words simply defers action, thus accelerating the approach of the economic and social chaos that is going to be the end product of ecological collapse.

The following question should haunt all of us: Why does this situation persist? If growth is leading us toward ecological collapse – or, turning this around so that the threat to human ambition is clear, if ecological decline and social conflict over access to increasingly scarce natural capital are going to derail the growth process – and if we are all truly interconnected and must now learn to live within the sustaining limits of global ecosystems that are at risk of collapsing, then why don't we change?

I think most people in the world know intuitively how much environmental harm human activity has already done. I think we are all aware of the vast potential for the unrelenting pursuit of present patterns of growth to precipitate a succession of ecological disruptions that will challenge human ingenuity, compassion, and fellowship. And I think most of us know we are running out of time. We know all this. Deep down inside, we also know that we have to somehow reorganize our national and global societies if we are to avoid the worst social and economic consequences of ecological decline. So why don't we?

Is it because of the siren call of some delusion that economic growth will solve the problem? Do we think, with some kind of circular logic, that a continuation of the present patterns of randomly generated growth will provide us with the wealth and technological capacity to deal with an underlying problem caused by aimless growth in the first place, and that it can do this in the less than twenty-five years available to us for finding and implementing solutions? Is it that we are motivated by good intentions and perhaps so blinded by the urgent requirement to meet the needs of the impoverished half of the world's people that we ignore the enabling role of ecological capacity? More critically, do we not understand that the world's less fortunate cannot ever hope to replicate the present consumption patterns of leading economies? Or have we been lulled into false expectations by the mantra of sustainable development? Have we come to believe that such development is possible, that the knowledgeable people who are working hard to make it happen will be successful, and that we can thus leave it to them to solve the problem? Perhaps our lack of action arises from the fact that we feel disenfranchised – that we feel helpless to do anything about it and so have just given up. Or are our diverse societies, with their cultural and religious precepts and social preoccupations, simply too resistant to change? In the case of the rich and powerful nations of the world, do we feel it is someone else's problem because we can out-compete others for access to scarce resources? Do we actually believe, when faced with conditions of global ecological scarcity, that others may become embroiled in famine, deprivation, human suffering, and conflict but we will be exempted? Or is it simply that in conditions of global competition for growth opportunities, individual nations are reluctant to jeopardize their competitive positions by taking independent action? Is it a situation where all nations must act in concert or none will act?

In my view, all of these perceptions contribute to the lack of political will to change, with the competitive dimensions of participation in the global economy weighing heavily. But there are more profound causes for the blockage that I am going to try to address in this book: we lack a clear understanding of the scale of the threat that ecological decline presents for our societies and of the short time available for taking decisive action. Furthermore, and of paramount importance, we lack a clear sense of what we can do about it. We know how to promote economic growth and are getting very good at it. We do not know how to move our economies and the global community toward conditions of ecological sustainability or how to rebalance the international agenda to achieve this. In this book I will be explaining in detail how this can be done (basically, by placing at the centre of political decision making in all nations of the world the binding requirement to provision societies with the natural capital that makes growth and social equity possible). To set the stage, there are several terms and concepts I will be using that readers should be familiar with before proceeding.

Natural Capital

The term 'natural capital' has been around for some time.[2] It is used here as a synonym for 'ecological goods and services,' 'environmental services,' or 'the human draw on natural systems,' and it embraces everything that humans rely on or extract from nature. It consists of both 'in-bound flows' and 'absorptive capacities.'

- *In-bound flows* of natural capital include everything required to support human life, from the air we breath to all sources of food and the biological resources on which food production depends. In-bound flows include the five-thousand-odd micro-organisms that are contained in a teaspoon of productive soil; all the sources of materials and energy that are required to feed, clothe, house, and provide amenities for people; and the water, land, and air used or consumed in human production and consumption processes. These in-bound flows account for everything made, used, or consumed by humans.
- *Absorptive capacities* are functions of ecological systems – or the services provided by them – that deal with human waste in all its forms, from the breath we exhale to industrial and urban air emissions, water effluents, and solid waste. They include the diverse air, water, and biological systems that operate on a local or bio-regional basis as well as the ocean, weather, and atmospheric systems that operate at the level of the biosphere.

Some might take exception to the depiction of ecological systems as providing 'services,' since this implies that the natural world is somehow proactively arranged to support the operation of human societies. This, of course, is not the case. On the other hand, in the same way that an individual can draw money from a bank account, human societies can draw on natural systems in a great variety of ways to meet their needs, within limits. It is in this sense that I use the term 'service.'

The Provisioning of Societies

I use the term 'provisioning' to refer to the processes through which human societies organize to access natural capital in all its forms, including both in-bound flows and the draws made on the waste absorption services of natural systems. In this book I will argue that human societies have gone through five overlapping 'rounds' in the organization of social provisioning arrangements, from early hunter-gatherer tribes to the present global economy, which relies on international business networks. I will also argue that relative wealth depends on which of the residuals of these organizational modes different societies or groups within societies now fit. Regardless, all must now make the transition to a new organizational pattern built around the technologies of the 'Sixth Round,' the age of global provisioning.

The Enemy Is Ecological Decline

I begin this book by talking about the fact that ecological decline is the enemy of all peoples – in fact, it is the only enemy that is *common* to all peoples. Some may argue that this depiction has it backwards: that it is human actions which are the enemy of ecological systems, since these are the cause of ecological decline. Thus some believe that we should make 'us' the enemy and that our approach to altering human behaviour respecting interactions with natural systems should be based on ethical or moral grounds and processes of cultural change and adaptation.[3] In the long run, if we had the luxury of time, this would be a defensible position. However, making 'us' or human behaviour the enemy tends to convert environmentalism into a type of religion or a political movement whose goal is to protect nature. When this happens the movement must then compete, like the Green Party, with all other religions or parties for people's allegiance.

On the other hand, even if ecological decline is an enemy we have created, it is still an enemy. It is an enemy that threatens all of human ambition: it can stifle growth, preclude the reduction of poverty, and constrain the human prospect. Defining ecological decline in this way and making the provisioning of human societies the goal turns the equation around. Defining ecological decline as the enemy rather than human consumption is a straightforward appeal to human self-interest. It leads to a call to organize to directly meet human needs. It is an attempt to force people to think differently about the nature of their dependence on ecological systems and how they must go about the task of reorganizing to meet their provisioning requirements.

Waging 'War' against Ecological Decline

The book is a call for all societies to wage war against global ecological decline. Admittedly, this is not a great metaphor. The war analogy immediately conjures up images of bloodshed, death, and sacrifice arising from a struggle against an enemy that is consciously mobilized to destroy our society. Clearly, ecological systems are not like this. Ecological decline is not arrayed in battle against human societies. Indeed, if anything, nature is supremely indifferent to the fate of humans: nature simply exists and will continue to do so whether ecological systems decline or strengthen and regardless of whether humanity survives. Nor is it possible to conceive of a war against ecological decline in traditional terms. This is obviously not an enemy against which we are going to lob hand grenades or launch rockets.

I accept that all of these perceptions have validity. However, I also believe that in its own way nature does draw lines in the sand that human societies dare not cross without incurring great suffering. We cross these lines when our actions precipitate ecological collapse and attendant human deprivation and when competition between societies for access to the same ecological goods and services escalates into open warfare. The book documents the extent to which these lines in the sand are now being drawn and the short time available to us to find ways of provisioning societies without crossing them. We have less than twenty-five years to find alternative ways of meeting our rapidly growing requirements for natural capital. In light of these considerations, it would be naive and misleading to think that anything less than mobilizing with the same intensity and commitment that we bring to fighting all-out war will produce the kind of effort required.

It is equally misleading to think that protesting against growth through 'active non-violence' or trying to adopt an environmental ethic as a guiding force for change will precipitate the aggressive response at the national level and the co-ordinated international effort required in the time available for taking decisive action. The world needs a clear strategy for dealing with ecological decline and is going to have to resort to weapons and tactics appropriate to the scale of the challenge. To change the interface with natural systems, societies must find and use new technologies that will enable them to meet provisioning needs from increasingly scarce sources of natural capital. If these technologies can be found, the ethical and cultural dimensions of the war effort will coalesce behind their use. To a large extent, technology determines patterns of culture and social organization. Thus to change our core provisioning technologies we will have to adapt both culturally and socially. In the same way that consumerism and the love affair with the car emerged in response to new technologies, a global environmental ethic will appear when new technology allows us to live in harmony with nature. Given the scale of the innovation challenge involved in developing these technologies and disseminating them around the world, mobilizing global effort as if for war is the only approach that offers a workable game plan for equitably provisioning the world's people.

Provisioning vs. Sustainable Development

Finally, I think you should have a clear idea right up front how an approach based on *provisioning* differs from the pursuit of *sustainable development*. Simply put, rather than striking a balance between environmental, economic, and social concerns – the three stools of sustainable development – securing access to the ecological goods and services on which social peace and economic progress depend must be made the overarching priority.

PART I

The Enemy Is Ecological Decline

The need for the global community to mobilize as if for war around the idea of provisioning societies with essential access to ecological goods and services in ways that avoid the violent and destructive consequences of ecological decline, which undermine growth and attempts to reduce global poverty.

Chapter 1

A Shift in the Angle of Vision

In a world fixated on the 'war on terrorism' and on a thousand other issues of varying consequence, we are losing sight of another enemy that is now in the advanced stages of mobilizing for a devastating assault on human societies.

The enemy is ecological decline. This enemy has given the world ample evidence of its lurking intent, but the scale of the threat it poses for economic and social security has yet to permeate the public consciousness. The following discussion is intended to make the nature of this enemy crystal clear and the case for mobilizing in specific ways to wage a global war against ecological decline both urgent and compelling.

The enemy is not nature: it is the erosion of ecosystem functionality. Humans, as a species, are part of nature. However, especially since the advent of agricultural communities, human societies have been created. They draw from ecological systems for everything they require in order to survive, to meet consumption requirements, to create wealth, to support economic growth, and to break down and absorb their increasingly diverse waste products. Human societies are *of* nature but are no longer part of natural systems.

When stress on ecological systems reaches the point where it constrains the ability to access or draw down the environmental goods and services required to provision societies – goods and services that are essential for all gains in human well-being – ecological decline becomes the enemy of all people.

The world is now in just such a position. As presently organized and using currently available technologies, human societies are drawing more from nature than ecological systems can provide: every major ecosystem in the world is now in some stage of human-induced decline. The peoples of the world have less than twenty-five years to find and implement new ways of organizing to vastly increase their ability to provision their growing populations and economies. And they must do so without further impairing ecosystem viability, lest they risk making the worst Malthusian nightmares a reality.

We have all heard the tales of woe, and the scale of human pressures on ecosystems is discussed in some detail in Part III. Nevertheless, to briefly illustrate:

- Over half of all the freshwater lakes in the world are now polluted.
- Most parts of the world are facing challenges associated with water availability and quality.
- Enormous groundwater reservoirs that support vast areas of high-yield agricultural production, as well as urban and industrial needs, are being drawn down well in excess of replenishment rates.
- The human-induced loss of biological diversity is reaching epic proportions – fully half the species of large mammals in the world are threatened with extinction; there may soon be little viable forest, coral reef, and other protective habitat left; and up to half the world's plant species are in danger of disappearing forever.
- The global catch of fish from the wild peaked in 1989 and has been in decline ever since; fish farming is now in direct competition with other forms of agricultural production for access to land and other land-based productive resources.
- Almost all of the world's agricultural land is now in use, productivity growth is levelling off, soil quality is declining, and there are no signs of a new 'Green Revolution' taking root.
- Awareness of the insidious, adverse effects on health of long-term exposure to low levels of toxics is growing.
- Human societies are now drawing on the outer reaches of the biosphere to absorb and break down human wastes.

The list goes on endlessly, with the most pressing issue being climate change: there is little prospect of preventing a rapid doubling of atmospheric concentrations of greenhouse gasses from human activity. This will only accelerate the relentless increase in global warming, which is already showing signs of bringing about great human tragedy.

The problem is more complicated than suggested by the simple compilation of long lists of independent examples of ecological stress.

Many changes already underway in the operation of ecosystems are probably irreversible, and societies will have to meet their future needs in conditions of ecological uncertainty and instability. Moreover, because the world is operating at the margins of ecological supply capacity, every new source of environmental trauma ripples across and between ecosystems and around the world. Everything is now connected. Feedback is immediate. The potential for environmental 'flips' to seriously impair the capacity to provision human societies with essential ecological goods and services is everywhere stronger than before.

From this already tenuous base, the global community will somehow have to find ways to address the vast incremental needs for ecological goods and services – needs that will all come to a head by 2025.

Within this timeframe, faced with the additional demands placed on already overstressed global ecological systems, humanity will have to find ways to:

- meet the provisioning needs of a global economy that will be two or three times larger (assuming annual growth of between 2.8 and 4 per cent);
- secure the incremental draws on ecological systems required to alleviate the poverty now afflicting half the world's people (the UN's goal of cutting global poverty in half cannot be achieved without sharply increasing the per capita consumption of natural capital by almost half of the world's people);
- meet the consumption needs of another 2 billion people – a 30 per cent increase over 2000 levels[1] – and, because urban growth will exceed that of the population as a whole, accommodate as many as 2.5 billion additional people in urban areas, where per capita demands on natural capital provisioning processes are greater (most of the increase in urban populations will occur in Third World cities, which will have to absorb again the number of people they took in over the past fifty years, in half the time, and on top of existing levels of poverty and inadequate infrastructure); *and*
- increase agricultural output in proportion to the growth in population (this amounts to matching the total productivity gains of the Green Revolution over the past fifty years, but in half the time and almost entirely from existing areas of cultivation and using existing, already stretched water sources).

When we add up the cumulative pressures on ecological systems that are a consequence of all this, and when we consider how most societies are now organized to meet their provisioning needs, we find that the demand for natural capital flows – including access to waste disposal services – could soon require the ecological resources of three or four worlds: in fifty years it could require ten worlds.[2]

But forget a fifty-year time horizon! Well before 2025 we are going to know whether continued growth is feasible. Long before that year all of the pressures now eroding ecosystem viability will have peaked: the full consequences of deforestation and global water stress, the insidious effects of pollutants, the loss of the global fishery, the failure of the world to feed itself, and the consequences of global warming will all be felt. Ecological collapse is not something to be avoided in the future: it is happening now. The global community has less than twenty-five years to organize itself to adequately provision the world.

Neither continued economic growth nor a reduction in poverty can occur without access to enormous incremental flows of ecological goods and services. This means that ecological decline is targeting the very foundations of the global economy and will strike with especially brutal force at the aspirations of the impoverished under-half of the world's still rapidly growing population. This new enemy, if not fought with deadly intent until defeated, will drive the peoples of the world into ever more difficult processes of adaptation to the consequences of ecological collapse and into ever more intense competition for increasingly scarce sources of natural capital. These growing constraints on the ability of societies to provision themselves threaten to become the catalyst for releasing stored up social tensions in explosions of conflict. The international community's response to these clear signs of a coming assault on human societies has so far been long on rhetoric and short on action.

Most recent efforts have been organized around the admirable concept of sustainable development, which has become the focus of concerted discussion and initiative since it was popularized by the Brundtland Commission 1987. This concept has set out broad goals for promoting harmony between the peoples of the world and between human societies and nature by organizing around the basic objective of meeting the needs of the present 'without compromising the ability of future generations to meet their own needs.'[3] The focus of sustainable development is on improving the quality of life for all the world's citizens without stretching the capacity of the environment to supply natural resources. However, the concept is not limited to ecological sustainability: it also emphasizes the economic and social dimensions of development. Agenda 21, the action plan that emerged from the 1992 Rio Conference on Environment and Development, is an attempt by the global community to implement the concept through efforts to balance economic, social, and environmental concerns in all dimensions of public- and private-sector decision making.[4] But so far these goals have not been translated into practical actions that have the potential to make a difference within time frames that matter.

Of course, plenty of creative thinking is being applied to these issues, and the concept has achieved some momentum. There is much that is progressive both in the international debate and in a wide range of initiatives around the world. Especially in the past few years, a growing range of intellectual analysis and practical action has emerged to provide a solid base from which to move forward.[5] However, although the list of positive initiatives is long and is genuinely suggestive of impressive global efforts to implement the principle of sustainable development, these efforts still only engage a sliver of the world, and the gains being made continue to be offset by the greater cumulative demands of growth.[6]

Part of the reason for the slow response is that the concept's implementation has had to take into account the diverse interests and perceptions of the global community. As a result, the international sustainable development agenda is now too broad and unfocused to summon the coherent, massive response required to deal specifically with the challenges presented by ecological decline.

The diversity of objectives now being pursued opens the concept of sustainable development to varying interpretations and conflicting actions. It is too easy to start out pursuing one purpose and end up pursuing another purpose entirely – for example, to push for the local engagement of people and end up dealing with issues of gender equity, or to argue for accelerated African development based on sustainable principles and end up with a narrow focus on employment creation and structural reforms to encourage foreign investment and fuller integration with the global economy. When translating theory into practice, it is too easy to forget the essential goal, which is to merge economic growth with environmental sustainability.

Furthermore, the concept lends itself to political posturing. Sustainable development has become the new opiate of our political elites: the rhetoric has become ubiquitous even while the meaning has become ever more oblique. The sense of real urgency in the formal pro-nouncements of many national leaders at UN forums is simply not matched by a comparable sense of urgency in national programs. Few politicians anywhere can articulate the specific actions they must take to move their societies toward a sustainable future, and few have the will or political capital to carry out the necessary reforms. Investments in education and health care, land claim settlements with indigenous peoples, equal rights legislation, urban renewal, stronger police forces and other dimensions of efforts to enhance human security, improved transportation networks, national competitiveness, and New Economy innovation are all defended along with environmental protection mea-sures as contributions to sustainability.

The endless repetition of the sustainable development mantra hides the fact that most of the debate now deals with the minutiae of eco-nomic and scientific analysis and with theories of how to promote growth and global equity as opposed to finding ways to maintain access to the ecological systems that underpin these processes. In the absence of a clearly defined game plan for sustainable development, politicians do as they have always done: they perpetuate the narrow pursuit of economic growth and the enhanced material well-being of their citizens.

The net result is that the agenda for international sustainable devel-opment remains overwhelmingly tilted in favour of growth while the assault on global ecosystems continues. Indeed, the push for ecologi-cal sustainability may be losing momentum as the pressures for con-tinued expansion of global economic activity and for spreading the benefits of growth more equitably around the world continue to mount.

In this respect, as captured in the Washington Consensus, in state-ments by G8 ministers, in policy positions released by the World Bank and the WTO, and more recently in the drafting of the agenda and the outcomes of the World Summit on Sustainable Development, the new international agenda has been kidnapped by the concept of the 'virtu-ous circle' of growth.[7] It is argued that economic growth, together with democratic systems of governance and open, transparent arrange-ments for encouraging trade and foreign investment, will eventually produce a virtuous circle of wealth generation, social advance, and increased investment in environmental protection.[8]

To put this result in perspective, it is helpful to remember that the birth of the modern environmental movement in the late 1960s that led to the first global Conference on the Environment in 1972 in

Stockholm was originally motivated by the narrow challenge of slowing or stopping the negative environmental impacts of growth. In the intervening thirty years the debate has gone almost full circle, from this initial concern over the consequences of growth, to the more complicated pursuit of sustainable development by achieving a balance between economic, environmental, and social concerns, to the new agenda of the WSSD, which has practically reverted to a fixation on growth as the cure for all that ails the world.

Again, it is important to be clear about what the enemy is: it is not growth, nor is it the global economy. Over the past two decades, economic development has brought more gains in the well-being of more people than at any other time in human history, and continued growth is essential if the dreary conditions of the world's poor are to be improved. The enemy is ecological decline; it is the rapidly increasing likelihood that shortfalls in access to global sources of ecological goods and services, or all-out ecological collapse, will derail the growth process.

Seen from this perspective, the serious lack of balance in the international agenda actually threatens human progress. It is indicative of a widespread belief that the world can safely delay taking definitive measures to deal with ecological decline until further growth has satisfied apparently more urgent demands – demands to augment the consumption wants of the wealthy and to address the consumption needs of the poor.

Well think again! The 'virtuous circle' argument is logical, powerful, and comforting, but fatally flawed. It can only work, as it did for the Western world, in conditions of ecological abundance. In the conditions of ecological scarcity that now confront the world, the single-minded pursuit of growth is not only misguided but also dangerous. If economic growth and ecological protection are pursued sequentially – if the imbalance in the global agenda is not remedied – the virtuous circle will become a vicious circle of mounting violence and human suffering that derails economic and social progress.

To break out of this conundrum, we need to narrow our angle of vision to focus our full attention on the challenge of provisioning continued growth and poverty reduction with the ecological goods and services they require. We can no longer proceed as if all agendas have equal validity: stopping ecological decline must receive top priority. If we reach the point where all of us are faced with unstoppable, irreversible ecological change or collapse, none of the other economic or social objectives in the diverse sustainable development agenda will be achieved. The international agenda must be squeezed down from all the things that *can* be done to promote growth, and that *could* be done in the name of social equity, to the few things that *must* be done to greatly increase the availability of ecological goods and services that will make possible continued growth and the pursuit of social equity. The simply stated objective of finding ways to provision societies with access to natural capital without further impairing the operation of global ecosystems must be made the great political challenge of our times.

Looking at the world through the lens of social provisioning could provide the small shift in the angle of vision needed to chart a new, more focused international agenda. This is a small shift, but vitally important, for seldom if ever do we articulate the economic development challenge in terms of the basic need to organize to provision societies and seldom if ever do we talk specifically about the need to sustain essential flows of natural capital as if this was the dominant priority for social survival and progress. Few people actually see, let alone discuss, meeting this most basic of all social requirements as a political priority.

Certainly, the concept of sustainable development is consistent with this approach; however, it falters as a result of the diversity of issues it tries to embrace. The environmental movement as a whole is based on this notion, but all too often the goal is stated as protecting the environment as opposed to meeting societies' provisioning needs. Concerns over provisioning arise when countries are faced with a potential disruption of energy supplies. They also arise in discussions of the impending 'water crisis.' The issue of flows arises when people draw attention to the astonishing differences in resource use between developed and Third World countries. It is also the unstated premise behind concerns over climate change, which is the ultimate expression of the outreach by human societies to the waste disposal services of ecological systems.

The closest anyone comes to incorporating the idea of 'provisioning' in a coherent theory is the idea of ecological footprints that measure the totality of environmental resources it takes to support the consumption and waste disposal needs of cities, nations, and the world.[9] The work of the Factor Ten Institute is also based on the limitations on provisioning. The Natural Step movement, which has developed a framework for implementing sustainable development at the organizational level, the idea of Natural Capitalism, which attempts to connect human institutions and businesses with the flow of natural cycles, including ecosystem services, and the efforts to develop zero-emission technologies are also highly relevant.[10]

However, none of these organizations or theories talks specifically about the need to meet provisioning needs as the dominant social priority. Nor does almost anyone else. No one outside of energy and military circles talks as if a big issue facing the United States or other advanced economies is their ability to maintain access to adequate flows of natural capital. The political leaders of Third World nations talk about foreign direct investment and access to markets for their primary products: they want to export their natural capital, but they do not describe it in these terms or express concern about their own access to flows of the essential ecological resources and services on which the expansion of their economies depends.

The biggest consumers of natural capital are urban dwellers. Yet no mayor of any city anywhere in the world talks as if the provisioning of the people whose well-being he or she is responsible for had anything to do with running a city.

No economic development textbook, no assessment of global economic integration, no national economic or social development strategy, no urban planning guide, no rural development handbook, and no book on corporate management talks specifically about the need to organize rural areas, cities, corporations, or nations around the task of maintaining the flows of natural capital on which their ability to function depends. It is as if provisioning is the essential but forgotten rationale for all forms of social organization.

In practical terms, what difference would it make if we shifted the angle of vision to focus on provisioning as the dominant social priority of all people, and if we defined ecological decline as our common enemy?

To begin with, looking at the long history of change in how societies have organized around the essential task of accessing ecological goods and services would help explain the roots of our present conundrum. It could lead to a slightly different understanding of the nature and causes of many of the cultural and equity issues and tensions that exist in the present global economy through a linking of these to differences in the ways that societies, and groups within societies, are organized to provision themselves. It could lead to a better understanding of the nature and causes of social and cultural tensions by showing why ecological scarcity and differences in the ways societies are organized to meet their provisioning needs are common catalysts for human conflict. Of paramount importance, it could lead to a different understanding of the limited options available to societies and the global community for coping with ecological scarcity. This could lead to a clear and binding commitment to bring about the technological and organizational innovations the global community must embrace if it is to avoid the worst consequences of increased competition for declining ecological resources and enhance the scope for continued human progress.

Responding to conditions of ecological scarcity is not a novel challenge for human societies. A simple progression consistently forced earlier societies to push the search for flows of natural capital to the edges of the known world. Better knowledge of local ecosystems and/or new technologies led to increased flows of natural capital that allowed population growth to take place until existing sources of natural capital were fully exploited and outreach to new sources was again a requirement.

The options available to societies to facilitate outreach to new, more novel forms of natural capital are extremely limited. In fact, there are only four things societies can do:

- All, or a portion of an affected population can migrate to a more favoured geographical region.
- They can trade for natural capital not available from local sources.
- They can take natural capital from others through war, colonial occupation, or the exercise of economic power.
- They can turn to technological advance to augment access, find substitutes, increase the efficiency of use, and reduce the scale of demand for absorptive services.

These options may be applied in combination. For example, technological advance can confer military advantage or enhance transportation capability that extends outreach capability, and migration and colonial occupation may occur in tandem. But aside from passive acquiescence to the consequences of shortfalls in natural capital, there are no other ways for human societies to cope with ecological scarcity.

In the long brush of human life on earth, successive societies organized around these options to increase their outreach in five dominant 'rounds of provisioning.' These rounds all overlapped with one another, and all five organizational patterns persist in to-day's globally integrated world.

The First Round, which took almost 200,000 years to run its course, saw hunter-gatherer societies fragment into highly diversified cultural groupings as they extended their search for life-sustaining natural capital to almost every corner of the world through migration and the slow accretion of new, differentiated local knowledge. It is likely that almost everywhere these tribal groupings engaged in perpetual war to protect their lands from incursions by their neighbours. It was this First Round that gave the world the vast base of cultural and linguistic diversity from which all present societies have evolved. At its peak, toward the end of the last ice age, all of the planet's people met their provisioning needs through hunter-gatherer practices.

Between 12,000 and 10,000 BC, the Second Round took hold as agricultural societies began to flourish. Spreading out around the world from their origins in the Eastern Mediterranean, the Indus Basin, and parts of China, they ruthlessly eliminated or assimilated untold numbers of earlier tribal societies. This Second Round reached its zenith in Africa around AD 500 at the end of the three-thousand-year, southward migration of the Bantu peoples and after AD 1500 when European colonizers brought advanced agricultural practices to the Americas, in the process wiping out or virtually destroying most indigenous tribal and nascent agricultural societies.

The Third Round involved the rise and spread of cities, whose administrations subjugated portions of rural economies to the task of provisioning growing urban populations and oversaw trade and military arrangements to meet other provisioning requirements. These arrangements were aided by technological advance. The ancient Greeks and, after them, the Roman Empire relied on colonization to absorb excess populations. Later, European cities struggled with one another for dominance during the commercial revolution of the Middle Ages, all the while creating the models of colonial possession that subsequent trade-based empires imitated. This round, which began in earnest by 3000 BC, is now basically over in advanced economies but accelerating in most developing countries. Indeed, the world fully entered the urban age only at the turn of the millennium, when for the first time a majority of the world's people were urban dwellers.

In the Fourth Round, nation-states replaced cities as the overseers of social provisioning by resorting to technological advance, migration, colonial occupation, and war. While nation-states first emerged in Asia, this Fourth Round really only took hold in the late middle ages in Europe. It then spread around the world, with the last surge of nation-states being created by the breakup of colonial empires after the Second World War and by the fragmentation of the former Soviet Union in the early 1990s.

Round Five involves reliance on private-sector corporations and the international business networks that tie the present global economy together. It has evolved slowly over the past three hundred years. It took firm hold after the Second World War and accelerated dramatically with the triumph of free-market economic theories over Marxist dogma in the mid-1980s. Today's advanced economies and wealthy enclaves throughout the Third World rely on the intricate organizational capabilities of private-sector networks and the use of leading-edge technologies to scour the world for sources of in-bound flows of natural capital; meanwhile, they extend their demands for waste disposal services to the outer edges of the biosphere.

This long progression of continuous outreach to more distant or novel flows of ecological goods and services produced the technological and organizational advances that have allowed the world to support vast population increases. In this respect, had it stuck to the simple technologies and highly sophisticated knowledge of local ecosystems that early hunter-gatherer societies relied on to provision themselves, the entire world would have been able to support only 20 million people. The technologies that underpin today's global economy have expanded provisioning capability to the point where we are now supporting, albeit imperfectly and at great ecological expense, a population in excess of 6 billion.

The history of outreach to provision societies has been marked by enormous suffering and by the creation and destruction of human cultures. During the first four rounds, competition for access to scarce natural capital often erupted into violent confrontations between societies – for example, on the borders of the territories of early hunter-gatherer societies. However, the greater conflicts over access to natural capital have occurred in the competition between societies with different modes of provisioning during the transitions between rounds. This occurred during the decimation of hunter-gatherer societies by agricultural peoples, during the subjugation of rural areas to the will of city-states and city-based empires, during the forced integration of city-states, rural communities, and ethnic and linguistic groups into nation-states, and during times when nations and city-states relied on military power to secure trade routes and colonial possessions.

In contrast, the technology- and trade-based provisioning arrangements of Round Five have been remarkably peaceful, at least when measured against earlier examples of competition for scarce natural capital. In large measure this is because trade and economic integration have displaced war as the most effective means of accessing necessary in-bound flows of natural capital. However, tensions over provisioning are mounting. The world has moved to embrace the organizational imperatives of the Fifth Round, and the effects of this have rippled back into the residual of the previous rounds. The consequences of this collision between rounds, and its uneven effects on people and nations, are very much in evidence today and help explain many of the tensions within the global economy.

In aggregate, there is a strong correlation between economic well-being (or social conflict) and the manner in which nation-states and groups within nations are organized to access flows of natural capital. Benefits accrue to societies in almost direct relationship to how their provisioning arrangements reflect the organizational characteristics of the five rounds. For example, hunter-gatherer societies tend to be at or near the bottom of the scale of relative affluence. Agricultural nations tend to be relatively worse off and more prone to violence than urbanized societies. Rural areas within nations are less well off than urban areas. Countries and groups within advanced urban enclaves that are actively involved in the technology-led growth dynamic and that are tied in most effectively to global provisioning networks are generally better off and less prone to violent confrontation than any other groups.

In terms of tensions over the erosion of cultural and social distinctiveness, the Fifth Round of provisioning continues a long trend. Human cultural and linguistic diversity had been squeezed by the expansion of agricultural societies, the cultural integrating power of cities, and the centralizing authority of nation-states. The activities of integrated business networks are now spreading the same technologies, policy frameworks, products, and ideas around the world. In doing so, they are 'levelling' all cultures. The past four rounds of provisioning have all moved the world away from highly differentiated tribal units back toward a common humanity. This process has been neither pretty nor fair. It has often been violent, and change at each step of the way has been constantly resisted by thousands of years of cultural conditioning.

Paradoxically, because economic growth is an urban phenomenon, the new global economy has not linked nations together so much as cities. The dynamic growth of urban areas has run lock-step with the

Fifth Round and with the spread of the organizational requirements and technologies of the Western growth model. Yet not everyone in urban areas is able to participate in the New Economy. The result is the global linking of well-off urban enclaves that are surrounded, in Third World countries, by vast peri-areas of urban poverty where most migrants from rural areas first settle.

Increasingly, common forms of work and social organization are shaping urban lifestyles, and it is in the formal economies of these advanced urban enclaves that the homogenizing power of technology is most evident. Cities and social interactions are shaped by the automobile. Urban lifestyles and consumption patterns are increasingly common across nation-states as mass advertising promotes the same products across national borders. A portion of leisure time in most countries now revolves around television, and much of the content is common across borders. Less obvious, but of considerable importance, infrastructure services help determine the urban form and remove urban dwellers both physically and psychologically from their roots in nature.

In sharp contrast, in the peri-areas of large urban centres the cultures of the impoverished masses are being shaped around the use of entirely different technological, infrastructural, and provisioning arrangements. The resulting gaps in economic well-being, human security, opportunity, and culture are now stretching the social integration functions of many cities to the breaking point.

These tensions are also testing the bonds of nationhood. Competition is being created within nations between hunter-gatherers, agriculturists, and industrial interests over access to the riches of bio-regions, and tensions of long standing persist between the requirements of urban areas for provisioning and those of small-scale farmers fighting to cling to their family farms and way of life. Many countries now find themselves facing demands for self-government or independence from tribal, linguistic, and religious subgroups.

National sovereignty is also perceived to be under attack from abroad. Growing reliance for provisioning on private-sector networks may not technically be eroding the sovereign powers of nation-states; that said, countries have been forced to relinquish considerable control over their own economic development in order to enjoy the benefits of private-sector initiatives. Common national policies and the creation of appropriate infrastructure are critical factors for integration into the provisioning arrangements of the global economy.

But there is a far greater concern than this. The growing demands for natural capital are making ecological scarcity an ever more volatile trigger for human conflict. Like ancient societies before it, the modern world has lost the capacity to control its interactions with the natural environment. Nation-states have either outgrown or despoiled local resources and all are now reaching out to more distant sources of natural capital. Remarkable gains have been made in the efficiency of resource use, but the cumulative human draw of natural capital is growing faster. This is eroding global ecosystem viability. For the first time, all the world's peoples are in direct competition for diminishing global, as opposed to local or regional, ecosystem goods and services.

The present-day options for augmenting access to useable flows of natural capital are few, and the consequences of different options are stark. We can no longer look to vast, untapped sources of natural capital to bail us out. Nor can people migrate to frontier lands, although millions of economic migrants are already trying to move to regions more favoured than their own. As in the past, some groups can simply take the resources they require from others through trade or war. In this respect, competition for access to environmental resources is not the only cause of conflict in our complex, interdependent world: considerations related to power sharing, national prestige and ambition, religious slights, economic gain or loss, and historical grievance can also play a role. However, the potential for ecological scarcity to be a catalyst for conflict, either on its own or as a contributing factor that causes opposing sides to coalesce along ethnic, national, or religious lines, is everywhere on the rise.

If history is any guide, this coalescing is likely to take place among groups that have similar provisioning processes, and competition is likely to take place either between groups that are organized in the same way to access the same resources or between those fully engaged in the dominant provisioning processes and those less effectively organized to participate.

Ecological scarcity has always struck the poor more directly than the rich, and done so with harsher consequences. Through the use of economic power backed by superior technology and military strength, wealthier societies have generally been able to maintain or expand their control over access to sources of natural capital and, in times of scarcity, to commandeer flows that are essential to their societies. On the surface, this continues to be the case today.

In the framework of how societies are now organized to provision themselves, those still tied to the first four rounds of provisioning are at a distinct disadvantage. People mired in poverty tend to rely on simple arrangements for provisioning themselves from local sources of natural capital and are immediately susceptible to the effects of shortfalls or changes in their relative ability to access these resources. They often live on the cusp of survival and are constantly faced with the prospect that ecological disruption will tip them from conditions of deprivation into total despair. As a result, they are more inclined to resort to violence if others threaten their access. It is those still trapped in the vestiges of provisioning arrangements left over from earlier rounds that now go to war, and most of these wars take place at the subnational level.

On a local basis, this type of competition for access to scarce natural capital is already boiling over into sporadic conflict. This can be seen in the assault by agricultural societies on the homelands of hunter-gatherers in tropical rainforests; in the attempts at ethnic cleansing between groups in overpopulated agricultural areas such as Rwanda and Bosnia; and, as in Zambia, in battles between advanced agricultural interests that are geared to provisioning national and international urban populations and those still locked into concepts of local provisioning, who are demanding that rural lands be redistributed.

In sharp contrast, the diverse and sophisticated provisioning channels that the wealthy have established to access global sources of natural capital provide a strong buffer against the types of localized ecological stress that cause so much hardship for the poor. Moreover, as international competition for scarce natural capital heats up, there is little reason to think that the economically and militarily strong will not once again attempt to divert essential flows of natural capital from weaker nations and societies.

On the other hand, the combination of global economic integration and global ecological scarcity places serious constraints on the ability of the world's wealthy nations to wield economic and social power in overtly self-serving ways. It is not simply that these avenues are only available as long as the people using them remain indifferent to the sufferings of the excluded. Economic integration has made Third World growth a condition of continued economic advance in leading economies, and this two-way interdependence constrains arbitrary action by advanced economies. As well, there is almost no way to mute the appeal of growth or to turn off the growth dynamic in Third World nations. Nor can the wealthy nations of the world do much to limit access by other nations to the resources of the global commons. Nor can trade or war increase the global availability of natural capital or the absorptive capacity of ecological systems. Unlike in the past, the better off and militarily strong can no longer ignore the plight of weaker societies and simply take what they need through trade, war, or conquest.

This new reality makes the well-off increasingly vulnerable to ecological 'flips,' which can now occur on a global scale. Localized wars over natural capital can spread to international arenas. In this respect, poverty equates itself with ignorance, hunger, unemployment, and bleak futures, and these conditions can breed envy, social tensions, hatred, intolerance, and – on the fringes – extremist views and terrorist groups. As we now know, the new weapons of terrorism allow extremists to wage different kinds of wars with the potential to inflict randomly brutal human and economic injury in hopes of advancing their cause, or simply to vent their rage.

These threats to economic and social progress will quickly become more acute if ecological scarcity is allowed to undermine the global growth dynamic, accentuate disparities between societies, and breed ever greater social discord. Should this occur, it is easy to imagine the world rapidly dividing itself into two warring camps: those who fully participate in the provisioning arrangements of Round Five, the global economy, and those who have been left out of the advanced integration processes or who are not well served by them.

To avoid such a rapid deterioration in the human prospect, and because ultimately on moral and practical grounds there is no other way to respond to conditions of global ecological scarcity, the world's people must now work together to make the transition to new ways of organizing to meet their collective provisioning requirements.

The scale of this challenge – the less than twenty-five-year time frame for taking decisive action, the complexity of the issues, and the fact that all societies are threatened and all must be equally engaged in finding solutions – means the world must mobilize as if for war. Nothing short of declaring a global war on ecological decline and mobilizing resources in a highly focused and co-ordinated manner at the level of nation-states as well as internationally will have much chance of preventing a descent into global anarchy. This new war must be fought to find and implement new ways of provisioning societies. This means the war must be fought on the battlefields of technological advance and social reorganization. Only vastly improved natural capital management technologies and practices will have the power to significantly enhance the ability of societies to provision themselves in ways that remain within the sustaining envelopes of viable ecosystems. Those technologies and practices must be developed and used.

The war against ecological decline will be over when the means have been found to provide all of the world's peoples with access to essential ecological goods and services, including those required to deal with human waste. When this goal has been achieved, the world will have entered a Sixth Round in the provisioning of human societies: the Age of Global Provisioning.

The peoples of the world now face this stark choice: compete with and eventually fight one another for privileged access to diminishing ecosystem resources; or commit collectively to wage war against global ecological decline. Humanity can begin a horrific conflict that will reduce the global population to levels that can be maintained from severely depleted ecological systems; or it can join in the common cause of dramatically augmenting provisioning capability.

This should be an easy choice. As history shows, however, with the exception of Round Five, for which the jury is still out, all past transitions to new modes of provisioning have been marked by inequities, the erosion of cultures, and intense human conflict. Thus, even if the world chooses to co-operate rather than compete, the transition to Round Six will still be enormously disruptive. Of necessity, changing the interface between human societies and natural systems will mean changing the ways in which societies are organized. Embracing social and cultural change is the price that must be paid to put in place, in relative peace, the new organizational arrangements and technologies required to provision the world's burgeoning population. The fact that technological and social adaptation must take place in conditions of increasing ecological instability adds enormously to the difficulties of this transition.

The rest of this book is an attempt to make the case for waging this war. It is a call to place the provisioning of human societies with necessary flows of natural capital at the centre of the political agenda of every nation on the planet, and it sets out the dimensions of a global battle plan organized around the global development and application of new provisioning technologies.

In the next chapter I explain the concept of provisioning societies in more detail. I begin with a simple question: Why does a cup of coffee cost more in an urban setting in Canada than in rural Turkey? The answer to this unlikely question leads to a discussion of how the ways societies are organized to provision themselves influence patterns of economic growth and poverty. It explains, in a very basic way, why all societies rely on access to ecological resources and how differentiated access underlies all forms of economic disparity.

The discussion in Part II shows how wealth creation and economic growth are offshoots of human efforts, aided by technology and forms of social organization, to extract and secure the essential flows of natural capital required for human survival and general well-being. It traces the 200,000-year progression in the organization of human provisioning efforts through five distinct rounds, which have now culminated, in the Fifth Round, in reliance for provisioning on the international business networks that tie our present global economy together. It explains how competition for access to scarce natural capital has shaped human cultures, and it shows how differences in the ways societies are organized to meet their provisioning needs help define the current roles of tribes, agricultural societies, cities, nations, and private-sector organizations in the global economy.

The five chapters in Part II are mini-histories that tell specific stories. Through these I offer insights into the long sequence of events that led us to our present global conundrum and provide a slightly different perspective from which to view the big issues that will be facing the growth process over the next twenty-five years. This part ends with a chapter that looks at how the current global economy is organized, the broad directions of technological advance now in train, and the enormous potential that a continuation of current patterns of growth and their extension around the world hold for the enhancement of human welfare.

Part III then provides a different view of the prospects for the global economy by looking at the twenty-five year challenge to economic growth and social order resulting from the bunching of ecological and equity issues that the world must urgently deal with. Chapter 9 looks at global equity issues from a historical perspective and then at present trends and their relationship to differences in the ways societies are organized to meet their provisioning needs. Chapter 10 provides an overview of the extent and nature of the human-induced erosion of global ecosystems. This discussion is especially concerned about cause-and-effect relationships and shows how, because competition for scarce natural capital is now taking place on a global basis and everything is connected, change in one area has unavoidable consequences else-where. This creates a dangerous situation as it diffuses and hides the potential for ecological 'flips' to derail human provisioning efforts. Chapter 11 then explains why the combination of global ecological decline and global inequity can be such a powerful catalyst for human conflict.

Parts II and III are written in a way that mirrors the broad divisions among perceptions of the global economy. Part II captures the opti-mism and hope inherent in continued economic growth, and Part III reflects the dark side. If you read Part II by itself, especially the last two chapters on the global economy, you will likely come away think-ing that growth really is the answer to all our social problems and that simply getting out of the way of the powerful growth dynamic is the sanest policy option for the world to adopt. On the other hand, if you read only Part III, you may want to slash your wrists or cancel plans to have more children, for you will think the world is on the verge of falling into the chaos of global competition for diminishing natural capital.

But don't stop there. Part IV sets out the elements of the battle plan for waging global war to equitably provision societies. It argues that the war must be fought on six specific battlefields of technological innovation, and that this approach can vastly increase the ability of societies to provision themselves in ecologically responsible ways. Suc-cess will also depend on the creation of specific political mandates for reorganizing societies around integrated bio-region and eco-urban man-agement practices. Ideas are advanced for how nation-states and the global community, acting together, can organize to wage this war. The last chapter shows how the war could lead to the Sixth Round, the Age of Global Provisioning, which could renew hope in the future of the world's people.

Chapter 2

Provisioning Societies

Politicians must be held accountable for addressing the looming issue of growing competition for increasingly scarce global sources of natural capital on which human well-being depends and the potential inherent in this competition to bring economic growth to a halt and precipitate a generalized descent into social chaos and war.

The idea of writing a book around the concept of organizing to provision societies had its genesis a couple of years ago, when I first penned these words. I was sipping a cappuccino in a cafe in Ottawa's Byward Market, having just returned from a meeting in Washington called to 'mainstream biodiversity.' The participants there had generally failed to make the protection of biodiversity relevant to representatives from several industry sectors. It seemed obvious that the global dialogue on sustainable development was being stymied by the binding requirement that all companies and nations must compete in the growth game. The immediate requirements of economic competition were taking precedence over the need to maintain the basic integrity of the ecosystems on which growth and human well-being ultimately depend.

As a result, the world seemed to be driving down an ever-narrowing and increasingly dangerous road. Growing pressures on ecological systems were eliminating exit ramps. If we were to continue, I thought, the world would soon trade competition for growth opportunities with competition for access to increasingly scarce natural capital, and the prospect of a bright economic future for one of increasing global conflict.

There was a pressing need to break the stagnation in this policy conundrum by grounding the debate over ecological decline in underlying constants that were more relevant to people's lives and that could provide a simple, compelling basis for strategic thinking. But how could the world coalesce around a more riveting concept than sustainable development? The search for common, underlying foundations that would enable us to harmonize social organization, wealth creation, and economic growth with ecological capacity had been going on for years. It was highly unlikely that I or anyone else was going to come up with something entirely new.

At that point, a friend dropped by and we ended up talking about a trip I had made to Turkey several months earlier. This led to the observation that we had just paid $3 for essentially the same cup of coffee that I had paid 25 cents for in up-country Turkey. After my friend left, I began to wonder what really accounted for the twelve-fold difference in the price of the two cups of coffee and what, if anything, this might indicate about how to break the impasse between growth and the environment. At first glance this question may seem trivial. However, it implicitly raises questions about the purpose and utility of economic growth, and the answers to those questions clearly illustrate why it is so essential that the world dramatically augment useable flows of natural capital.

Is there merit in how the benefits of growth are distributed? Are Canadians better off because they enjoy all the trappings and comforts that cause the price of a coffee to be so much higher? Is the environmental stress associated with the provision of all of these trappings worth the apparent social gains? Flipping the question around, are the people in rural Turkey going to be better off when they are paying $3 for a cup of coffee? If technological advance and economic growth continue, will we in the now affluent societies still be paying $3 for our coffee, or much more? Will the people in rural Turkey actually be better off, or will the distribution of the benefits of growth always involve gaps in relative wealth and social well-being?

Moreover, will the people of Turkey – and for that matter people in the rest of the world – be better off when faced with the additional ecological stress associated with making the technological and social changes required to inflate the price? Does the global assault on ecological systems have to be an uncontrollable accompaniment to the spread of economic growth? And more to the point, is the growth process inevitably self-limiting because it is leading to ecological collapse and to increasing competition among inherently unequal groups and nation-states for access to shrinking sources of natural capital?

The coffee shop seemed like an odd place to be asking these dismal questions. It was located in the midst of one of the most affluent societies on earth and just across the street from market stalls filled with the produce of the world. As such, it was a place that was synonymous with the social gains derived from growth.

To be able to live freely in a sharing, tolerant, and politically open society that is largely indifferent to race, creed, or religion, to be able to sit and watch steady streams of generally happy, healthy, well-dressed people walking by or driving past in their SUVs, to be able to enjoy the foods of the world stacked in low-cost abundance in the market stalls across the way, to breathe clean air and drink clean water directly from the tap, to be rewarded after receiving the gift of a good education with steady, satisfying employment, to be able to connect electronically to friends and colleagues, to be able to travel anywhere, are all benefits derived from growth.

The levels of wealth, comfort, health, and general welfare enjoyed by Canadians exceed those achieved in any previous age, including that of the Roman Empire at its height. Yet in contrast to Roman times, these levels have been attained without resort to slave labour and with a feeble military capacity that is focused on international peace rather than on conquest.

Affluence, comfort, social harmony, and security: these are not trivial benefits! By any yardstick, it would be hideously poor judgment to suggest otherwise. If growth can create the same increases in societal wealth described above and confer the same diversity of opportunity and the blessings of choice on other peoples as it does in leading economies, then 'globalization,' to the extent that it helps spread these benefits around the world, clearly holds enormous promise for improving the lot of humankind.

Yet there I was, sitting in the coffee shop puzzling over these questions and visualizing the cataclysmic bunching of ecological and equity issues that are now making the world a more dangerous place and putting at risk the impressive gains of economic growth. So, why the difference in the price of a cup of coffee, and what does this have to do with these big issues?

Obviously, the gap in prices can be explained in terms of differences in the costs of production – different wage structures, energy costs, tax levels, social service levies, and so forth. But a more useful explanation is provided by the diversity of employment categories that ultimately support the production of a cup of coffee in each location and by the implications of employment diversification on requisite flows of natural capital. Economic growth is based largely on the role played by technology in diversifying employment opportunity. At the same time, growth cannot take place unless societies enhance their capacity to increase the volume of in-bound flows of natural capital and to access environmental or ecosystem services to assist with the disposal of waste. Thus, the differences in the price may reflect the greater number of specialized occupations involved in the production of the two cups of coffee; ultimately, it may also reflect the greater total draw of natural capital used in their production and sale and the costs and benefits associated with organizing to secure these flows.

How Much Natural Capital Does It Take to Make a Cup of Coffee?

The first step in generating wealth and economic growth is to initiate the processes leading to specialization and the diversification of employment opportunity.

Technological advance is critical to this process – without it, the potential for diversification shrivels. A limited specialization of functions occurs in hunter-gatherer and purely agricultural societies; that said, these functions are essentially communally organized activities and the pace of technological advance is exceedingly slow. Thus, generalized economic growth does not take place in these communities. Technological advance and economic growth are primarily urban phenomena. Both are rooted in the demands made by denser urban populations for products, technologies, and services, and diversified employment is a result of these demands.

Simply putting more people and products between the producer and the final consumer is not the objective. Loading up people at points along production chains simply leads to a lowering of average wages and overall well-being. To be effective, employment diversification must be based on the ability to add value, or it must be a response to an unavoidable market requirement.

Service industries play a key role because they add layers of value-added costs to transactions by inserting more specialized services and products at every stage in production chains from initial concept to sales and after-sales service. This tendency is clearly evident in the area of advertising: in 1989, global corporate spending on advertising was estimated at $120 for every person in the world, or over half as much as the world spends on public education.[1]

In modern economies, employment diversification and technological advance are also influenced by mundane things such as standards and government regulations. In the food chain, for example, production and service functions and technologies have become more varied as a result of the introduction of standards and regulations respecting food quality, working conditions, sanitary considerations, packaging and labelling, transportation codes, advertising transparency, and waste disposal requirements. Each individual standard or regulation creates a new, sometimes very small and other times huge incremental technological or service requirement that adds to aggregate employment.

In terms of the number of people involved in operating the two coffee shops, the Ottawa facility wins hands down. It is located in a building designed by an architect to satisfy stringent building codes. A restaurant specialist was called in to design the interior space and arrangements for seating customers. Reliable water and energy providers service the shop. The staff use hygienic coffee-making technologies that comply with municipal regulations, and the facilities are regularly inspected. An outside contractor cleans the shop, and the owners employ the services of a lawyer and an accounting firm in managing their business. On all these fronts, the service providers required by the Ottawa shop are more diverse than those required by the Turkish coffee shop. The same is true of infrastructure services and related employment streams. In the case of water, this is no contest since the Turkish shop is not connected to a water main or municipal sewage facility. In addition, the Ottawa coffee shop pays taxes whereas the shop in Turkey operates in the informal economy and pretty much avoids this requirement. As a result, the Turkish shop does not require a related stream of services and employment functions – tax collectors, accountants, messengers, the providers of forms, and the like.

In simple terms, then, a cup of coffee is more expensive in Ottawa because the shop has to fold the costs of more services into the price of its coffee. If you want to sip coffee in Byward Market, you have to be able to pay for the infrastructure and services that create this amenity. The natural capital dimensions to the difference in price between a coffee in Turkey and a coffee in Ottawa arise from the fact that the services and forms of infrastructure supporting the production of the two cups can only be provided by drawing on flows of natural capital.

Both shops use the same amount of coffee, water, sugar, and milk to make the coffee. However, every infrastructure element and service built into the Ottawa operation involves a flow of natural capital exceeding that used in Turkey. The buildings that house the shops use vastly different volumes of materials in their construction. Ottawa's water purification facilities and the water mains into the Ottawa shop are all made of natural capital and are regularly maintained and upgraded. The electrical grid in Ottawa is more extensive and reliable and consumes more natural capital than the simple lighting system in the Turkish shop. Also, the relative draw of the two shops must incorporate a minute share of the ecological demands associated with the generation and distribution of power.

Additional flows of natural capital are associated with the provision of architectural and design services and also with the provision of government inspectors, cleaners, lawyers, and accountants. Sanitation and garbage removal services keep the premises and surrounding areas clean and neat. The provision of all of these services requires offices, equipment, and materials as well as communication and transportation facilities. All of the service people need personal accommodation and their own access to necessary infrastructure and services. Again, a small portion of each of these requirements for natural capital supports the operation of the Ottawa coffee shop.

When we aggregate all of these various employment functions, it becomes obvious that the Ottawa coffee shop requires far more natural capital than the Turkish coffee shop and thus must reach out much farther around the world in order to secure these flows.

In sum, the total flow of natural capital to support the Ottawa operation vastly exceeds the flow required to support the Turkish shop. The cost of the extra diversity and quality of infrastructure and services, and thus the cost of the total flow of natural capital incorporated into the price are ultimately what accounts for the difference in price between the two cups of coffee.

The same applies in all areas of economic activity: every production or service chain creates its own unique demand for access to flows of natural capital. The training of a teacher requires a huge investment in infrastructure. The legal profession cannot expand without a parallel expansion of office, communication, transportation, and other facilities and services. The development, installation, and use of advanced communication technologies requires the provision of a wide array of service occupations, and all of these imply a need for additional infrastructure and flows of natural capital.

Even in the New Economy, natural capital is essential to growth. People can't eat information or build offices out of it. Nor is there any evidence that the new wealth is leading to more resource-sparing lifestyles. Quite the opposite: it is leading to more opulent lifestyles, more consumption, more travel, and bigger ecological footprints. Silicon Valley and all of its imitators around the world rely on flows of natural capital, and their success has increased the demand for ecological goods and services.

Every person born increases the demand for natural capital. Every job that is created increases the demand for natural capital. Every innovation that leads to increased specialization of employment increases the demand for natural capital. The world lives on natural capital. Jobs and economic growth depend on it. This is a binding and inescapable fact. And it has always been this way.

As the example of the two cups of coffee illustrates, reliance on natural systems increases with wealth. It is often assumed that people living closer to nature – the Inuit of the North, the Yanomamo in the Amazon Basin and so on – depend more on natural systems for their survival than those living in modern societies. When the full implications of the natural capital draw of modern economies are taken into account, it is actually the other way around.

The farther people are removed from nature, the more they come to depend on it to maintain their lifestyles. The availability of natural capital is as fundamental to allowing a lawyer, a doctor, or a biotech executive to earn a living as it is to creating jobs for miners, foresters, and farmers, and it is vastly more important for the ability of all of these professions to earn a living than it is for people who live on the basis of what they can extract directly from their local environment.

Organizing to Provision Societies

As I sat in the coffee shop watching the people in the market across the street pick through the produce of the world, it was obvious that there isn't much in life more basic than the task of provisioning human societies. But how did all this stuff get to be in the market? For that matter, how does milk get distributed to everyone in New York, and how do food, building materials, clothes, and TV sets reach the 21 million inhabitants of Mexico City or the teeming megalopolises of Southeast Asia?

Looking only at the food chain, it obviously took an incredibly sophisticated organizational capability to arrange at one end for the provision of inputs into agricultural production units around the world, and then to move produce from farms through local collection networks, then through food processing, refrigeration, packaging, and storage facilities, then through specialized global transportation networks and marketing and sales organizations, then through wholesale outlets and then, eventually, through local distribution networks to the market stalls across the street.

Knowledge and technologies have to be applied to the management and maintenance of agricultural land. Communication networks have to be established. Energy has to be made available throughout the chain. The relevant service industries have to be tied in. The people involved in these diverse occupational areas have to be trained. And there has to be a built-in management capacity at every stage and spread throughout all the related industry sectors to ensure access to systems that will accept the diversity of waste products generated during all of these operations.

Seen in this light, the market across the street reflected the global economy operating at its most basic yet complex level – providing food and organizing the total related draw on ecological resources from around the world required to feed the people of Ottawa. The food chains, in turn, are only a portion of the provisioning arrangements that make up the total global economy and that create access to the full range of ecological goods and services the people of Ottawa draw from nature.

Extrapolating from this example, it is clear that the organizational arrangements that create access to ecological goods and services for the people of Ottawa extend to the far corners of the world. These provisioning channels are built around a sophisticated array of technologies and businesses that are interlinked and networked across national borders; eventually, these channels narrow themselves down into the specific hard and soft infrastructure services that directly support the Ottawa coffee shop. These networks as a whole and their cumulative draw on natural capital provide the provisioning capacity to support all the many services and jobs that go into making the cup of coffee in Ottawa.

In contrast, the processes involved in producing a cup of coffee in rural Turkey are much less complicated and rely far more on access to purely local resources. As a result, the total draw on ecological systems is much lower. Differences in infrastructure services also help explain why the Ottawa coffee shop contributes to the employment of far more people than the shop in Turkey. In this respect, if it wants to charge $3 a cup, the Turkish shop will have to establish access to and incorporate a comparable level of infrastructure amenities and services into its operations. In the process, it will have to access significantly more natural capital and connect itself to the organizational networks that facilitate this outreach.

Third World Jobs, Natural Capital, and the Global Economy

The progression through which the Turkish coffee shop might acquire access to these more diversified forms of infrastructure can be illustrated by looking at how workers migrate from informal to formal sector employment. This continuum of change also suggests how wealth and job creation increase the scale of provisioning requirements by adding to the per capita consumption of natural capital.

Both hard infrastructure (water mains, sewers, roads, communication facilities, etc.) and soft infrastructure (education, legal and financial services, etc.) are essential for diversifying employment opportunities, and the availability of these services is a precondition for generating wealth. Wealth is generated directly through the creation of jobs related to the provision of core services and indirectly through the employment-generating effects of standards, regulations, and the more specialized job functions created by access to more sophisticated technology. The availability of physical infrastructure creates demand for social, personal, and corporate services.

The reverse is also true: there are infrastructure limits to growth and thus to the pursuit of equity goals. Without access to infrastructure, it is difficult to increase the value of landholdings and to upgrade the quality of services and amenities provided to clients. When there is no access to clean air and water, to energy services and communications links, to adequate educational and training facilities, to health services, a lot of other things have to be forgone.

These observations have particular relevance for Third World development and patterns of natural capital consumption. In this respect, Hernando De Soto makes the point that the poor actually have significant assets. He estimates that 'the total value of real estate held, but not legally owned by the poor of the Third World and former communist nations is at least $9.3 trillion,' or about twice the total circulating money supply in the United States.[2] However, he argues that because the poor do not have clear legal title to their 'property,' they cannot capitalize their assets or use them as collateral to raise money to improve or expand their businesses. He makes a strong case, but the argument I am advancing here suggests that the challenge involves more than just resolving the question of ownership. The availability of infrastructure services – preferably tailored to the needs of the rural and urban poor – is essential to the processes of job and wealth creation and ultimately to the ability to access natural capital. Without these services, it is not possible to augment property values or to raise the sophistication and diversification of service jobs. These more diverse forms of infrastructure are also essential to the processes of diversifying provisioning channels.

Poverty in the Third World is concentrated in informal-economy sectors located mainly in smallholder agricultural regions and, increasingly, in the peri-areas of cities. There are serious difficulties involved in measuring the number of people actually employed or living in these sectors; that said, it is fair to say that up to two-thirds of the populations in some countries may still depend on informal-sector employment.[3]

Much activity in the informal economy is related to basic provisioning. In the food sector, for example, the supply chains linking small-scale rural producers to consumers in the informal portions of the urban economy involve the same sorts of functions as in the formal economy; these chains require people to grow food, transport it, and sell it to intermediaries (e.g., food stall operators) or final customers. Similar employment is generated in other low-level infrastructure services, such as the delivery of water in old Coke bottles, transportation by rickshaw or tuck-tuck, communications (e.g., sharing of a cell phone), low-level sanitation and waste removal services, and the recycling of clothing and basic building materials.

A diversity of informal employment also arises in the areas of personal and business services. Examples include Joseph, a barber who plies his trade with only a wooden chair, scissors, a comb, and a pocket mirror in an open-air market in Botswana, and Ahmed, a travel agent who operates his business from a table in the street across from the entrance to a hotel in Delhi that caters to international travellers. Ahmed also has an umbrella in case it rains and offers a range of services, from guided tours to local sites to standing in line to validate flight reservations.

In many ways, these jobs are similar to all but technically specialized jobs in the formal economy. The main differences relate to the technologies and skill sets being used, the lack of infrastructure support, and, of course, the pay. Also, those who are employed in informal activities must organize themselves in distinct ways to meet their provisioning requirements insofar as they lack access to the more extensive and diversified provisioning arrangements that serve formal economies. There is obviously some spillover here. Shanghai still apparently gets almost all of its vegetables from the surrounding region, and there is certainly informal-sector involvement in the supply and consumption of these flows. Nevertheless, the essentially separate structure of the formal and informal economies is real.

The transition from informal to formal sector employment tends to begin in the food chain, when agricultural producers sell to consumers in wealthy urban enclaves or produce for export and thus begin to establish ties to national and global networks, technologies, and standards.

The transition in other occupational areas can be illustrated by a progression that has often occurred in Third World countries. Many desperate people who live by scavenging in garbage dumps begin to recycle materials they find in the dumps. Moving into the cities, some of them begin to sort through residential and commercial garbage put out for collection. Small contracts for garbage removal are then struck, perhaps with shop owners or wealthy home owners who aren't satisfied with the regular garbage collection system in their neighbourhood. Eventually, other contracts are secured and a more formalized service is organized.

This type of progression in employment from informal to formal sector activity, which creates wealth for the urban poor, involves ever greater access to infrastructure services and to sources of natural capital flows. We can see these relationships by looking at Ahmed's ambitions for the growth of his travel business. His priorities are to get a motor scooter to cut travel time, then an office, and finally a computer.

Ahmed's scooter will link him to the energy and transportation infrastructure of the formal economy. These links may be a little indirect, as initially he may get his gas from a local reseller who carts fuel in rough containers from the nearest formal-sector gas station and may have his scooter repaired by a local mechanic who uses cannibalized parts and recycled tires discarded by or 'borrowed' from formal-sector users.

In terms of upgrading his office, he plans to get a tent or awning and hopes eventually to build a more permanent structure. When he does this, he will in all probability have to deal with the legal system, as thorny issues of land ownership and rental payments are likely to arise. Let us assume he is able to get over this hurdle, perhaps with the aid of someone offering paralegal services to informal sector individuals, and having arranged financing through an organization geared specifically to informal-sector realities. In terms of creating further asset wealth, his next challenge will depend disproportionately on the availability of other forms of urban infrastructure. As he upgrades his office facilities, Ahmed will have to draw more and more on urban infrastructure and service industries such as water, sanitation, electricity, and telephone lines. At this point he will be in the same situation as the owner of the Turkish coffee shop in terms of increasing the value of his property and the profitability of his business.

By finally getting a computer – the key to being able to provide a wider range of services such as booking international flights and hotels – Ahmed will be linking himself to the global information networks and to the education and training services of the formal economy. He will have to upgrade his skills in order to manage his new business functions. He may need more sophisticated legal and accounting services, and he will probably have to advertise in order to expand his client base.

As these progressions take place, he and his employees will likely tie in to health and other social service networks, and his operations will increasingly have to comply with industry standards and regulations. His children may receive a full education – during which they will be exposed to the knowledge of the world – and, of course, he will have to deal with the tax system.

The problems inherent in the coming assault on natural capital that is going to result from a successful push to reduce global poverty are almost intuitively self-evident. As occupations move up the scales of income and technological dependence, personal consumption grows. But this is only part of the reason that reliance on flows of natural capital increases.

As the example of the cup of coffee illustrated, the key factors influencing the natural capital intensity of employment relate to the number and diversity of other support jobs that are required and the infrastructure links that are essential to carry out job functions. In other words, the overall effect of technological advance on the diversification of employment is the real driver of natural capital consumption, and it is the total outreach through changing forms of organization to meet provisioning arrangements that ultimately determines the total draw on natural capital.

In this respect, it seems that disproportionate increases in the demand for access to natural capital take hold in association with the transition from predominantly rural to more urban societies and as people migrate up the job curve from informal to formal sector employment. The transition from informal employment is especially important as this involves forging links with the full range of diversified employment opportunities provided by the formal economy and with the more extensive outreach to sources of natural capital provided by the formal economy's more diversified provisioning arrangements.

This suggests that efforts to cut poverty on a global scale, which must be based on the creation of urban employment (see later chapters), could have a dramatic impact on flows of natural capital over and above the impact that accompanies normal processes of economic growth. It also indicates why, in conditions of constrained global access to essential flows of ecological goods and services, neither growth nor poverty reduction can continue unless societies radically alter the ways in which they provision themselves.

It was this line of thinking that led me to conclude that finding ways to halt ecological decline while still meeting the provisioning requirements of societies must be made a political priority in every country of the world. But my line of thought did not end there. If growth and equity depend on access to natural capital, and if relative wealth varies with the intensity of consumption, the most successful societies must be the ones best organized to access ecological goods and services. But how do societies come to be organized to meet this basic need? Who arranged for this to happen? And how do we account for the differences that exist in how these provisioning functions are organized among today's societies?

Somehow the world has lost sight of the simple reality that all societies rely on natural capital flows and in order to survive and prosper must organize to access these flows. Perhaps this lack of awareness reflects the fact that our present arrangements to meet provisioning needs evolved so slowly and over such a long time that it is hard to trace the underlying rationale for much of what we do and for how our societies are organized. Regardless, the answer to these questions lies in the past, in the long history of the evolution of provisioning arrangements, and in the story of how past societies responded to conditions of ecological scarcity that constantly forced them – in an uneven manner and often with the assistance of new technologies – to move to new ways of organizing to meet their provisioning needs.

Thus we turn, in Part II, to a discussion of how competition for access to scarce natural capital compelled earlier societies to organize their provisioning in various ways, and how this led to the present mélange of provisioning arrangements and cultures. The discussion of how past societies coped with ecological scarcity also lays the groundwork for understanding humanity's compelling need to find new ways to provision itself in the face of ecological decline – this time on a global rather than a local or regional basis – and the very limited options for doing this.

PART II

From Common Genes to the Global Economy

How human societies evolved through five overlapping rounds in the organization of provisioning processes to reach their current situation, and the prospects for the global economy.

Chapter 3

Round One: The Spread of Hunter-Gatherer Societies

Some 3.8 to 3.9 billion years ago, long before the formation of the ozone layer that allowed land-based life forms to survive lethal ultraviolet radiation from the sun, life on earth began under water. It then took some 3 billion years to create the profusion of plants and animals that now occupy the oceans of the world. It was not until around 450 million years ago that the first plants appeared on land, followed quickly by spiders, mites, and insects. It took another 350 million years for this planet to develop the tropical rainforests in which half of all species now live.[1]

Throughout this great unfolding, biological diversity has suffered five massive global extinctions, with a sixth – human-induced eradication – now building momentum. The most notable of these, what palaeontologists call 'the great dying,' occurred 251 million years ago and eliminated an estimated 90 per cent of all ocean species and 70 per cent of all land species. This was likely caused by the after-effects of an asteroid collision. This cataclysmic event cleared the way for the evolution of dinosaurs, which were themselves wiped out – apparently by another asteroid – in the last of the extinctions some 65 million years ago.[2]

The first proto-humans appeared about 5 million years ago, and about 200,000 years ago *Homo sapiens* – or humans as we know them today – arrived on the scene.

Species are populations whose members are able to interbreed freely under natural conditions and produce fertile young. Conservative estimates of the number of known species now top out at around 1.8 million – about one-tenth (and possibly only one-hundredth) the number that evolutionary biologists believe actually live on this planet.[3]

Impressive as these numbers are, they become even more remarkable when we take into account the interactions between them. All species are linked in some way to food chains. In these chains the primary food species – the ones at the bottom – are by far the most numerous. The larger organisms above them in the chain – especially the largest or keystone species – owe their existence to the smaller life forms on which they feed. In turn, the food chains are part of complex, geographically defined ecosystems or interconnected webs of life that have taken hundreds of millions of years to evolve. Not surprisingly, given the imperfect documentation of species, the interrelationships both within and between ecosystems are not fully understood by the scientific community.[4]

Throughout these billions of years, all the species that have emerged have been the product of specific environments. The diversity of species is a result of processes that enabled established species to adapt to meet the rigours of new environments to which they migrated or were carried by ocean currents or winds or by the shifting of continental plates. This eventually led to genetic modification and to the creation of new species. As differences in micro-environments are often encountered within very short distances, most species do not have to migrate far before problems of adaptation arise. Thus, for example, 'the 10,000 known endemic species of insects on Hawaii are believed to have evolved from only about 400 immigrant species.'[5]

This adaptation process is heavily weighted against success, with the result that the survival rate of species has been almost zero – only 1 in 200 by one estimate.[6] Yet amazingly, the species that perished have been replaced by even larger numbers drawn from the survivors, and life forms, species, and ecosystems have grown steadily more complex. Despite the remarkable combinations of interacting life forms that now exist, they have not emerged in response to some preordained design; this diversity is the product of hit-and-miss processes driven by short-term survival needs and happenstance.

The drive for survival predisposes all species to spread as widely and abundantly as possible within those regions of global ecosystems to which they are genetically capable of adapting, and they survive in those regions as long as they are able to compete successfully for their food sources. This explains why many species develop highly effective forms of territorial behaviour. This is especially striking in the case of social insects, and ants in particular.

Across many parts of the East African savannah, anthills are found in seemingly geometric patterns. The reason for this is that deep underground, soldier ants from each colony are in constant battle to protect their territory and its food sources against troops from other colonies.

Ants have been around for a long time. They handily survived whatever cataclysmic event occurred to eliminate the dinosaurs. The result is that there are now some 20,000 species of them, from the Arctic Circle to the tip of South America. They comprise nearly 10 per cent of the animal biomass in the Amazon rainforest and are only slightly less abundant in the grasslands, deserts, and temperate forests of the rest of the world.[7] So it is possible to look on ants as being engaged in constant warfare with other colonies and species under the surface of every portion of open ground on which humans walk in every corner of the world.

These processes of species evolution, differentiation, and conflict over food sources and natural capital are precisely the same ones that led to the emergence of humans, the splitting of the human species into competing groups, and their eventual occupation of the planet. This global spread of hunter-gatherer societies in search of natural capital to meet the needs of their growing populations constitutes the First Round of provisioning.

While there is much scientific uncertainty about dates and classifications, it would seem that the original ancestor of humans, *Australopithecus afarensis*, emerged with a brain about the size of a chimpanzee's in the savannas and woodlands of Africa, and there began the long, slow process of co-evolving with the rest of life. About two million years ago, several man-ape populations emerged, one of which, *Homo habilis*, survived for another million years. It developed into the intermediate species *Homo erectus*, which expanded its range from Africa to Asia over one million years ago (fossils found in Java may be 1.8 million years old). *Homo erectus* had appeared in western Europe by about 500,000 BC and in China by about 400,000 BC. Shortly after that, the populations of Africa and Eurasia began to diverge with the appearance in Eurasia of Neanderthals, whose brain size exceeded that of modern humans but who still ranked as less than human.[8] Only recently, through DNA testing, has it been established that *Homo sapiens* – that is, modern humans – originated in Africa about 200,000 years ago.[9]

It has yet to be determined how humans actually evolved from primeval life forms; that said, there is no uncertainty regarding our roots in natural systems and our dependence on them. As David Suzuki points out, humans are, literally, made of air, water, soil, and sunlight.[10] Moreover, we are neatly placed in the ecosystems we inhabit by our dependence on all of these elements and by our position in food chains.

We are also linked to all of these sources of sustenance though our use of various energy forms that allow us to access, process, consume, and dispose of all that we draw from nature. 'Sunlight pours energy on the earth, and the energy gets converted from one form to another in an endless cycle of life, death and renewal.'[11] For example, photosynthesis allows plants to capture and transform solar radiation to support their growth. This process allows animals and humans to meet a portion of their food requirements. Vegetation also provides humans with vital sources of energy for cooking and heating. For thousands of years, fire (from the burning of vegetation) and human muscle power were the only energy sources available to human societies. This remained the case until agricultural and coastal societies succeeded in harnessing animal, water, and wind power. Eventually, after the mid-1700s, the world's leading economies made the transition to fossil fuels and electricity.[12]

Fire and the energy forms that followed it had a profound impact on human societies. But it took more than the mastery of fire for humans to position themselves to occupy the world. Not until 50,000 to 100,000 years after the initial migration of early humans out of Africa did the human vocal tract evolve to the point where rapid spoken language was possible (the jaw had to be shortened, the tongue had to be moved forward, and a right-angle bend had to be developed where the mouth turns down into the throat). It was only then that humans, armed with various attributes to offset their physical disadvantages (a large and versatile brain, which allowed for reflection, and speech, which expanded social interaction – the two prerequisites for rapid technological advance as well as for artistic expression, religious thought, and cultural development), could assert their full potential in the natural world.[13]

This process began about 100,000 years ago, when *Homo erectus* left the African continent. It seems that *Homo sapiens* followed in their tracks, migrating across Europe by 40,000 BC (the first fully modern people in Europe were the Cro-Magnons), through the eastern Mediterranean region and across central Asia into Australia by 40,000 to 30,000 BC, to the other islands of Southeast Asia by 33,000 BC, and to Siberia by 20,000 BC.[14]

Recent evidence suggests that humans may have reached the east coast of the Americas – presumably by boat across the Atlantic – as many as 18,000 years ago. Theories related to the origins of some languages suggest that humans may have occupied portions of these continents as many as 30,000 years ago. There is long-accepted evidence that the Clovis people crossed the Bering Strait either by boat or on foot (during the Ice Age, when a land bridge existed) to arrive in Alaska by 12,000 BC. Then, the theory goes, they spread southward at the rate of about eight miles a year until they arrived in Patagonia some two thousand years later. However, one site, at Monte Verde in Chile, suggests that people lived there at least a thousand years before the Clovis people first crossed the Bering Strait.[15]

Regardless of exactly when, the end of the First Round of provisioning was completed when hunter-gatherers arrived in New Zealand about AD 1000. In about 1/35,000 the time it took to create the tropical rainforests, humans had become the most widely dispersed keystone species in the world.

The First Round was important for the later development of human societies, because this was the time of the creation of the basic cultural and linguistic diversity from which all subsequent societies evolved. The original human settlers were likely organized into family units, clans, and possibly even tribes of hunter-gatherers, and they lived off the land by scavenging. As they developed primitive weapons and hunting techniques, they were able to hunt game animals.

The number of people able to live off a given area of land was determined by the relative abundance of food sources, the technology and hunting skills in use, and seasonal variations in climate. Once the population of a clan or tribe reached this limit, further population growth could only be accommodated through migration. As this process endlessly repeated itself, the new 'colonialists' had to adjust to their new environments. For people migrating short distances, the adjustments might not have been significant, However, as migrations took them out of forest areas and into grasslands, or across mountain ranges or bodies of water into new ecosystems, the émigrés had to acquire and master new local knowledge in order to survive.

This knowledge led to new ways to access natural capital, new words and concepts to describe and give meaning to natural phenomena, and eventually to entirely new languages, beliefs, and customs. As the ages passed, the common ancestry of these now diverse clans and tribes was forgotten, and they evolved as completely separate entities.

We will never know just how culturally diverse humans came to be during the First Round, but judging from modern-day language differences, that diversity must have been impressive. There are still some six thousand languages in the world, and some small but geographically diverse areas exhibit astonishing linguist divisions. For example, there are around 250 surviving aboriginal languages in Australia and over 100 native languages in California. At present, the absolute champion in the language diversity game is Borneo, whose people speak over one thousand languages, most of which are more distinct from one another than the eight major language groups that still persist in China.[16]

Cultural and linguistic diversity should not be confused with racial differences. Genetic variation between humans is so minuscule as to make the entire issue of race – or biological differentiation between peoples – virtually meaningless.[17] Geographically linked genetic variations exist, but most of these can be accounted for by genetic adjustments to environmental factors. For example, dark skin protects against cancer caused by higher levels of UV radiation. Overall, about 85 per cent of the limited genetic variation that does exist occurs within the same populations; variations among populations on the same continent account for another 6 per cent; differences in populations from different continents account for the remaining 9 per cent.[18]

Even so, genetic uniformity has not prevented conflict between different groups. Cultural and language differences can be strong barriers to peaceful co-operation. Certainly the relations between hunter-gatherer groups were not peaceful. Competition between peoples for access to natural capital was endemic, and conflict on the edges of tribal territories was likely a persistent reality. In this respect, most anthropologists believe that the Cro-Magnons probably wiped out the Neanderthals with whom they were competing as they spread out of Africa and that many hunter-gatherer groups learned to kill non-members on contact.[19]

This tension between culturally different groups of humans, especially in the context of competition for access to natural capital, continues to be one of the major causes of war and human waste. Indeed, even today, the prevention of conflict requires serious cultural conditioning backed by strong social confidence in the ability to secure access to requisite natural capital.

Hunter-gatherers have been described as 'the original affluent society': 'With small populations, low levels of need and expertise in a particular landscape, humans could eat well, enjoy much leisure and evidence great health of body and mind.'[20] However, with the technologies and forms of social organization available, it took virtually the entire resources of the world to allow a very small population to achieve this standard of living. With an average population density of around 0.4 per square kilometre (the density for current hunter-gatherer societies is 0.1), the world as a whole could only have supported a population of around 20 million.[21] In comparison with present population densities, this is an amazingly small figure. What is even more remarkable is that the spread of these small hunter-gatherer clans and tribes led to the greatest flowering of cultural and linguistic diversity the world will ever know.

Hunter-gatherer societies did not, of course, all continue in a pure form. The latter stages of Round One overlapped for thousands of years with the rise of agricultural societies. Indeed, by the time the last surge of hunter-gatherer expansion reached New Zealand around AD 1000, the momentum of this Second Round of provisioning – the spread of agricultural societies – had been building for some 11,000 years. In many parts of the world a spectrum of societies emerged as hunter-gatherer societies began to supplement their food requirements through agricultural activities.

Pure hunter-gatherer societies and many mixed societies were overwhelmed by the spread of stronger agricultural societies. This process would eventually eliminate hunter-gatherers from all but the most remote regions – the ones that cannot support agriculture. The squeezing down of these original clan and tribal groupings has left the modern world with a very difficult legacy: the few remaining hunter-gatherer tribes find themselves having to struggle constantly to hold on to their cultures, languages, and lands. Their efforts have generated considerable sympathy and international support. Even so, it is highly unlikely that they will succeed because of how the world is evolving. In simple terms, the needs of the world's huge population simply do not allow the luxury of providing these groups with access to the large territories they need to support their traditional ways. For example, in South Africa, after the end of apartheid, the remaining

Khoisan – the Bushmen of the Kalahari – regained some 50,000 hectares of their original territory through a successful court challenge. But this is only a fraction of the land they require, and they must rely on state charity to survive.[22]

Elsewhere, the same story prevails. Australia's aboriginal peoples are still arguing with the descendants of European settlers over land claims. In Colombia, hunter-gatherer tribes are moving toward having the government recognize their right to tribal lands and are involved with the government in mapping their claims. In Canada, land claim issues have been before the courts since 1973, and those courts are now beginning to grant aboriginal title and, in some cases, to grant extensive rights of self-government. Similar initiatives are under way across South America, the United States, Africa, and Siberia.[23] Yet few of the tribal groups involved in these negotiations have the capacity to survive in their limited domains without extensive public support.

As the world enters the urban age, the contribution of indigenous peoples to modern cultures is becoming ever harder to define. As a result, their efforts to retain their way of life are likely to run up against the shoals of widespread public indifference. In this respect, much is made of the contrast between the worldview of hunter-gatherers, which revolves around keeping the Earth as it is, and that of farming communities, whose relationship to the natural world is defined by their power to change it. Because indigenous knowledge is derived from direct experience with the natural world, it is seen as having special relevance for current attempts to reduce human impacts on the environment, and considerable effort is going into cataloguing this knowledge on a local basis. In a similar manner, the attempts being made to protect and preserve indigenous languages are often defended on the grounds that their loss would constitute a diminution of what it means to be human.

Without wishing to detract from the merit of these arguments – indeed, as discussed in Part IV, local environmental knowledge is indispensable to bio-region management – much of this thinking runs counter to the fact that the ascent of human civilizations has been based on technological advances and on what humans have created. In many respects it is this capacity to create that separates the human species from all others. Indeed, it was human ingenuity that gave the first hunter-gatherer societies the capacity to survive in formidable circumstances: it was technological innovations and the ability to gather knowledge of local ecosystems that allowed the first humans to devise methods for provisioning themselves from diverse and often harsh environments. It was also hunter-gatherer societies, not some alien population from another planet, that made the transition to settled agriculture. Moreover, many peoples across the Americas were involved in agricultural production by the time the first Europeans arrived. They were already in the process of changing their cultures. It is reasonable to assume that, had they been left to their own devices, they would eventually have converted more fully to agricultural lifestyles, with all that implies for cultural change and the elimination of hunter-gatherer options.

Thus, while a failure to advance technologically caused many hunter-gatherer societies to remain static and unchanging for long periods – to become, in Toynbee's phrase, 'arrested civilizations'[24] – many others made the adjustment to new technologies, adopted new forms of social organization, and made necessary cultural and linguistic adjustments. Many of the issues surrounding indigenous peoples, then, relate not so much to cultural change *per se*, but rather to the pace at which it happens and, more importantly, to who controls or drives it and why. And it is in this regard that the challenges facing indigenous peoples are so formidable. As population growth adds another 2 to 3 billion people to the planet's already swollen ranks, as technology ties them ever more tightly together, and as competition for access to shrinking sources of natural capital accelerates, the ability of indigenous peoples to remain outside the mainstream will be severely tested.

The world has moved away from vast tribal diversity toward greater social homogeneity through the spread of agricultural societies, the culturally conforming requirements of city life, and the centralizing power of nation-states. Some even argue that the world is about to be divided into only a handful of 'civilizations.'[25] These pressures for conformity add enormously to the challenge of maintaining older cultural values, lifestyles, and languages.

The world cannot address the needs of current and future generations by returning to simpler times. The global community must move forward to address the enormous ecological and social issues that are about to affect the well-being of billions of people. This is going to mean adopting technologies and forms of social organization that will allow humanity to address the increasingly complicated task of provisioning huge populations in conditions of global ecological scarcity.

The urban age is a scientific age. Moreover, in a world tracking toward a common humanity, the expansion of the definition of what it means to be human will come powerfully and productively from the next iterations in the evolution of technology and from forms of social organization that address the unfolding challenges to the provisioning of societies. The structured assembly and evaluation of vast quantities of data on natural systems – and especially the knowledge emerging from the operation of global ecosystems – must now shape the directions of technological and social advance.

The merits of the case for cultural survival are constantly challenged by the ever-changing demands of human survival. As populations expand, societies will have to change how they are organized to provision themselves. If indigenous cultures are to survive, they must be made relevant to these overarching global conditions. The challenge is, of course, a continuation of a long story that began thousands of years ago, when the spread of hunter-gatherers around the world was brought to a crushing halt by the Second Round of provisioning – the emergence and spread of agricultural societies.

Chapter 4

Round Two: The Rise and Spread of Agricultural Societies

Around 10,000 BC, shortly after the Clovis people crossed from present-day Siberia into Alaska and began their southward migrations, the first settled, agricultural societies began to compete with hunter-gatherer clans and tribes for the control of land. Within the space of a little more than 12,000 years, the Second Round of provisioning – the organization and spread of societies that relied on agricultural output to meet social requirements for natural capital – had eliminated much of the linguistic and cultural diversity of hunter-gatherers and confined the few surviving groups to diminishing pockets of land – land that is generally unsuitable for agriculture.

This Second Round was driven by the same processes as the first – advances in knowledge of local ecosystems and technology that led to surplus production and population growth, followed by the need to access additional natural capital to accommodate the needs of surplus populations. With rare exceptions, hunter-gatherer societies either adopted the new technologies and ways of life or were eliminated: there were few options in between.

This Second Round began in prehistory, when hunter-gatherers were first scavenging food from the wild. Over many centuries, their knowledge of local plants expanded, and they began developing a range of simple techniques for harvesting them. But it was the knowledge of how to actually plant, cultivate, and process crops and how to domesticate and breed animals that drove to the transition to settled agricultural communities.

Knowledge of how to cultivate one or two plants was not enough for societies to live off agricultural output alone. This awaited the domestication of a wide range of plants, or a wide range of plants and animals, sufficient to supply all the requirements of specific communities. This seems to be why food production arose independently only in the few regions of the world that were well stocked with plants and animals that could be domesticated. All other regions awaited the arrival of imported agricultural plants and animals – only then could the full transition occur.[1]

The evidence suggests that there were only five regions in the world with a sufficient variety of plants and animals to allow agriculture to develop independently. The first region out of the gate was the Fertile Crescent between the Tigris and Euphrates rivers, where the transition began for plants around 12,000 years ago, and for animals a few centuries later. The process began in China (notably in the Yangtze and Yellow River basins) almost as early. Then followed Mesoamerica (Mexico and northern parts of Central America) and the Andes (and possibly the adjacent Amazon Basin) around 3500 BC, and finally eastern North America around 2000 BC, some 6,000 to 8,000 years after the first agricultural societies were formed.[2]

It is possible that agriculture emerged independently in four other regions: the African Sahel (5000 BC), tropical West Africa (3000 BC), Ethiopia (indeterminate dates), and New Guinea (perhaps as early as 7000 BC). But in these cases the advance may have been triggered by the arrival of imported crops and animals. Regardless, all of the important crops and domestic animals on which modern agriculture is based were being farmed somewhere in the world by Roman times.

Agriculture brought with it profound social changes. The first and most obvious was population growth, a result of secure and surplus food supplies. Farming allowed population densities ten or even one hundred times higher than before.[3] This alone gave agriculturists a major advantage in the confrontations that subsequently arose between agricultural and hunter-gatherer societies.

Food surpluses and population growth also led to settled societies, new forms of social decision-making, and new structures of governance.[4] In densely populated agricultural communities, the egalitarianism of hunter-gatherer societies was quickly replaced by more hierarchical systems – by the leadership of chiefs and, in larger communities, of kings who ruled a number of settlements and their clan and tribal groups.

The transition to settled agricultural communities accelerated the pace of further innovation, initially in terms of farm implements. Metallurgy also began to evolve around this time. These innovations led to the diversification of labour and the creation of new occupations. For example, weaving, which dates as far back as 7000 BC, was given a tremendous push when the Mesopotamians began breeding woolly sheep a little before 4000 BC. This was followed by innovations in weaving technologies, such as the warp-weighted loom developed by the Trojans in Turkey. These advances changed the social life of agricultural societies; the making of cloth and clothing came to occupy roughly half of human labour hours in preindustrial societies.[5]

Agricultural technologies and crops did not spread quickly, and often this spread was peaceful. For example, emmer wheat, first domesticated in the Fertile Crescent around 8500 BC, took almost two thousand years to reach Greece and over three thousand years to reach northern Europe. Ancestral chickpeas, originally found only in Turkey and first domesticated around 8000 BC, took five thousand years to reach the Indian subcontinent. Sheep were first domesticated around 8500 BC in southwest Asia and pigs about a thousand years later in China, but it may have taken until around the birth of Christ for them to reach Taiwan.[6]

By and large, the globalization of agriculture was an ugly process during which huge migrations of agriculturalists and pastoralists confronted pre-existing societies and either eliminated or absorbed almost all of them.

In Europe, the impact on earlier societies was intermixed with social change arising from the further domestication of animals – in particular, from the harnessing of the traction power of oxen and (later) horses. This led to the cultivation of new lands and also to the emergence of nomadic herdsmen who were able to live off large herds of cattle, sheep, and other ruminants.[7]

Earlier hunter-gatherer societies had, of course, lived off wild herds of animals for thousands of years. The Plains Indians of North America culled buffalo, and the Lapps relied on the vast reindeer herds of northern Scandinavia. Both groups may extend back to 12,000 BC. In the mid-1900s, 30,000 Lapps still lived off a herd of over 300,000 animals.[8] But neither of these societies actually controlled or managed the herds: they merely lived off them, moving when the herds moved. In contrast, the domestication of animals involved managing them as a permanent food source, and the cultures of herdsmen were built around this changed relationship.

Horses were first domesticated in what is now Ukraine around 4000 BC. Saddles and bits to control them evolved soon after and provided nomadic herdsmen a more secure life than farming in their particular environment. The management of great herds meant that people had no need for other livelihood. Wheeled carts appeared on the steppes north of the Black and Caspian seas before 3000 BC and led to the intensive occupation and exploitation of most of the Eurasian grasslands, along with ways of life able to support large populations. The wheel added enormously to human mobility; together with the horse and metal weapons, it conferred significant military advantages on these societies.[9]

For thousands of years, waves of marauding nomads from the steppes were the scourge of peoples from Hungary to China. Perhaps these waves were induced by droughts or other natural disasters. The first such wave, around 4000 BC, when horses were still ridden bareback, involved the westward expansion of Indo-European speakers from the Ukraine. This wave seems to have replaced all earlier western European languages except Basque. Another wave occurred around 3000 BC with the founding of Troy in western Anatolia by horse-riding barbarians, ancestors of the Huns. In 1674 BC, horses enabled the Hyksos to conquer the Egyptians (who had no horses) and establish themselves temporarily as pharaohs. The Huns attacked China repeatedly for thousands of years; by 400 BC they had forced the Chinese to adopt horses as instruments of war in order to fight them. The Huns then moved westward in the fifth century AD followed by the Avars (Turkic invaders of sixth to eighth centuries AD who were eventually evicted from Hungary by Charlemagne), the Bulgars (Turkic speakers who invaded the Balkans in the seventh century), the Magyars (Finno-Ugric ancestors of modern Hungarians, in the ninth century), and Seljuk Turks in the eleventh century. Finally, the Mongol hordes overran Russia and reached and burned Budapest on Christmas Eve of 1241.[10]

These invasions, combined with the steady extension of animal and plant husbandry, dramatically changed the composition and size of European populations and the bases of European societies, languages, and cultures.

The Dark Ages in Europe that followed the collapse of the Roman Empire were marked by an almost total absence of technological advance. This contributed to the 'fossilization' of feudal agricultural practices. This most rigid form of agricultural society was based on the consolidation of land ownership in the hands of local lords and great ecclesiastical estates; clusters of dwellings were surrounded by agricultural lands cultivated by serfs.

However, major advances took place in medieval Europe. Scratch ploughs gave way to heavy, ox-drawn ploughs, which had curved mouldboards capable of turning the heavy, wet soils of northern Europe. These ploughs, initially developed by the Slavs in the sixth century, were in use in Germanic areas by the seventh century, in Viking areas by 800, and soon after that in England and Normandy. A second leap forward took place in the eighth and ninth centuries, when horseshoes and the chest harness allowed horses to be substituted for oxen. This led to a three-field system of crop rotation, which reduced the amount of land left fallow by the earlier two-field system.[11]

The development and transfer of these and other agricultural practices were aided by monastic orders, which were the medieval equivalent of agricultural R&D centres and agricultural extension services. The abbeys, of which there were an estimated 40,000, were 'models of agricultural, industrial and commercial organization ... They conducted research into agricultural and mechanical technologies, such as wind and water mills, which they were quick to adopt and share with sister organizations throughout the West. They ran schools and model farms, passing on their knowledge of breeding, crop rotation, water power and metallurgy to their surrounding communities.'[12]

These innovations, which generally involved the use of more efficient energy systems, be they animal, hydraulic, or wind, were accompanied by significant increases in food production. This led to significant increases in population density and to the migration and occupation of empty lands across Europe by surplus populations. The serfs were being freed in a process as dramatic in its day as the later colonization of America.

Europe's population surged from 40 million in AD 1000 to 48 million in 1100 and 60 million by 1200. The gains in agricultural productivity and population growth during these years freed people from the soil, led to the founding of towns and cities, and created a demand for skilled labour in the towns: for leather workers to make horse harnesses; for foundry workers to make farm implements; for masons and carpenters; and, later, for lawyers. It also broke the restrictions of feudal land management systems, which cleared the way for family farms.[13]

The same dynamics were at work across Asia. Until around 3000 BC most of tropical southeast Asia was still occupied by Stone Age hunter-gatherer societies. However, as Chinese-derived crops and technologies spread south with the migrations of Burmese, Laotians, and Thais from southern China, they overwhelmed and eradicated almost all former practices.[14] Korea and Japan maintained their cultural integrity and languages, in part because of their greater geographical isolation.

The next surge began in Africa south of the Sahara around five thousand years ago. By then, agricultural societies had been established in northern Africa based on crops and animals first domesticated in the Fertile Crescent. These had spread as far south as the Ethiopian highlands, where local peoples had also domesticated a number of plants that were unique to the region (e.g., the ensete banana, oily noog, finger millet for brewing beer, and teff, the cereal used to make Ethiopian bread).[15]

In the case of cattle, there were pastoral tribes in the Sahara between 9000 and 4000 BC, when the region was much wetter; these same peoples may have begun domesticating sorghum and millet. Cattle herding had spread south from Ethiopia into what is now northern Kenya by around 2500 BC; further expansion westward was halted by the tsetse-fly-infested areas of central Africa. Cows, sheep, and goats arrived on the northern edges of the Serengeti plain in the third millennium BC, but it took another two thousand years for them to reach southern Africa.[16]

In sum, no indigenous crops or animals had been domesticated in Africa south of the equator; agriculture had to await the migration of non-indigenous crops and livestock. The primary agents in this process were the Bantu, who had domesticated sorghum, pearl millet, and other crops in the Sahel zone of western Africa just south of the Sahara. When their population increased beyond levels that the land could support, some Bantu were compelled to move elsewhere. They began to migrate. By the last three or four centuries BC they had reached the Indian Ocean coast; by AD 500 they had reached the Fish River, some five hundred miles east of the present site of Cape Town.

The outcome of this migration was the emergence by colonial times of a number of significant, agricultural-based empires, which brought tribal clans together under the rule of chiefs or kings, who resided in central agricultural villages or towns. These groupings were made up of Bantu offshoots and local tribes that had made the adjustment to agriculture. The great cities of these empires included Kumbi-Saleh, the capital of the ancient Ghanaian empire, which had a population in medieval times of around 15,000, and Timbuktu, Djenne, and Gao in the empire of Mali. Benin and Katunga in Nigeria, both much older, emerged as capitals of territorial empires in the late sixteenth and seventeenth centuries. In the seventeenth century, Kumasi was the capital of the Asante Confederacy and Abomey was the capital of the Kingdom of Dahomey. Other cities in western and central Africa included Mbanza Kongo, capital of the Kingdom of Congo (founded before 1530), Great Zimbabwe, capital of the Rozvi Mutapa empire founded in the fifteenth century, and Bulawayo, capital of the Matabele empire.[17] These agriculture-based chiefdoms, kingdoms, and empires largely displaced the earlier inhabitants from almost all areas suitable for Bantu farming. Those displaced included the Khoi herders or Bushmen, and the San, hunter-gatherers better known as Hottentots.

By the time these agriculture-based empires were taking shape in Africa, cities dotted Europe and the boundaries of most modern nation-states were beginning to assume their present configurations. Pure agricultural societies no longer existed in Europe, and much agricultural output was being consumed in urban areas. These new nations were spreading European agricultural practices around the world and further subjugating many indigenous populations.

The last stage in this Second Round of provisioning, the arrival of fully developed European agricultural societies in the Americas, was equally cataclysmic for indigenous hunter-gatherer societies and even for those at relatively advanced stages of agricultural development, such as the Mayas, the Incas, and farmers in southeastern North America. Everywhere in the Americas, first by the Spanish and Portuguese and later by the English and French, indigenous peoples were overwhelmed, in Jared Diamond's phrase, by 'guns, germs and steel.' The few survivors were squeezed into isolated pockets of marginal land, where they struggled to survive.

As Diamond relates, agricultural societies were 'armed' with plaguelike diseases, most of which were mutations of animal diseases. Over the millennia, agricultural societies had developed resistance to these diseases. When they then introduced these diseases to populations that had never been exposed to them, the effects were catastrophic. In some parts of the Americas they eliminated up to 95 per cent of the pre-Columbian native population.[18] Disease, combined with Europeans' hierarchical forms of social organization and their military application of superior technologies, made the elimination or transformation of hunter-gatherer societies almost inevitable.

European agriculture arrived in the Americas with the colonial settlers, most of whom were farmers and brought bring their own crops with them. That said, several crops native to the Americas were exploited by the settlers and eventually found their way around the globe; these included potatoes, yams, and corn. With respect to domesticated animals, there were none in the Americas except the llama, the alpaca, the dog, and possibly the turkey. These aside, all the domestic animals currently farmed in the Americas were imported by colonial settlers.

The patterns of land ownership and exploitation established during the period of colonial occupation had profound implications for the structure of the economies of these territories, on subsequent patterns of urban growth, and on the borders of nation-states. They also strongly influenced efforts to promote economic growth. Especially in Central and South America, the Spanish and Portuguese *encomienda* system of granting local political authority to privileged settlers concentrated land ownership. This was an extension of European land-owning patterns of the time, and it led to the organization of agriculture around huge blocks of land known as *latifundia*, which relied on the semi-feudal exploitation of peasant labour.[19] The colonial intrusions into Africa and Asia were less apocalyptic but still highly disruptive of the pre-existing political and economic order. European settlers occupied prime agricultural lands, controlled decisions on crop production, and totally dominated the production of cash crops for export. Links between the large European farms and European enclaves in urban areas were tight, and investment in infrastructure was highly settler-oriented. As a result, the European presence disrupted local patterns of land holdings and production systems while producing little spin off benefit for surrounding peasant economies.[20]

The process by which agricultural innovation leads to population growth and the forced geographical expansion of elements of affected societies continues today in the form of highly mechanized, energy-intensive agricultural practices in the developed world and the transfer of these technologies in the guise of the Green Revolution to countries of the Third World. The resulting increases in food surpluses have contributed to the enormous growth in population that has occurred since the Second World War and have led to the migration of displaced rural workers into ever more marginal agricultural lands and into urban areas.

These final stages in the Second Round of global provisioning – the extension of European agricultural practices through colonial expansion and the spread of Green Revolution technologies – were completed in less than four hundred years. They ended the long, inexorable process that pushed all societies, at some point in their evolution, into heavy reliance on roughly similar agricultural technologies and practices. Pre-existing societies that made this transition by adopting the new crops, livestock, and technologies survived. The ones that didn't – those that either resisted innovation or were not given time to make necessary adjustments – were 'out-bred' and then displaced, conquered, or eliminated by force of arms or imported diseases.

Reliance on agriculture to meet provisioning needs – in particular, the way societies came to organize to meet this requirement – has left the world with unresolved challenges. The agricultural technologies that now dominate global agricultural practices have pressed the world into a Faustian bargain. They have brought about enormous increases in agricultural productivity and output, without which it would be impossible to feed the world's people. At the same time, the increased availability of food surpluses has allowed the human population to soar to its current bloated levels – levels that condemn almost half the world's people to conditions of acute or marginal poverty.

The technological advances required to feed billions of people are now an important driver in the consumption of natural capital and are wreaking havoc on regional and global ecosystems. Around 70 per cent of human water consumption goes to support agricultural production, and this draw is compromising the ability to channel water to meet urban and industrial development requirements. Chemical fertilizers and pesticides are seeping into groundwater reservoirs in every agricultural area of the world and contributing to massive algae blooms that are affecting the productivity of freshwater and marine ecosystems. The extension of agricultural lands is threatening rainforest and other biodiversity habitats and the existence of isolated indigenous populations. And agriculture contributes about 25 per cent of the greenhouse gas emissions that are contributing to global warming.

Furthermore, patterns of land ownership and agricultural production are contributing to distributional inequities within and between countries. This, as the discussion of Round Four will illustrate, has led to years of experimentation with policy approaches designed to reverse the deteriorating terms of trade facing most primary resource producers; to land reform initiatives designed to break the monopolistic control over land and allow more egalitarian development to take place; and now to an emphasis on small-scale agricultural production for export as a means of sopping up surplus rural populations.

Again, as I will explain in more detail later, the time for these kinds of approaches to deal with rural poverty and employment issues may well be over. The world has now entered the urban age; for the first time in history, more people live in urban than in rural areas. At the same time, almost all of the world's available agricultural land is now under cultivation or being used to graze animals. In these conditions, the overarching social objective must be to maximize output. As important as rural employment objectives are, the higher need for agricultural areas is to organize to produce sufficient surpluses to feed the world's people, and this means feeding urban populations. Rural development approaches that ignore this reality are likely to be frustrated by the political power of urban areas, with their growing demands for increased flows of natural capital.

Indeed, since the end of the Second World War, the most fundamental economic development challenge facing the world – and the challenge is still growing – has been how to accelerate the transition of the largely agricultural economies of newly emerging nations to modern, urban-based industrial economies. In the next section I look at the roots and nature of this challenge by tracking Round Three, the role of cities in the organization of efforts to augment flows of natural capital.

Chapter 5

Round Three: Urbanization

The Third Round of organizing to meet provisioning needs is the story of the emergence and global spread of cities and their role in securing inbound flows of natural capital and in drawing on other ecological resources to absorb urban wastes.

There is nothing natural about cities: they are human constructs. Everything in them is made from natural capital, and everyone living in them is totally dependent on access to ecological goods and services. Cities are the ultimate concentrators of natural capital consumption. They are scavengers that live off flows of natural capital derived from other regions. The relative success of cities depends overwhelmingly on how well they and their agents meet this requirement for natural capital consumption. For most of their 11,000-year history, cities have consciously organized around the task of securing inbound flows of natural capital; through migration, commerce, and war, they have both co-operated and competed with one another for access to necessary flows.

Cities are also enormous generators of the waste products that result when natural capital is processed and consumed. These wastes must be absorbed by natural systems. Problems relating to the disposal of urban pollutants have been a persistent management issue since ancient times; municipal waste disposal systems can be traced as far back as 3000 BC.

The world is now entering the urban age. For the first time ever, most of the world's people are living in urban areas, and as a result, urban demands for natural capital are the main source of stress on regional and global ecosystems. It is a paradox, then, that cities no longer play much of a role in provisioning. Round Three has long since ended, and city agendas everywhere now tend to focus on the built environment, urban infrastructure, and factors that contribute to the cultural and social well-being of residents. Most cities isolate and separate their residents from nature so that urban dwellers have little sense of their links to nature. Those who live in cities have forgotten that their lives rely on flows of natural capital.

The first permanent human settlements were established more than 15,000 years ago as fixed ceremonial meeting places. Ten to twelve thousand years ago, clusters of families began gathering in the first agricultural villages. However, for serious population growth to occur, for cities to take root, and for economic growth to begin, the world had to await advances in animal and plant husbandry that produced enough surplus to feed urban dwellers who were not directly engaged in the production of foodstuffs.

We know little about the origins of the oldest known city, Jericho, on the Jordan River, which dates from around 9000 BC.[1] It seems to predate local agriculture, although by around 6000 BC it was the centre of a vibrant agricultural region. Similarly, the ruins of Çatal Hüyük in southeastern Turkey suggest that the city flourished between 6500 and 5700 BC. Why it did is another enigma lost in the mists of time.[2]

The more certain knowledge of established cities dates back to 3000 BC in Sumer, in what subsequently became Babylonia and is now Iraq. By about halfway through the third millennium BC, other cities had appeared in the basin of the Lower Indus in Pakistan and on the islands and coastlines of the Aegean. By 1300 BC a city had been established at Anyang in China, and presumably there were others.[3]

The emergence of the first cities was a defining moment in economic history. They made it possible to create wealth through employment based on functional specialization, trade and commerce, and generalized technological advance. They also played a key role in promoting cultural and social cohesion by shaping new forms of centralized political organization and management.

Human attachment to cities is due in part to the fact that denser urban populations encourage and support the growth of specialized occupations and thus create the opportunity for mass employment. This in turn is largely attributable to the role played by technological innovation and by the effects of greater population densities on the diversification of employment opportunity. Indeed, the birth, organization, and evolution of cities have all been influenced by technological innovation and by the division of labour: specialization and its links to technologically induced productivity are urban 'inventions' that predate Adam Smith and neoclassical economics by thousands of years.

In this respect, the blossoming of the Sumerian city-states was preceded or accompanied by a wave of innovation and by the supply and use of technology-based products and services throughout society, including 'grain cultivation, the plough, the potters wheel, the sailboat, the draw loom, copper metallurgy, abstract mathematics, exact astronomical observation, the calendar, writing and other modes of intelligible discourse in permanent form.'[4]

Of perhaps even greater importance, the processes of technological innovation were given a dramatic impetus by the emergence of cities. Indeed, the systematic technological advance that the world has now come to expect would not exist without the catalytic role played by cities across the millennia in creating educational institutions and other conditions favourable to innovation.

Cities' dependence on surrounding rural areas and the need to exchange urban services for flows of rural produce influenced the initial structure of urban employment. This is revealed in the patterns of employment in Athens in the fifth century BC. Occupations ran the gamut: there were the construction trades involved in public projects; there were metal workers, who churned out implements for farmers and miners; there were 'forwarders' who helped access essential flows of natural capital; there were sailors, shipwrights, road builders, wagon makers, and drivers, who helped convey materials by sea and land. There were also weavers, cobblers, and clothiers, who dressed the citizens, and soldiers and arms makers, who helped maintain civic order and the security of trade routes.[5]

The growth and density of urban populations also created the capacity to support specialized service providers. Thus, for example, Herodotus on his visit to Egypt in the fifth century BC noted the existence of physicians for the eyes, the head, the teeth, and the belly.[6]

All cities have always had to deal with the tensions between population growth and the quality of urban life. Their relative wealth has always been a magnet for rural migrants seeking to improve their lot, yet growth adds to the challenge of provisioning. As larger populations co-opted local food and other natural capital supplies, cities were forced to secure ever larger flows of essential natural capital from more distant sources. The motto for early cities in dealing with these ever-expanding provisioning requirements and their associated tensions might be summarized thus: trade of necessity, migration when possible, war if required.

Trade quickly became the lifeblood of urban survival. The earliest cities grew around trade, and the need to protect trade routes contributed to the development of the military power of cities. From the little that is known of both Jericho and Çatal Hüyük, for example, it is clear that both were important trading centres. The Sumerian city of Ur was tiny, but its commercial and trade relationships extended from the Persian Gulf to the Indus River and up the Euphrates and Tigris into Anatolia and Kurdistan. It was characterized as 'many-tongued,' which suggests a broad range of outside contacts.[7]

A key element in these early trading arrangements was water transportation, which provided the basis for a succession of trade-based civilizations around the Mediterranean basin. These included the Minoan civilization, which flourished in Knossos and other cities and towns of Crete for almost 1,500 years before coming to a mysterious end, and the Mycenaean civilization of warrior merchants, which reached its zenith around 1250 BC in Greece.

The provisioning efforts of early cities gave the world money, writing, the principles of financial management, the mechanisms for the global exchange of ideas and technology, and the concentrations of people and wealth that were the first essential steps toward the creation of empires and nation-states.

By 3300 BC the Sumerians were exchanging clay tokens for goods. This led to the development of commercial economies based on the use of money.[8] Coin minting was developed in western Asia Minor and the Aegean around the last decade of the eighth century. The use of coinage spread to Greece in the seventh century and to Sicily and southern Italy in the sixth century. By around 500 BC Athens had an important mint.[9] The use of money to facilitate the exchange of goods led to the introduction of interest, which allowed the financing of trade. By the end of the fifth century Athens had banks, stock exchanges, pawn and personal credit facilities, and a primitive double-entry bookkeeping system.

The need to record trade transactions may have led to the invention of writing.[10] It seems the earliest 'writing' was Sumerian cuneiform, whose logograms were initially restricted to the naming, numbering, and measuring of things. The oldest recovered cuneiform tablets are mainly clerical records. One of the first alphabetic scripts was developed by the Phoenicians around 1100 BC. The Greeks developed their own alphabet around the middle of the eighth century BC.

Trade relations between cities helped spread ideas and technologies between cultures. The earliest benefits of this exchange involved the spread of agricultural crops, domestic animals, metallurgy, and maritime and weaving technologies. These transfers became an integral part of all trading arrangements. The Mongols brought Chinese inventions like gunpowder to Europe. Nowadays, technologies, scientific information, and cultural exchange are all facilitated by global trade and intercity electronic communication networks.

As greater demand forced outreach to more distant and diversified sources of natural capital, the organizational requirements of provisioning became more complex. As it became more difficult to manage these flows on a centralized basis, the focus of effort shifted to meeting differentiated market demand. This required a merchant class, and the concomitant rise of the profit motive in daily life. No longer did cities consciously organize to mange the task of provisioning in ways that contributed to the quality of urban life.

But cities are more than mere crucibles of economic growth. They are also places where people mingle, live, and enjoy life. When people in early societies began living closer together, it altered the cultural and political landscape. The expanded social interaction that takes place in cities tempers antisocial behaviour and contributes to a sense of common humanity. Thus, cities became the great cultural integrators.

The first cities were the inheritors of earlier tribal divisions and had to devise means of governance capable of overcoming these divisions. Cities can tolerate diversity, but only within limits: people can speak a thousand different languages in a well-functioning city, provided they also speak a common language. Thus, city life breaks down the narrowness and ethnic cohesion of village and rural life.

It was in cities that individuals could transcend the ties of tribe in exchange for a broader allegiance to king or city or empire or religion.[11] It is not surprising, then, that hierarchical forms of political and religious authority quickly evolved to meet the requirements of more structured urban economies.

The loose chiefdoms and kingships of decentralized agricultural village communities were replaced by the concentrated power, wealth, and privilege of urban kings and by the harmonization of diverse religious beliefs into greater unities. All the new forces of civilization were 'brought under the control of the palace and temple ... Power was incorporated in the military and in the organized control of communal life: kings assumed the power to command, to seize property, to kill or destroy and to extract wealth from trade or through the spoils of war.'[12]

The concentration of wealth and the will to use it helped build commitment to the city and helped, also, to shape urban cultures through investments that gave expression to civic pride and cultural and religious beliefs. Many of these investments were in public works and architecture. The evidence of this can be seen in everything from the vast irrigation systems developed by Ur, by regions in China, and by the Mayan and Aztec civilizations, to public investment in the art and culture of Athens, citizen sponsorship of gladiatorial contests in Rome, the building of palaces to reflect the glory of nobles and royalty, the construction of cathedrals, mosques, and temples to reflect the glory of religion, and the civic sponsorship of Michaelangelo and the Renaissance.

Strong reminders of this once dominant cultural attachment to cities are visible today with respect to public and philanthropic support of the arts and investments in recognizable architectural accomplishments. These have become sources of civic and national pride. The Empire State Building in New York, the Eiffel Tower in Paris, the Guggenheim Museum in Bilbao, Spain, and the Petronas Towers in Kuala Lumpur are such symbols. In Shanghai, an 1110-metre Bionic Tower is now being designed: the three-hundred-story complex will house 100,000 people. If built, it will be a public works project on a scale not seen since the construction of the Great Wall of China.[13]

The shaping of culture and political organization, the hosting of technological advance, the creation of wealth through trade and commerce, and the generation of mass employment through functional specialization are common attributes of all cities, and always have been.

Provisioning Cities: From Ur to the Fall of Rome

The relationship between a city's success and flows of natural capital to it has become more obscure as cities have grown and as urban management issues have become more diversified and challenging. However, the relationship can be seen clearly in how cities were organized in the 3,500 years between the emergence of the first Sumerian city-states and the fall of the Roman Empire.

Throughout this period, cities were largely defined by their relationship to nature. They were in theory, if not always in practice, designed to maintain harmony with their hinterlands, and their history was very much the story of how they organized people's energies so as to secure necessary flows of natural capital. In this respect, the primary challenge they faced was how to assemble and discipline peasant labour on a grand scale. This required the centralizing authority of kings, supplemented by the moral authority of religion – the omnipotent power of a god-king.[14]

Egypt, the first city-based civilization, and Sumer and Akkad, the world's first city-based empire, both came into being in response to the organizational requirements of living 'within' nature. The task of 'provisioning' their growing urban populations required that land management be placed under the control of strong, broadly supported political entities. The results were the first efforts in history at integrated bio-region management.

Geographically isolated by deserts and hills, Egypt was a self-contained society that depended on agriculture. Survival demanded that large pools of labour be mobilized to build dikes, canals, and irrigation ditches to regulate the flow of the Nile. Thus, when King Narmer united the communities of the upper and lower Nile around 3100 BC, the primary task of governing was to organize people in a common effort to irrigate and cultivate the land. The ancient Egyptian civilization was created around the world's first river basin management system.[15]

In contrast to the relative peace in Egypt, the cluster of sovereign city-states in Sumer were constantly engaged in disputes over access to land and water that often led to war. This situation prevailed until it was brought to at least a temporary halt by the dominance of one city-state, Ur, and the creation of an empire. This was quickly followed by the construction of large-scale irrigation works that allowed the communal sharing of water on a regional basis. By 2700 BC, irrigated fields were sustaining tens of thousands of people.[16]

But it was in the organization, philosophical underpinnings, and challenges of the Greek city-states that the social consequences of outreach were really clarified. Between the eighth and sixth centuries BC, a new urban fabric took shape in the Aegean. This was the time when the Greeks developed the ideas of art and politics that would so influence Western civilization. These ideas found expression in the *polis*, or city, 'the place where people come together ... consciously, in pursuit of a better life.'[17]

The Greek cities were states in the sense that they legislated, levied taxes, spent public money, had borders, and waged war. City and state were one and the same. It was in the *polis* that political power was located and that the arts flourished, and it was the *polis* to which people owed their allegiance. The Greeks believed that human creativity and productivity required, almost as a matter of human nature, that people live in cities – albeit cities of limited size. According to Aristotle, direct democracy (the precursor of modern representational democracy) could only be exercised by fairly small populations. Thus he defined his notion of the appropriate size of a city as 'the largest number which suffices for the purposes of life, and can be taken in at a single view.'[18]

In more practical terms, the size of the original Greek *polis* was also a result of geography. Greek cities tended to be small, and isolated from one another by mountains. They were based on the unity of city and countryside, and most were self-sufficient in the sense that they could draw their food and necessary resources from the surrounding region, thus maintaining the urban/rural balance that is lost with large-scale urban growth.

The Greeks' preferred approach for dealing with the limitations of local agriculture and other resources was the forced emigration of poor peasants, who established new towns and colonies that paid tribute to the sponsoring city-state.[19] The point of controlling city growth by orderly colonization, to take place as often as numbers warranted, was to prevent conflict over land while maintaining the quality of urban life.

Beginning around 775 BC, agricultural pressures and commercial ambition spread the Greek *polis* and culture from Nauxratis in Egypt to Marseille in Gaul, and from Sicily to the farther shores of the Black Sea.[20] The biggest colonizing cities were the great commercial centres such as Rhodes and Miletus. Émigrés from the latter apparently set up seventy urban colonies. In the fourth century BC, Alexander the Great established colonies and founded towns and cities built on the Greek model from Alexandria in Egypt to such far-flung places as Gandhara (Peshawar) in the Indus valley in Pakistan and Bactria in Central Asia.[21]

By around the middle of the sixth century BC, most accessible land in congenial climates was already occupied, deforestation had altered much of the landscape, and cities had no option but to turn to trade in order to provision their bloated populations. By 775 BC the Greeks were already engaged in limited but widespread trade throughout the eastern Mediterranean and with the Etruscans in Italy. Trade expanded rapidly between the sixth and fourth centuries BC, when the economy of the region was booming.[22] The success of these provisioning efforts was aided by a number of innovations, including the lever, the pulley, the cogged wheel, and the vertical axle, which enabled rotating mills to grind flour using animal power.[23]

As a matter of principle, foreign trade was only permissible if the city lacked natural resources. Trade was looked down on, and citizens, by definition, could have no part in commerce. Thus responsibility for trade was lodged with foreign traders or 'Metics.' As the requirements for trade grew, it was the non-citizens – the craftsmen and the traders – who created the surpluses that allowed the aristocracy to lead its leisured life.

The tensions between population growth, the requirements for natural capital, and the quality of urban life eventually caught up with and radically altered many Greek city-states. Ideas about ideal city size broke down in the face of the relentless dynamic of urban growth. There were hundreds of city-states in Greece, but most were small. In the fifth century BC, a city of 10,000 was considered 'great.' Only a handful ever had populations over 40,000. Athens, where the greatest achievements of the Greek city-states were found, experienced the most rapid population growth and itself became the core of a great trading empire, especially after the fourth and third centuries BC. [24] At its peak around 42 BC, Athens had a population between 215,000 and 300,000: 110,000 to 180,000 citizens, 25,000 to 40,000 resident aliens and Metics, and between 80,000 and 110,000 slaves.

As the regional farm population declined and the problem of provisioning citizens became more acute, Athens began importing vast quantities of foodstuffs and materials from diverse sources – fish from the Hellespont, beef from Italy or Thessaly, fruit and spices from a variety of sources, grains from around the Black Sea, Egypt, Sicily, and Italy, and timber from Macedonia. Attica as a whole imported three-quarters of its cereal needs.[25] As summed up by Pericles, 'because of the greatness of our city, the fruits of the entire earth flow in upon us.'[26]

The Athenian ideal of citizenship weakened dramatically as the city's population grew and trade expanded. The Sophists began to preach the doctrine of individualism. As early as the fourth century, Plato, a precursor to today's antiglobalists, complained that 'they have filled the city with harbours and dockyards and walls and tributes instead of with righteousness and temperance.'[27]

It seems that the focus of effort had shifted away from commitment to the *polis* and managing its relationship with the hinterland toward meeting the need for natural capital through trade and deriving wealth from it. But it was not the pursuit of profit or trade that eroded the ideals of Athenian democracy. Rather, it was the loss of local self-sufficiency and the need to access ever more distant sources of natural capital to provision a growing urban population.

The Roman Empire, which was initially motivated by Greek ideals, followed the same course: it established colonies that sent their surplus production back to Rome. However, the Romans relied more heavily than the Greeks on slave labour to meet their provisioning requirements. One estimate suggests that in AD 28, some 3 million slaves (versus only 4 million free people) maintained the agricultural and road infrastructure of the Romans' predatory provisioning system.[28]

In imitation of the Greek ideal of local self-sufficiency, important Roman cities and colonial towns were deliberately planned for around 50,000 people. As part of a policy of wide dispersal, the empire became a huge city-creating machine. Many of the more than 5,000 civic bodies it established were little more than villages; the total population of all of them likely peaked at around 17,500,000. Yet the growth of Rome, like that of Athens before it, could not be contained, and at its peak the city contained around one million people.[29] As this happened, the civic ethos shifted from social harmony to commerce. And, like Plato before him, Cicero railed against those tempted far from home by 'soaring hopes and dreams' of commercial profit and blamed the 'lust for trafficking' for the downfall of Corinth and Carthage.[30]

To provision this population, besides exacting tribute from its colonies, Rome traded to the far corners of its empire and far beyond. Early in Roman times, for example, the Silk Road became an established trade route linking the Empire to the Han Dynasty (202 BC to AD 220). Chinese silk, fashionable among the patrician women of Rome, was exchanged for among other things multicoloured glass vessels (developed about 3000 BC in Mesopotamia) and blown glass (invented by the Romans in the first century BC).[31]

From the perspective of social provisioning, the outreach model established by the Greeks and Romans is one of the lasting legacies of the early cities. It is also one of the most unflattering, as it involved exploiting distant territories while allowing the balance and harmony of nearer relationships with nature and the land to languish.

Provisioning Cities: From Feudalism to the Information Age

After the Roman Empire collapsed around AD 400, other civilizations rose to fill the leadership vacuum. Byzantium, the eastern portion of the empire, operated out of Constantinople (now Istanbul) and remained a major commercial centre for another thousand years. Islamic civilizations flourished throughout the Arab world and North Africa, and other civilizations came and went across the Old World, Asia, and the Americas. In Christian Europe the chaos left by the fall of Rome led eventually, and painfully, to the establishment of feudal societies by around AD 800. From this point on, the role of cities in provisioning societies was influenced most strongly by events in Europe; however, the provisioning process is more difficult to identify. The evolution of cities was driven more consciously by commercial and political interests than by any direct concern with provisioning or with the quality of urban life.

As noted in the discussion of Round Two, after the tenth century, static feudal societies were broken by the technological innovations spread by monastic orders. The productivity gains and population surges accompanying these innovations led to the colonization of much of Europe as freed serfs sought to claim land for themselves. As this process unfolded, Europe found itself covered with towns and agricultural villages, which quickly evolved into the cities that gave Europe its urban definition.

These new towns developed slowly during the tenth and eleventh centuries and then at an astonishing rate through the twelfth and thirteenth centuries – three thousand popped up in Germany alone. They were generally small. Some were little more than walled villages, most likely had populations of around 3,000, and few exceeded 10,000. But many, such as Venice with a population of 64,000 and Paris with 30,000, grew to become towns of a new and unprecedented kind. This was the medieval city, which 'like the yeast in some mighty dough, brought about the rise of Europe.'[32]

These cities differed from agricultural settlements in terms of both their permanence and their organization. Most were built around trade and industry and were located conveniently near roads and waterways. They became centres for exchanging goods, and this led to the rise of a new merchant class, the beginnings of a new era of specialized production, and the appearance of a new class of skilled craftsmen, the freest of which were the 'masons' who built the buildings, bridges, and infrastructures of the towns. These masons also roamed Europe building the cathedrals that were the architectural expression of the new wealth of the age and of the continuing role played by religious orders.

Strong intercity trading networks were established that linked the cities of the eastern Mediterranean with Italy and northern Europe. At the same time, a trade route through Kiev linked Scandinavia with the Mediterranean. 'This expansion of commercial life, supported by agricultural prosperity and combined with the increase in population, brought a renaissance of urban life unparalleled since the days of the Roman Empire'[33] – one that would not be replicated again until after the Industrial Revolution.

In every sense, the economic awakening of the West that accompanied these dramatic changes and that led to the breakdown of feudal society was a small business revolution.[34] It was aided by the idea of 'incorporation,' which first took hold in northern Italy and Flanders in the ninth century, spread slowly across Europe, and finally reached England in the twelfth century. Incorporation allowed the creation of independent enterprise, for both individuals and towns. It meant that workers were free to sell their labour and farmers their produce. It led to family farms and the emergence of entrepreneurial craftsmen (saddlers, armourers, tailors, glazers, cutlers, and so on).

This process led to the creation of guilds, which quickly became the basis around which city governments were organized. The guilds were originally syndicates 'of the town's business owners incorporated to defend their privileges, maintain prices and keep out competition.'[35] They first emerged in Florence in the tenth century, and from there spread rapidly, reaching England in the early 1200s. The guilds divided and subdivided into specialized craft units as the economies of towns grew; each guild reflected the relationship between the 'master' who owned a shop and the journeymen and apprentices who lived and worked in that shop. During this era, the merchant class of 'owners' gradually evolved into a new middle class. The fortunes of this middle class became entwined with 'the churchmen, anxious to appropriate the new wealth to God's purpose and the noble men, eager to profit from and control the new economy.'[36]

This small business era was soon enough overtaken by the Commercial Revolution, which began in the twelfth century with the regional dominance of trade by city-states and ended on the eve of the Industrial Revolution with the initial trading networks of colonial empires. Trade associated with cities reached its peak in the late thirteenth and early fourteenth centuries as the older Mediterranean trading networks were increasingly tied by land and sea to the newer, intercity trade networks of northern Europe.[37]

This period was marked by the division and co-ordination of production functions across borders and by the establishment of civic trading activities and large, family-owned companies backed by the power of both city-states and the church. The growth of these trading enterprises was supported by the emergence of sophisticated banking and investment mechanisms, by new forms of corporate organization, and by technological advances – especially in navigation and shipbuilding.

The transformations of the commercial era began in Venice at the end of the twelfth century during the early years of the Renaissance. One of a number of city-states in northern Italy, Venice was a modest trading centre for the exchange of goods between Europe, Constantinople, Syria, and Alexandria, as well as a regional shipbuilding centre. Its commercial and trading activities were highly centralized under the control of the Doge and a dozen or so leading merchant families.

An innovation that helped transform this city-state was a novel method for sharing risk in the financing of ships and expeditions. 'Merchants divided the cost of the vessel and expeditions into twenty four carets (shares), taking some themselves and selling the rest to other merchants,' who would then share in the risk and in the profit of successful ventures.[38]

Through its involvement in the Fourth Crusade, which led to the sacking of Constantinople, Venice gained a series of outposts that gave the city control of the eastern Mediterranean shipping lanes and a monopoly over trade with the East. This model of empire allowed for the protection of trade routes; it also provided 'colonies, including the fertile island of Crete, which became consumers of Venetian products and providers of wines, grains and materials.'[39] Following on the invention of the stern rudder and the example set by Genoa, a rival city-state, Venice began to trade with northern Europe by sailing out and around the Strait of Gibraltar to Britain and Flanders. With its monopoly of eastern Mediterranean trade, ensured by its outposts and colonies, it remained a world power well into the eighteenth century.

While Venice was laying claim to its empire in the Levant, the Renaissance was helping propel Florence into the front ranks of mercantile powers. In contrast to the highly centralized, state-run Venetian model, the commercial revolution that emanated from Florence toward the end of the thirteenth century was more democratic. It was led by a new class of merchant bankers. 'About 1275, a number of highly successful patrician merchant families, among them the Bardi, Peruzzi and Frescobaldi, expanded into banking, establishing networks of agents, or factors, in the Italian city-states and throughout the East and Europe.'[40] Others joined this group, including the Albertis and then, in the early 1300s, the king of banking families, the Medici. Originally one of seventy-two merchant banking firms in Florence, the Medici levered their close association with the Catholic Church into 'not only the most successful commercial enterprise in Italy, but the most profitable family business in the whole of Europe.'[41]

The Medici banking business is often referred to as the first MNE. However, by the end of the fourteenth century there were as many as 150 Italian banking companies operating in the international arena. By 1340 the Bardi family had 1,209 foreign agents representing it in cities from Seville to Bruges in Europe and around the Mediterranean, and a Prato merchant had records showing he did business in two hundred cities.[42]

Key to the success of Florentine merchants was their domination of Europe's wool and cloth-finishing industry. Wool was imported from England, finished in Florence to a high standard, and then re-exported for consumption by the wealthy across Europe. The innovation in all this came not so much from technology but rather from organization. The work was performed at different stages by unrelated companies, all of them co-ordinated by an entrepreneur.[43]

During this period, the wealth of these mercantilist cities vastly surpassed that of the greatest business centres of the classical world. However, even while the urban character of Europe was being confirmed, the boundaries of nation-states were being stabilized. The centralization of political power in nation-states necessitated the creation of capital cities, and external trade links were increasingly between these national cities, which slowly came to command the main trade routes. Thus, the capital cities became great commercial centres as well as the locus of military and state planning. During this period, city-based enterprises were literally scouring the globe to access natural capital and other industrial inputs.

Amsterdam was one of the first national capitals to benefit from the commercial revolution. The city was linked through canals to the world's most efficient agricultural system; it was further linked, through other provisioning routes, to central Europe in one direction and to the sea in the other. By the mid-1600s the Dutch fleet 'was larger than those of Spain, Portugal, France, England, Scotland and Germany combined.'[44] The city had a stock exchange and a banking system, both modelled on their Italian precursors; it also had investors willing to finance expeditions. To support these ventures, local businessmen had developed a system of newspapers to provide investors and traders with information on commercial developments elsewhere in the world.

By the eve of the Industrial Revolution, London had become the great merchant city of the world. The city's dynamism was increasingly being driven by the rise of a new commercial middle class that was anxious to partake of economic opportunity and thus focused on breaking down the monopolistic control of kingly rule and aristocratic cliques as well as the trade-shackling constraints of the guilds. The British commercial fleet doubled in size between 1580 and 1630 and had undergone a further three-fold increase by 1690,[45] when its ships were exploring the known limits of the globe and drawing bounty from it. Not surprisingly, the growth in the numbers of the rich and the privileged during these years was impressive. One estimate has it that between 1576 and 1642 their absolute numbers 'rose by about 70 per cent and by about a quarter as a proportion of the total population.'[46] Thus, as had happened with Athens and Florence in earlier times and more recently with its rival Amsterdam, commercial success was leading London toward a new urban system based on merit and private enterprise – tendencies that were accelerated by the Industrial Revolution.

The roots of the Industrial Revolution in Britain are to be found in the wealth garnered during this brief but intense commercial revolution that preceded it. Necessity also played a role, for Britain was engaged in a 'desperate quest for alternatives to rapidly diminishing timber resources [and was forced to turn] to iron as a substitute building material and to coal as a substitute fuel.'[47] Britain was not alone in having to find alternatives to wood, an increasingly scarce energy source. In France, regulations requiring the replanting of harvested trees had been introduced in the mid-1500s and 'the cutting, transport and sale of wood was regulated by city ordinance in 1672': by 1723 'a royal edict banned the cutting of trees less than ten years old.'[48] However, in the race to exploit coal as a new energy source, England had a distinct advantage, as its reserves were both abundant and easily accessible.

The dramatic shift in the mid-1700s toward industrial and civil reliance on coal to meet energy needs marked the beginning of the modern era's dependence on fossil fuels. It also helped inspire the invention of the steam engine, which symbolically signalled the beginning of the Industrial Revolution. The enormous potential of this technology to power factories and to revolutionize transportation ushered in a new age that continues today – one in which wealth and economic development are created mainly through technological innovation rather than through the exploitation of land and natural resources. Furthermore, in the first century of economic and population growth following the onset of the Industrial Revolution, the increases in provisioning requirements did much to drive the competition among European powers for the acquisition of colonial possessions.

While technological change had always played a part in social transitions, the sheer scale of innovation that occurred after 1780 had no precedent. Nor did the scale of wealth that this technological revolution created and the extent of social change that flowed from it.

As the process of replacing human labour with steam-powered machinery began in earnest, invention spawned invention with dramatic results. A 300 per cent increase in worker productivity between 1750 and 1825 led to massive increases in cotton output. Similar increases in coal, iron, and other sectors followed. Meanwhile, the mechanization of agriculture had begun. The new technologies precipitated dramatic changes in the structure of industry: decentralized, highly structured and organized handicraft industries gave way to large-scale factory production in specific industrial towns.

The growing importance of international commerce from the fifteenth century on had begun to break down the monopoly of city-based craft guilds and the prerogatives of the aristocracy; the Industrial Revolution destroyed both. This led to the final overthrow of feudal estates, the increasing separation of church and state, and – of paramount importance – the abolition of the guilds and the rise of the middle class.

The impact of all of these changes on cities was enormous. On the one hand, they helped ring the final death knell of city autonomy by turning cities into dependencies of states. On the other, they elevated the place and importance of cities and launched the world toward an urban future. In the Middle Ages, cities had blossomed as a result of population surges accompanying gains in agricultural productivity. The changes brought about by the Industrial Revolution now caused cities to explode.

Based in large part on the wealth generated by commercial success and on the increases in food supply made possible by new agricultural technologies, Europe experienced another huge population surge. From about 200 million Europeans at the time of the Napoleonic wars, the population had tripled to 600 million by the First World War. Europe's population rose from about one-sixth of the global total to about one-third in a little over a century.[49]

As agriculture was mechanized and output per acre rose, rural populations drained into the rapidly growing industrial cities in search of jobs in the huge new factories. After 1830, the railways accelerated this process by massing urban growth around coal-producing areas and by promoting a thickening of populations around main railway junctions and export terminals. European societies were transformed from predominantly rural to overwhelmingly urban.

As the full effects of the Industrial Revolution took hold in Britain in the latter half of the nineteenth century, London became the greatest city the world had ever seen. From perhaps 200,000 people in 1600 (roughly 4 to 5 per cent of the total population) it had passed the one million mark by around 1810, hit 2,363,000 forty years later, and doubled again to 4,536,000 in 1901. If the full area of Greater London was included, the population was 6,500,000, or about 20 per cent of the country's total population. Paris grew almost as quickly. From perhaps 450,000 on the eve of the Industrial Revolution, it grew to 1.3 million in 1850, to nearly 2 million in 1870, to 3.3 million in 1900. In 1800 there were no cities in the world with populations over a million. By 1900 there were eleven, including Berlin, Chicago, New York, Philadelphia, Moscow, St Petersburg, Vienna, Tokyo, and Calcutta. By 1930 there were twenty-seven.[50]

A tidal wave of immigrants from Europe doubled America's population between 1870 and 1900, with most of the immigrants settling in the continent's rapidly expanding cities. At the same time, America's home-grown population was migrating toward the same urban areas. American cities were strutting their stuff in a dramatic illustration of the capacity of cities to generate mass employment. 'In 1870, more than two-thirds of America's workers were engaged in occupations other than manufacturing – agriculture, forestry and fishing. Ten years later these pursuits claimed only 59% of the workforce. By 1910 only one-third of the workforce was still farming, logging or fishing for a living. The number of wage earners in manufacturing grew from 1.3 million in 1860 to 5.3 million in 1890.'[51]

The effects of these changes on the rural/urban population distribution were equally dramatic. In 1870, only one out of every five Americans lived in a city with eight thousand or more inhabitants. By 1900 the proportion was one out of three; by 1920 fully half of Americans were living in cities.[52] This process has been accelerated by all subsequent technological innovations, so that today over 80 per cent of Americans are urban dwellers.

Innovation, like private enterprise, takes root in the social fabric of cities. The Industrial Revolution again reconfirmed the place of cities as the loci of technological advance. The unique characteristics of cities such as Manchester and Glasgow were instrumental in shaping the innovations that led to the Industrial Revolution. Again, during the later stages of that revolution, unique urban characteristics favoured Detroit in the competition for the home of the automobile industry.[53]

In a similar fashion, but more by conscious design, Berlin grew in the early twentieth century to become the most concentrated locus of R&D and technological innovation in the world. This won it global leadership in technological innovation – a position it enjoyed until the Second World War.[54]

As the Information Revolution began to take hold in the late 1970s and older manufacturing centres began to move investments into advanced technology manufacturing and service industries, technology growth poles again led the processes of economic advance. These new growth poles create comparative advantage through their concentrations of people skills, R&D capacity, and investment capital. These tasks are facilitated by the existence of educational facilities, relevant supplier industries, and communication and transportation infrastructures that link the growth poles to markets.

As in the past, the present global economy ties cities together in the framework of business networks far more than it does nations. Commerce and technology tie growth poles together in ways that now define the great challenges facing cities as the world enters the Urban Age.

Between 1950 and 1990 the population of the world's cities grew ten-fold, from roughly 200 million to over 2 billion, with most of the growth occurring in the Third World. The pace of growth of specific Third World cities has been mind-numbing. In less than a hundred years, for example, Mexico City's population has soared from around 100,000 to over 20 million, with most of the growth taking place since 1950. In the 1990s the world saw the number of cities with populations in excess of 5 million grow from thirty-five to fifty-seven, with all of the increase in the Third World.[55]

Not surprisingly, this rate of growth has overwhelmed the urban infrastructure of most Third World nations and has polarized urban populations on the basis of relative wealth. Most Third World cities, and some cities in industrialized nations, are being divided into well-off enclaves linked through advanced infrastructure and investment to global business networks and markets and vast, sprawling, un-planned, filthy, impoverished, and unhealthy peri-areas where most people work in the informal economy. The growth of these peri-areas is largely uncontrolled and outside the framework of normal city plan-ning. The people living in them lack potable water and access to hard infrastructure. They are poorly supplied with municipal services from education to health care to policing.

The divides between wealthy enclaves and the peri-areas are taking on cultural overtones: people are becoming separated not only by differences in lifestyles and amenities but also by technology, educa-tional achievement, economic opportunity, and expectations.

Rapid population growth in Europe and America after the onset of the Industrial Revolution had similar effects. The Poor Laws enacted in Britain in the mid-1800s and the need to provide housing for the poor in New York attest to the difficulties these cities faced in adjust-ing to rapid industrialization and population growth. However, the scale of urban growth now taking place is simply unprecedented, and the challenges facing the world's exploding cities defy comparison with past urban challenges.

The population of New York, for example, more than doubled from 1.5 to 3.4 million between 1870 and 1900, in part through the annex-ation of adjacent municipalities. It doubled again over the next forty years when another 4 million where added.[56] In contrast, Shanghai may add 5 million people to its base population of 13 million in a little over a decade.[57] In 1996, Mexico City added 70,000 people per month, or 840,000 people over the year.[58]

Estimates of the numbers of people now living in abject urban pov-erty generally exceed 600 million. There may be as many as 100 mil-lion unemployed roaming the streets of China's cities. Yet the imbalances, apparent misery, and often poor employment prospects have not dampened the irresistible lure of city life and wealth, and often with good reason: urban growth is producing huge benefits for enormous numbers of people.

And that, in a nutshell, summarizes the dilemma facing the world with respect to the place and role of cities in enhancing human welfare. It is only in cities that the needs of huge populations can be met. It is cities that give hope for a better future for the impoverished masses of the world. Yet it is also in cities that the great social, economic, and above all ecological challenges of the coming decades will arise, and it is in cities that solutions must be found.

These challenges begin with the fact that the current projections of global population growth, together with the expected rise of urban populations to 60 per cent of the total, could add 3 billion more urban residents by 2025. Almost all of this growth will occur in Third World countries, and especially in the already bloated cities of Africa and southeast Asia.

Most of those migrating to cities will begin their transition to urban life in the impoverished peri-areas of major cities. Thus, most of the growth in urban populations will have to be accommodated in those portions of urban areas already seriously deficient in infrastructure, social services, and job opportunities and separated from their more favoured neighbours in wealthy enclaves by growing cultural divides. Moreover, this growth will have to be managed in roughly half the time it took for the world to add the previous 2 billion urban residents.

As the example of Shanghai illustrates, there are hopeful signs that some cities may be able to absorb these increases. However, the ability of global ecosystems to supply the flows of natural capital to support urban growth and to reduce urban poverty is another issue entirely.

Cities of the twenty-first century will be the dominant habitat for humankind, yet they are imprisoned in the legacy of ancient times. Like hunter-gatherer and agricultural societies before them, cities were born and continue to exist in the tight relationship between humans and their technological and organizational capacities to secure flows of natural capital. Cities are now the great concentrators of natural capital consumption. Like Athens and Rome before them, they have outgrown local sources of natural capital and are reaching out to global ecosystems to meet their provisioning needs. Cities are driving the environmental crisis. Like ink blots spreading out over the world from thousands of black wells, cities are obliterating local sources of natural capital and extending their ever-lengthening provisioning tentacles into the distant edges of global ecological envelopes.

It is in cities that the great equity and ecological issues of the next twenty-five years will arise, that solutions will have to be found, and that the challenge of global ecological decline will eventually have to be addressed. Yet, primary responsibility for provisioning human populations long ago passed from cities to nation-states and then to global, private-sector business networks. To show how and why this situation arose, in the next section I look at the origins and evolution of Round Four, the rise and spread of nation-states and their role in provisioning societies.

Chapter 6

Round Four: From City-States to Nations

The Fourth Round of global provisioning involved the rise of nation-states and the evolution of their role in securing access to essential flows of natural capital.

The first 'nation' in the modern sense of the word may have been China, whose autonomous regions were forcefully united under Emperor Ch'in Shih Hwangti in 211 BC. A similar transition may then have occurred in Korea, followed by Japan, which framed its first national constitution in AD 604.

The global spread of nations truly began with events in Europe in the Middle Ages. The gains in European agricultural productivity that led to population surges and the founding of cities after AD 1000 prepared the ground for the subsequent division of the continent into nation-states. At the end of the fifteenth century the nation-states of Europe were still more geographical configurations than the generalized national cultures we associate with nation-states today. The boundaries of these nations were not 'natural' in the sense of containing coherent, unified peoples. The task of moulding ethnic diversity into unified national cultures and creating a strong sense of national identity took many more generations, and the powerful influence of the Commercial and Industrial revolutions, to accomplish.

The spread of nation-states accelerated rapidly after the Second World War as colonial territories were granted full independence and began trying to replicate the institutions and infrastructures of strong, sovereign nations. The collapse of the Soviet Union in the early 1990s added another group of nations to the global community and a number of nation-states are still grappling with the demands of their ethnic minorities for autonomous statehood. Nevertheless, by the end of the twentieth century the idea of nationhood had swallowed up all of humanity. Everyone on the planet now belongs to one nation-state or another.

All nation-states are cultural mixing pots. They seek to cultivate a sense of common cultural identity, which means that minority languages and cultural diversity cannot flourish within them. Like the rise and spread of agricultural societies and cities before them, the global spread of nation-states has further reduced human diversity and is putting constant pressure on the diversity that remains. The broad outline of change has seen the five hundred proto-states of Europe reduced to around twenty-five nations, and the thousands of clan and tribal cultures and languages that exist around the world have been integrated into around two hundred nation-states and a much smaller (and shrinking) number of official national languages.

Throughout this evolution, nation-states gradually assumed primary responsibility for provisioning their citizens. Cities fought against this, but the complexity of the arrangements required to access ever-more distant sources of natural capital came to require greater economic and military capability than cities and surrounding regions could mobilize. Nation-states slowly took over control of these outreach arrangements and extended their national provisioning efforts through trade, war, and colonial acquisition.

The role of nation-states in provisioning processes was also encouraged by an almost universal consensus in Western societies that the main purpose of governance was to secure economic growth and social well-being. This view began to crystallize during the transition from the rule of nations by kings to more democratic forms of government that occurred in the late 1700s. This led to the ongoing debate between advocates of free trade and those seeking to impose protectionist policies. This debate hung in the balance until the demise of communism in the late 1980s. In leading economies, these ideas are now encapsulated in the tenets of neoclassical economics and in the belief that human welfare is best served by patterns of economic growth that result from private sector initiative. This 'victory' of the principles on which the social legitimacy of the nation-state is based also signalled the transition from the Fourth to the Fifth Round: reliance on international private sector networks to meet inbound provisioning requirements.

It was against this international backdrop that the modern environmental movement was born in the late 1960s. Efforts to place ecological decline on the agendas of the world's nations were compromised by the primacy of neoclassical economic thinking in political decision making. By the time global environmental degradation and provisioning issues became acute, nation-states were already ceding inbound provisioning responsibility to private-sector networks, and limiting their role in maintaining ecosystem productivity to regulatory actions. This reality was subsequently enshrined in the principle of sustainable development, which tempers ecological protection with the need to address economic and other social priorities. This inadequate framework is now the defining characteristic of the international provisioning arrangements of Round Five – our present global economy.

The Rise and Spread of Nation-States

In this age of strong nationalist sentiment, it is hard to imagine that nation-states have not always been the primary and often exclusive focus of allegiance for most people in the world. There is nothing in history to indicate that national sovereignty reflects some underlying natural order or that nation-states and a strong sense of nationalism will or should survive. As we saw in the discussion of Round One, the differences between people are artificial constructs that developed thousands of years ago in response to environmental diversity. The nation-state is a relatively recent phenomenon, one that emerged only after five thousand years of struggle between many competing interests.

A case could be made that tribal and regional groupings of linguistically similar peoples have always evinced feelings of group solidarity. Thus, even if nations did not exist in a physical sense, then surely they existed in terms of some underlying emotional pull toward tribal or group solidarity that was just waiting to erupt into nationhood once awareness reached a critical threshold. However, throughout history, human allegiance has attached itself to many constructs: certainly to family and tribe, but also to chiefs, to pharaohs and kings, to city-states, to emperors and empires, to a common faith or a religious leader (Islam provided the basis for a broader political culture, and the Holy Roman Empire linked diverse regions of Europe under the Roman Catholic Church), to class, to race (as in Nazi Germany), to political ideals such as communism, to nation-states, and to some kind of broader global community as advocated by the World Federalists.

On the other hand, in the same way that the need to organize to provision societies shaped the social structures of hunter-gatherer, ag-

ricultural, and urban societies, the evolution of provisioning requirements has helped determine the role of nation-states.

The story of the long, slow concession of city autonomy and self-
reliance leading to the creation of nations and the spirit of nationalism
began in ancient times, when concerns over the management of natural resources caused city-states to band together to strengthen their
provisioning capability. Even at this early stage, the role of cities in
provisioning was mixed up with the creation of broader political entities and empires. But it was only around the integrating power of
cities of sufficient scale and continuity that the interactions between
diverse peoples could develop into civilizations[1] and, eventually,
nation-states. This was certainly what happened in China and elsewhere in southeast Asia; and we have already seen how the ancient
Egyptian civilization and the world's first 'empire' – that of Sumer
and Akkad – both came into being in response to the organizational
requirements of living in harmony with nature, and how Sumer and
Akkad only emerged after a period of intercity warfare. Indeed,
Toynbee argues that most of the civilizations 'that have arisen and
have run their course within these last 5000 years have started, like
the Sumerian civilization, as constellations of local sovereign independent city states that ended up being encapsulated politically in a world-
state as the culmination of a series of devastating wars.'[2]

This tendency to form broader political entities to better address
provisioning requirements was also evident in Hellenic Greece. Centres of cultural and learning activity – places like Olympia, the Oracle
at Delphi, and the theatre at Epidaerus – gave the entire region a sense
of unity. Moreover, while the development of the *polis* was based first
and foremost on separateness and self-sufficiency, a movement in the
direction of political federation was evident as early as the sixth century BC among at least some of the 158 Greek city-states.

The most enduring federal state in Greece, the Boeotian Confederacy, survived from 447 to 386 BC as 'a well organized federal system,
with a board of magistrates, a large representative council, a treasury
and a command of income, even a federal court or courts: and it was
strong enough to impose uniform local governments upon the member cities.'[3] This confederacy was eventually broken after the fall of
Athens by Spartan edicts which decreed that all cities were to be free.
Nevertheless, by the time Athens and other city-states were submerged
within the Roman Empire, some twenty-odd confederations of city-
states had emerged.

The Incas had united Peru a few decades before the Spanish arrived, and the Aztecs were just about to unite Middle America when they were interrupted by the conquistadors. Kingships and empires were also well advanced in Africa by the time the first European powers arrived in the late 1300s, and they might have evolved into tribal or language-based nation-states had colonialism not interrupted the process.

All this aside, the story of nation-states is really the story of their rise in Europe and their global spread from this base. While the origins of European nation-states go back much further, one can say that they really began to emerge after the fourteenth century. At that point, Europe was still splintered into a thousand independent 'statelets'; five hundred of these would persist into the sixteenth century. Indeed, even in 1500, on a global scale, 'less than twenty percent of the world's land area was marked off by boundaries into states run by bureaucrats and governed by laws.'[4]

Modern European nations can be traced back to the efforts of agricultural communities to form alliances based on language and ethnic groupings in order to counter threats from marauding nomads. A notable example was the union of the seven Hungarian-speaking tribes under King Stephen in 1001 to battle invading Mongol hordes. But Hungary, as a nation-state, emerged only after hundreds of years of continued Mongol invasions and internal conflict. Well into the fourteenth century, Hungarian kings were still fighting to crush the independence and eradicate the feudal privileges of the aristocracy, who ruled as virtually independent potentates or 'little kings.'[5]

Further west, the roots of nationhood go back to the breakup of Charlemagne's empire. At this time, northern Europe was split roughly into Latin- and Germanic-speaking sections and into territories roughly contiguous with the administrative units that the Holy Roman Empire had established in order to deal with church matters and collect tribute. These units included the old Roman administrative regions of Gallia, Germania, Italia, and Anglia.[6]

In the early Middle Ages, competition for territory among feudal aristocrats led to the emergence of royal families and kingdoms, which began to compete with the church for people's allegiance. The power of these aristocracies and princely dynasties was local in nature. However, through marriages and alliances they were able to conduct their political intrigues on a European basis.

With the rise of medieval cities, and as the Commercial Revolution took hold, the struggles between kings and nobles and between the secular and religious authorities were overlaid on more basic tensions between autonomous cities and the centralizing impulses of kings, nobles, and the church. But once begun, the processes of national consolidation took on a life of their own. European nations evolved in response to the competitive pressures of the times: when one nation began to take off, all other nascent groupings had to adopt the same organizational norms and attributes – and even some common cultural characteristics – to avoid being left behind.[7]

The amalgamation of cities into nations under kingly rule was an ugly and uncertain process driven by personal, ethnic, and civic ambition for power and glory. The process involved a crazy quilt of competing jurisdictions and power arrangements, of privilege and ancient custom, and it resorted to war and conquest, diplomacy, marriage, inheritance, purchase, and outright theft. Royal authority and the institutions of centralized governance were extended piecemeal until kings had established effective control over lands approximating today's national boundaries. By the end of the fifteenth century (later in Italy), the Catholic Church, local medieval communities, and the diversity of city-states and regional federations had all been overwhelmed by nation-states under the rule of often despotic and militaristic kings – notably Louis XI in France, Henry VII in England, and Ferdinand and Isabella in Spain.

In the welter of conflicting pressures that gave birth to European nations, it is easy to lose sight of provisioning. These links are revealed in the conflict between kings and free cities regarding how best to organize for commercial success – or, in our parlance, how to organize the flows of natural capital on which social well-being depended. The core issue was whether the welfare of communities was to be enhanced through free unions of cities and regions or through the centralized authority of kings and a small privileged class.

Cities' struggles to remain independent eventually failed as a result of commercial and military realities. Sporadic surges in population growth and the need to constantly extend outreach to new sources of natural capital through colonization, trade, and conquest pushed European societies to organize around broader coalitions – ones capable of providing centralized political and military power that could deal with the challenges and complexity of outreach.

As outreach efforts became more demanding, and as nation-states began to develop, concerns rose regarding the security of trading routes and networks. Cities began banding together to protect themselves. 'Leagues' of cities became common across Europe. The Hanseatic League, for example, was organized in the fourteenth century by German merchants to facilitate their trade with western Europe and the eastern Mediterranean. Other coalitions included the League of Swabian Cities, the Rhenish League, and arrangements between English merchants to control the sale of wool and cloth to the Low Countries.[8]

To be effective, the new commercialism required territorial unity, internal peace, freedom of movement, effective transportation systems, and in many instances the military capacity to extend and protect trade routes. All these things required more resources and political power than cities could summon. The efforts of cities to retain their independence by creating federations and leagues ultimately proved too weak to succeed.

The steady movement toward the creation of institutions of governance – institutions able to shape and unify society and to enhance the public good, protect borders, and create access to flows of natural capital – eventually centralized political power in national organs of governance. The cost of this centralization was the death of local municipal freedom and the transformation of cities into dependencies of states.

Yet this outcome was by no means certain: between the twelfth and fourteenth centuries 'it looked as if the Western world, like the former Graeco-Roman world, might become a galaxy of city-states, instead of becoming the mosaic of nation states that it did become and continues to be today.'[9] The last holdouts were the city-states of northern Italy, which had united as the Lombardy League to fight the hegemony of Rome. In 1300 there were eighty self-governing city-states in northern Italy. This number had shrunk to ten larger political units by 1500 – a condition that persisted until their eventual integration into the Italian nation in the mid-1800s.[10]

The Commercial Revolution had profound implications for nation-states; it created a huge demand for natural capital flows as inputs into production processes and thus accelerated the development of colonial empires. Stronger imperialist attitudes led to greater efforts to access offshore natural capital to feed home industry and to create foreign markets for manufactured goods. All of this led to more aggressive forms of colonialism and to nationalistic empires that relied heavily on military power to achieve what could not be directly negotiated.

The links between commerce and government were tight during these years. Especially in Spain and Portugal, all commercial activity was entered into on behalf of the sovereign. Then, during the seventeenth and eighteenth centuries, national organizations to manage trade and colonial conquest began to replace the earlier trading leagues established by cities. As Holland, Britain, and France got into the game, and with the recent Florentine model of large-scale, transborder enterprise as a guide, monopoly trading companies were formed that operated under strict government direction and in concert with the military to exert political and administrative control over colonies and to extract appropriate supplies of resource wealth.

The Dutch, who were still trying to gain their independence from Spain, set up the Dutch East India Company in 1602 to conduct wholesale trading operations in colonial areas. In many respects this company was 'a shadow government, with the power to make war and peace, coin money and establish colonies.'[11] Its links with government were similar to those between the commercial classes and cities in the era of city-states, only now the links were with the national government.

Besides the Dutch East India Company, the most notable of these national trading companies were the Moscovy Company, created by Britain in the mid 1500s to, among other things, find the Northwest Passage; the Hudson's Bay Company, whose charter gave it a monopoly on the Canadian fur trade; the Royal African Company; and the British and French East India companies.[12] Of these, the British East India Company was the most successful. Between 1600 and 1887 it fought off incursions from other colonial powers and extended British influence over trade from Persia, through India, which it basically conquered and ruled, to enclaves in Singapore, Hong Kong, and elsewhere in Asia.

By the mid-1700s, just before the commercial era gave way to the Industrial Revolution, private entrepreneurs were beginning to compete for the lucrative international markets that had until then been a monopoly of the national trading companies. The growing political power of these new merchant classes contributed to the growth of mass political movements seeking more democratic forms of government and to an assault on the privileges and prerogatives of monarchs and the nobility. The absolute power of kings was directly attacked and replaced by more representative forms of democracy in three ground-breaking confrontations: the American Revolution (1783), the French Revolution (1795 and after), and the English pursuit of Parliamentary reform after the Napoleonic Wars (1830–46).

The decline in the power of kings marked the transition to the idea that nations are composed of citizens and that political decisions should be based on the nation's welfare. It was through the umbrella institutions of the nation-state that political freedoms and the right to vote were granted. The spirit of nationalism, which reached its peak in the nineteenth century, grew out of a political commitment to the right to self-determination based on the idea that personal freedom and the sovereign rights of people reside in the nation and that it is the national government to which one owes total allegiance. At the same time, the growing complexity of cultural, social, and economic needs became such that only a strong central power could address them.[13]

Some nationalists took the concept much farther. They argued, for example, that humanity is divided naturally into communities or peoples, which can be differentiated on the basis of race, language or religion; and that self-governing nations by and for these unique 'peoples' are the only legitimate form of government. For these early theorists, '*la loi naturelle*' or '*Naturtrieb*' underpinned nationalism even though no such law exists in nature! To push the point, notions of racial superiority were often built into expressions of national culture, buttressed by national myths, a shared history, distinctive cultural attributes, national symbols, and the creation and protection of cultural industries. The nation also became the guardian of generational continuity, as if it was some independent, primeval life force.[14]

These attitudes were modified somewhat with the evolution of the melting-pot societies of the Americas. As a result, modern notions of nationhood are now less tribally configured and more generically defined along the lines of a body of people residing in a defined geographical area and obeying the same government.[15]

Cities, Nations, and the Global Economy

By the end of the eighteenth century, the push to expand colonies and establish empires had taken deep root in the public consciousness of Europeans. Also at this time, the role of nation-states in provisioning processes peaked. Round Five then began, with a slow devolution to reliance on private enterprise to meet national provisioning requirements. The growing political power of the new merchant classes forced a slow shift in the role of nation-states: they began to withdraw from direct involvement in provisioning societies and to focus on developing policies favourable to the commercial success of private enterprise.

This transition was accelerated by the publication of Adam Smith's *'Wealth of Nations'* in 1776. Smith's assault on the monopolistic trading policies of colonial powers led to the enduring idea that social welfare can best be served through individual effort and the operation of free markets – provided, of course, that competition is fairly managed. At home, he argued, state power should be used to create domestic production units; abroad, trade and colonial expansion should be pursued through support for business initiatives. He also argued that the ultimate objective of state power was national advantage, not the welfare of individual businessmen.

As an outcome of Smith's arguments, government policies began to focus on trade policy. This led to years of jockeying by national governments, which took different approaches to achieving economic and trade advantage. Most policies involved either opening or restricting international trade. Britain followed mercantilist or protectionist policies until 1840, when it replaced them with free trade. At the same time, the government finally revoked the charter of the British East India Company.

Europe, especially Britain, was by then living off flows of natural capital from distant sources. America, on the other hand, was still largely untapped territory with vast natural wealth to be exploited. Thus, American perceptions of free trade differed from those of the British. In the United States, the prevailing view throughout the nineteenth century was that manufacturing was vital to national security and that all the essentials of national supply needed to be under national control. This view drove government policy after the Civil War, when the Americans raised duties and tariffs on foreign imports in order to encourage infant industries and home manufacture.

Most other countries followed the American example. England, in contrast, repealed its free trade policies only after the First World War. By that time, the use of border measures to control trade had become more complex with the addition of national quota systems and exchange control mechanisms; these included a joint initiative by the British, French, and American governments to introduce the gold standard along with greater national control over privately owned banking systems.

By the mid-1920s, the momentum had started to shift back toward free trade as large American companies began trading and investing internationally. America found itself having to reach out to the far corners of the world for additional sources of natural capital and for markets for its manufactured goods. (The Europeans had long had to do this.) This laid the groundwork for a strong push to open national markets to foreign goods – a push that was led by the United States at the end of the Second World War.

The United States emerged from the Second World War as the un-questioned global superpower. It was the leading industrial nation, and its production capacity and commercial strength were backed by the largest domestic market in the world. As the strongest military power, it provided the political leadership and deterrence muscle for the free world in the face of the intransigent threat of global commu-nism. These factors contributed to the success of America's role in reconstructing Europe and rebuilding the economies of its former en-emies, Germany and Japan.

America's leadership position also gave the country enormous le-verage in shaping international political and economic organizations, including the United Nations and its specialized agencies, the World Bank, the International Finance Commission (IFC), and the General Agreement on Tariffs and Trade (the forerunner of the World Trade Organization). These organizations were instrumental in guiding in-ternational relations, fostering economic development, and setting the terms of trade in the ensuing decades.

The economies of the West were committed to economic growth based on free enterprise, and beginning in 1948 they launched succes-sive rounds of GATT negotiations with the goal of reducing or elimi-nating barriers to trade. However, their efforts to expand the global economy based on the tenets of capitalism was hampered by the mor-tal ideological combat of the Cold War, the emergence of new domes-tic challenges, and the confusing array of forces unleashed by the arrival on the international scene of a host of Third World nations.

The new role of governments in international trade policy was ac-companied by new domestic challenges associated with industrializa-tion and rapid, unmanaged urban growth. These problems included inadequate housing and social support systems for the urban poor and unemployed. The persistence of hazardous and exploitative work-ing conditions perpetuated labour union activity resulted in signifi-cant social legislation.

Concerns over impoverished living and working conditions in industrial cities were augmented by opposition against the inequities generated by colonialism, uncontrolled capitalist competition, and the imperialist policies of wealthy nations. These were not new issues, and since the early 1800s dissent had gradually been crystallizing around theories of communism, which had come to compete with those of capitalism for the allegiance of the world's peoples.

Communism called for total state control of provisioning processes, and emphasized the role of the state in creating conditions of self-sufficiency. The take-over of the Russian government by communist factions during the First World War and the rise of communism in China led to a continuation of this great debate under the cloud of the Cold War.

A number of the newly established nations of the Third World were heading in a different direction, towards a third way that viewed development being fostered by an expanded role for nation-states. Development economics, as propounded by theorists after the Second World War and into the 1970s, was influenced by the experience of the Great Depression of the 1930s, and by the earlier emphasis in Europe and America on creating national production units and securing within national boundaries all of the production capacity required for national well-being. The model provided by communist regimes helped influence this approach; so did the belief that capitalism had perhaps run its course. However, for many countries the driving concern was the deteriorating terms of trade in raw materials (especially agricultural products, of which there were many producers) as opposed to manufactured goods (of which there were monopoly suppliers). This issue was closely tied to the challenge of provisioning high-consumption countries, although it was seldom talked about in those terms. Rather, the deteriorating terms of trade were generally seen as a hangover from colonial trading patterns, and many argued that this was inevitable under conditions of free trade.

Countries following this third way looked to governments to level the playing field and to enact import substitution strategies to promote industrialization. It was believed that countries, not industries or companies, were responsible for economic growth. National economies had to go through stages of growth, and only governments could mobilize the political, financial, and other resources necessary to force the growth process. This return to an emphasis on national self-sufficiency necessarily involved blocking or limiting foreign investment and restricting imports so that domestic infant industries could grow. If countries were too small to support domestic industries, then narrowly configured regional trading blocks were the answer.

The appeal of this approach was enhanced by the apparent success of national planning exercises in the Soviet Union and China. Even World Bank and UN agency investment strategies from the 1950s through into the 1970s were often mounted on the basis of comprehensive three- and five-year national development plans, which imitated the centralized planning approach of communist countries.

Among national revolutionary groups, extreme views on the structural imbalances constraining growth gained widespread acceptance during the 1960s and early 1970s. In general terms, these groups felt that the established social order had to be destroyed and the old ruling classes and landed aristocracies eliminated as preludes to the nationalization of industry and production facilities. Again, although not discussed in these terms, the objective was to place provisioning processes under direct national control.

Yet not all developing countries adhered to these ideological prescriptions. A handful of emerging economies began to compete aggressively with the developed world for market position. Huge changes in the nature and directions of technological innovation were also afoot: the Information Age was at hand.

Following the example of a number of Japanese companies, and to a large extent aided by Japanese investment and market linkages, a handful of newly industrialized countries (NICs) began flexing their economic muscle and competing with the West in the domain of large-scale, standardized production for mass markets; they also began competing with the West in the mining, mineral processing, and forestry sectors. Western producers were suddenly faced with competition from countries with plenty of low-wage workers, higher-quality ore reserves, and more productive forest resources. Production advantage began to flow toward these newly competitive economies. By simply copying what was done in the developed world, Third World producers were able to convert what had become 'commodity operations with low rates of return and low growth prospects in the developed world [into] high return, high growth opportunities' in low-wage economies.[16]

And it was not simply a matter of other countries catching up: much of the production capability of advanced economies was actually moving offshore. The mobilization, financing, and management of this new competition was made possible through transfers of technology and know-how from the more advanced economies. Huge portions of American industry were affected, as were the industrial sectors of Britain and other advanced economies, and the consequences were often harsh. The decline in American industry was evident before the end of the 1970s. By then, a handful of rapidly industrializing nations – the Asian Tigers (Korea, Singapore, Hong Kong, Thailand, Indonesia, and Malaysia), Brazil, Mexico, and, a few years later, China – were exporting more manufactured goods than primary materials.[17] As industries began to move offshore, many American factories closed and 'rust belts' began to appear. The United States lost its leadership position in a number of sectors (e.g., copper to Chile, cars to Japan, consumer electronics and electronics assembly to Asian producers) and was being seriously challenged in others.

With standardized production processes becoming entrenched, and with national markets becoming saturated, the obvious next move was to raise profits by lowering production costs. Thus, intra- and inter-company trade began to emerge based on cost differentials and the use of specialized production technologies. In practice, this meant that investment flowed into new manufacturing plants in low-wage economies that were tied to international marketing networks. The global restructuring of production had begun again.

American and European industry responded to these new competitive challenges by focusing on productivity gains and cost-competitiveness. They achieved these things through aggressive cost cutting and downsizing and through the use of new microelectronic and information technologies. These productivity measures came hand in hand with rounds of mergers and acquisitions and with the forming of strategic partnerships.[18] Corporations' efforts to improve their market position often added to labour and political woes: at first, the use of new technologies raised fears of higher unemployment and worker displacement.[19] The fears were somewhat justified: in the 1980s, 'two-thirds of the (American) workforce took 20% cuts in their real wages.'[20]

National governments responded to the out-migration of industry with deregulation, privatization, and trade liberalization. In effect, governments were attempting to 'unleash' their industries. This process was initiated in the United States in 1975 by President Gerald Ford and was pursued with a vengeance by President Reagan and the British prime minister, Margaret Thatcher. These efforts resulted in changes in the organization and conduct of international business on a global scale not seen since the dismemberment of the old mercantilist system almost two hundred years earlier.

The outcome of all this was a bit of a paradox. Productivity gains were rapid, and American and European industries were able to regain much of their competitive strength. However, international trade became a requirement of continued growth, since the restructured, lean-and-mean industries of Western economies could no longer survive on the basis of domestic markets alone. Access to growing Third World markets had become a necessity. As a result, the processes of corporate rationalization through mergers, acquisitions, strategic partnerships, and investment in new plant were rapidly extended into the international arena. The cross-border business networks that are the distinguishing characteristic of the current global economy were born.

Despite the public furor over the perceived negative social repercussions arising from the push for gains in productivity and competitiveness, these changes were only the front end of an even more massive change in the structure of Western economies. Almost unseen beneath the gloom surrounding the apparent demise of America's industrial might, the country was organizing its vast innovative muscle to launch the Information Age.

The Second World War had unleashed a flood of new technologies with the power to transform industrial organization and the way the world operated. Atomic energy, jet aircraft, rocketry, computers, and solid-state electronics – 'these were the triggering technologies of the revolution soon to get underway,' and America was the hothouse for producing and using these new technologies.[21]

Governments poured research money into the economy. Initially, most of it was earmarked for defence; commercial applications for the new technologies followed quickly after. Innovations flowed from government and university labs, from private R&D centres and new entrepreneurs. An incredible flow of new technologies began to reshape the organization of work, industry, and society as a whole.

In the mid-1950s, television was the most visibly compelling of these innovations. This electronic window spread awareness in new and important ways and quickly began sending 'highly polished American programming' to even the poorest countries of the world. In the process it 'began reducing national characteristics to a common global denominator.'[22]

The most substantial technological innovations were those relating to the computer, and in particular to microchip technology. These new computer and communication technologies were the most powerful drivers of change in almost every aspect of industrial, commercial, and social activity. No sector was left untouched. These new information technologies began to shrink the world. Their use in aircraft such as the Boeing 707 and the Lockheed DC-8 beginning in 1957 reduced travel times to Europe to six hours. They also precipitated constant advances in communication technologies and services – advances that accelerated for more than four decades before coming to an abrupt (but likely temporary) halt at the end of the 1990s as installed capacity began to exceed growth in demand.

The profits being made by the new IT companies soon dwarfed the economic losses from migrating industries. Within a few decades, most Western economies were wealthier and more advanced than ever. At least symbolically, the Information Age began in 1975. Although computer use did not become ubiquitous until into the 1980s, that was the year that over half of American workers were already employed in the new information economy. America was the first nation to enter the Information Age, and it has maintained its leadership position ever since.[23]

Nor were the changes limited to the Western economies: 'Espionage spread the new technology to Communist countries. Licensing arrangements, strategic partnerships and cross-border investments brought it to US allies. Piracy, fakes, knockoffs and counterfeits brought it to the Third World.' A combination of all of these helped augment Japan's own significant research efforts: 'Nothing could contain it.'[24]

In most industrialized countries, technological advance virtually eliminated opposition to neoclassical economics. By the end of the 1970s, most Western economies and many emerging economies around the world viewed government intervention and the resulting price distortions as the major impediment to wealth creation, and saw unfettered free markets and efficient pricing mechanisms as the solution to development problems. The ripple effects took longer to be felt around the world, and debate continued in development circles regarding whether free trade, open borders, and increased foreign investment could offset the competitive advantages of scale, technological sophistication, and market leadership – advantages enjoyed by the developed economies. However, the collapse of the Soviet Union in

1991, and with it the demise of communism, completed the rout of opposing theories. Neoclassical economics was the new orthodoxy, and the Fifth Round in the organization of social provisioning was firmly entrenched.

In large measure, the application of the theories of neoclassical economics to the governance of national economies has gelled around the ten market-friendly policy objectives encapsulated in the so-called Washington Consensus: fiscal discipline; investment in education, health, and infrastructure; broadening the tax base and cutting marginal rates; moving to market-determined interest rates; competitive exchange rates; trade liberalization; openness to foreign direct investment; privatization of state enterprise; deregulation to increase competition; and strong legal protection of property rights.[25]

The upshot of this long ideological battle is that in the matter of provisioning societies, direct control or oversight no longer relies on nation-states and their designated agents; instead, it relies on private enterprise operating through global business networks. In this transition, the role of governments has shifted: their sole responsibility is to control the environmental and socially harmful side-effects of industrial and municipal activity. They no longer control inbound provisioning.

The Rise of the Environmental Movement

In the late 1960s, against the backdrop of this broad restructuring of global provisioning mechanisms, the modern environmental movement was born. A catalytic moment in its formation was the appearances of Rachel Carson's book *Silent Spring*. Then in 1971 came the Club of Rome's report, 'The Limits to Growth,' and a flood of publications on various related themes: the population, growth, and environment paradigm; steady-state economics; 'small is beautiful'; environmentally appropriate technologies; 'the population time-bomb'; and the diminishing human prospect.[26] A subset of issues arose around the theme of 'environment and development,' with analysts and politicians struggling with the challenges presented by 'the pollution of poverty' – that is, the Third World's reduced enthusiasm and capacity for investing in environmental protection.

These publications and the Stockholm Conference on the Environment, held under UN auspices in 1972, contributed enormously to public awareness of environmental issues. They also led to the creation of the UN Environment Program and environment departments or ministries in national governments. Detailed environmental regulations to temper human and industrial impacts on the environment soon followed.

However, the environmental movement immediately faced stormy weather; the world's economies were already overstressed by new forms of international competition and structural change. Not surprisingly, there was heavy opposition from industry and politicians based on the perceived costs of compliance, the effects of regulation on competitiveness, and the views that even more industries would relocate to 'pollution havens' in low-wage economies. The result was that regulatory approaches slowed. Environmentalists were increasingly forced to justify the need for regulations by providing detailed impact assessments and quantifying costs and benefits. For almost two decades environmental issues stayed on the front pages of the newspapers, but progress in terms of reducing environmental degradation was painfully slow.

Spurred by growing scientific evidence of a large-scale decline in global ecosystems – that biodiversity was being lost, that the ozone layer was being destroyed, that forests were being depleted, that fish stocks were declining, and that the world's climate was changing – a second Global Conference on the Environment and Development was held in Rio de Janeiro in 1992.

Not surprisingly, the approaches that emerged from the Rio conference were framed largely in terms that reflected the political orthodoxy of the time. Two streams of thought did much to shape the discussions. First, the conference was held in the context of the emerging global consensus around neoclassical economics and the importance of free markets to economic well-being. Second, the Third World nations were almost unanimous in repeating the mantra about the pollution of poverty and arguing that growth and the elimination of poverty were essential preconditions to the ability to eliminate or reduce pollution. These views helped shape the principle of sustainable development, whereby the well thought out integration of economic, social, and environmental concerns in decision-making by present generations is supposed to somehow maintain growth options for future generations.

A second concept, the 'precautionary principle,' was also put forward. This concept, which reflects the lack of scientific certainty around many ecological issues, basically says that once a legitimate possibility of risk to humans is identified, nations should proceed with the utmost caution until the risks are fully assessed. Thus, in the case of climate change, for example, human actions that seem to contribute to global warming should be curtailed.

Sustainable development and the precautionary principle are elegantly simple and potentially powerful guidelines for governing both public- and private-sector decision making. However, both have substantial shortcomings when applied in real-world situations, and the elusive nature of these concepts has significantly compounded the challenge of defending ecological protection measures against the expanding pressures of global growth. Despite the engagement of policymakers in attempts to translate the concepts into practical initiatives, the global agenda remains dangerously unbalanced.

For example, the precautionary principle is a double-edged sword: the identification of a possible risk can precipitate action, but at the same time the existence of scientific doubt that is implicit in its use can provide sound arguments for delaying action.[27] Furthermore, the complexity of decision-making processes makes it harder for societies to apply the principle of sustainable development. It is difficult enough to simply measure changes in ecological systems, let alone allocate responsibility for them. Cause-and-effect relationships are hard to prove. The evaluation of economic, ecological, and social trade-offs is a demanding exercise, especially compared to normal, free market decision-making practices. Similarly, with global issues such as climate change, it is not always possible to defend proposed regulations by referring to quantified benefits from specific actions.

No nation is organized to manage its affairs with the degree of sophistication required to develop and consistently use analytical tools that balance economic, social, and environmental concerns. In these circumstances, there is a tendency to rely on economic quantification to guide social and environmental decision making. And there is the rub. The principle of sustainable development, when it devolves to economic assessment, accepts that environmental damage can be justified if the economic and social benefits that result are greater than the value of the environmental loss. This approach can only work when there is room for environmental trade-offs. As the discussion in Part III will illustrate, we no longer have this luxury: global ecological systems are already stressed to the point that the ability to provision further growth and wealth creation has been compromised.

The world has evolved from conditions of local and regional competition for access to scarce natural capital by tribal or urban-based societies and civilizations to competition between nations over diminishing global sources of declining ecological goods and services. At the same time, the transfer of provisioning responsibility from nation-states in Round Four to global, private-sector networks in Round Five has placed the assault on natural capital in the hands of hundreds of thousands of individual decision makers, all of whom are in the business of maximizing their investment returns. Governments can control the levels of environmental impact arising from the actions of each of these individual organizations through regulation, but they cannot manage the cumulative total of all residual impacts on a global basis. Like the ancient Greeks and Romans, the modern world has again lost its capacity to control its interactions with the natural environment. But, unlike ancient civilizations, which had vast portions of the globe left to exploit, our world is now full: the peoples of the world have precious few untapped sources of natural capital to which they can reach out.

To fully understand how the world reached this precarious position and the capacity of the global economy to deal with it, in the next two sections I look more closely at how private enterprise came to be the preferred vehicle for accessing and managing essential flows of natural capital and at the emergence and functioning of the global economy, which is the full expression of Round Five.

Chapter 7

Round Five: Reliance on Global Business Networks

The Fifth Round in the global organization of arrangements for provisioning societies is the story of how private-sector companies came to be the preferred vehicles for securing the inbound flows of natural capital required to meet the consumption needs of societies, for overseeing the processes of technological innovation and the diffusion of technologies and management practices required to augment these flows. It is also the story of the growth of free-market economies and in the size of corporations, and of the emergence of multinational enterprises (MNEs).

In discussing this transition to Round Five, I have focused on the period since the Industrial Revolution and on how neoclassical economics came to dominate global thinking regarding the place of open markets in promoting economic growth. While this period is critical, Round Five is also the story of how, despite five thousand years of persistent efforts to exert centralized control over provisioning, the task has always come to rely on individual and corporate initiatives. During Rounds Two to Four, societies always started out trying to control the provisioning process directly. But in every case, as the scale of provisioning needs increased or the complexity of the task grew, responsibility was turned over to private initiative.

Seen in this light, there is a powerful sense of inevitability about the rise and operation of cross-border business networks, which are the hallmark of the current global economy. Reliance on private-sector initiatives and MNEs to create and manage these networks is a rational and even necessary organizational response to the complex challenge of provisioning the world's huge and growing population.

It is worth retracing some of these events in order to see the pattern in this cycle of centralized control followed by the devolution of responsibility to private interests.

Private-Sector Initiatives during the First Four Rounds of Provisioning

In hunter-gatherer societies, provisioning was generally directed by clan and tribal chiefs. In agricultural societies, it was directed by kings, who controlled the collection and distribution of all communal crops. This centralized control continued in the earliest cities and for thousands of years afterwards, albeit without as much concern for equity in distribution. A central issue in the organization of these early provisioning arrangements was the need to mobilize and control peasant labour in collective enterprise. The usual result was demogogic kings wielding opportunistic religious authority.

The first cities had to meet the need for inbound flows of food and amenities. As we have seen, even the earliest cities involved themselves in two-way trade in order to access and pay for these flows. As far as we know, the trading arrangements of the ancient city state of Ur, and those of other trade-based civilizations in the Mediterranean basin, were made by individual merchants (and possibly families) who operated under the direct control of civic rulers.

The Greek city-states, with their philosophy of rural/urban balance, looked down on trade and preferred to meet their needs for natural capital by establishing colonies. Eventually, however, the pressures of population growth could no longer be contained, and cities – especially Athens – were forced to meet their provisioning requirements through trade. Plato's rant against the excesses of profit-seeking merchants and his lament at the decline of democracy merely acknowledged the fact that Greek society had come to rely on the Metics (i.e., on individual merchants or merchant families) to organize essential flows of natural capital.

The cities of the Roman Empire flourished on flows of tribute, encouraged by the presence of the Roman Legions. Eventually, however, Rome and other cities in the empire came to rely on a similar class of merchants to secure from the far corners of the known world the food and supplies required to provision urban population growth.

Skipping ahead to the early medieval period in Europe, the next major transition in social provisioning occurred under the centralized control of the church, which had become the primary carrier of wealth and technological know-how. Through its monasteries and orders, the church participated actively in local economies; it was practically the only organization trading widely across the continent. The church's success in introducing new agricultural technologies led to increased farm output, huge population surges, and the founding of villages and cities, which ushered in the small business era. These changes led to a transition from the centralized control of economic activity to the highly decentralized activity of small entrepreneurs.

The huge growth in individual entrepreneurship, small industry, and family farms was then slowly brought back under the centralized control of the recently founded medieval cities. Through the creation of guilds – initially intended to protect the privileges of leading merchants – the control of commerce was effectively placed under municipal authority, often with the church as a covert partner. By restricting access to trade and by regulating profits, the guilds helped create the powerful merchant families of Venice, Florence, and other city-states in northern Italy. Like the Metics of Athens and the merchants of Rome before them, these families developed the risk-sharing facilities and merchant-banking operations that enabled large-scale commercial enterprise to take hold.

Many of these merchants were eager to move beyond the confines and restrictions of the guilds and to operate outside of the restrictions of municipal control. In political terms, private companies could often do what cities could not, and the greater flexibility the new merchants enjoyed allowed them to experiment with new forms of cross-border investment and business organization. Florentine bankers, for example, began to finance the activities of foreign kings. Indeed, some lost money when England's King Edward defaulted on loans extended during the 1340s in exchange for export licences. Despite such setbacks, private initiative prevailed, and the activities of leading merchants led to the first cross-border rationalization of production involving flows of intermediate or semiprocessed goods, which supplemented flows of primary resources and finished products. The small business era then morphed into the Commercial Revolution, which created the wealth that financed the Renaissance.

As mentioned in the discussion of Round Four, cities attempted to deal with the growing complexity of provisioning arrangements by joining forces in leagues, or trading networks designed to control and monopolize intercity trade. Eventually these efforts also failed, partly because of the success of the new merchant class but also because civic autonomy disappeared under the centralizing weight of nation-states.

The first approach these nations took to organizing provisioning efforts was direct state control. As we have seen, the first nations to benefit in the early years of the colonial era were Portugal and Spain, where the Crown enjoyed a monopoly over settlement and trade in the colonies. Holland, Britain, and France then got into the game by creating monopoly trading companies, which operated under government-granted charters to administer the colonies and to sustain the flow of resources from them. Although the royal monopolies continued for some time – national trading companies were still operating well into the 1800s – their control over international trade began to erode as the Commercial Revolution took hold in the late 1600s. As both populations and wealth grew in the years leading up to the Industrial Revolution, so too did the independence and political weight of the merchant classes.

The growing power of commercial interests in Britain led to a number of changes in government organization – changes that gave further impetus to private enterprise and that helped lay the groundwork for the Industrial Revolution, for more democratic forms of government, and for the rise of capitalism. The most important of these changes:

- Parliament rather than the king was made responsible for the nation's debt. This led to the issuing of treasury bills to raise funds for government initiatives.
- In 1694, the Bank of England was founded, with a monopoly on the issuance of bank notes and the authority to set the discount rate and control money supply.
- A press was established on the Dutch model, in order to increase the flow of information on global commerce.

These changes led to an explosion of joint stock companies (150 were founded between 1692 and 1695) and the creation of the first modern stock exchange – in London in 1698.[1]

These things also led, on the eve of the Industrial Revolution, to a serious assault on centralized government control over international provisioning, the rise of the middle class, the erosion of the monopolistic position of kings and aristocratic elites, and the introduction of the institutions of representative democracy.

The response of most governments was to seek to control the activities of private-sector entrepreneurs by directing investment and trade for national advantage. This sparked the 'great free trade versus protectionism' debate, which began in the mid-1800s and continued well after the Second World War in the confrontation between free enterprise and communism. However, the Industrial Revolution and subsequent technological advance had unleashed such huge population increases that the scale and complexity of provisioning requirements simply overwhelmed the capacities of nation-states' governments.

After five thousand years of periodical recourse to private initiative to meet ever-expanding provisioning needs, the Industrial Revolution irrevocably launched the world on a trajectory of increased reliance on the private sector. It also accelerated the long trend toward increased corporate scale required to deal with the rapidly growing challenge of provisioning economic growth and the expansion of the world's population.

The Rise of MNEs

By the mid-1800s, British technology had spread to other countries in Europe (notably Holland, France, and Germany) and to North America. These countries, benefiting from lower wages, large markets, and mobile human and financial resources, began to catch up to Britain in productivity and, ultimately, in wealth.[2]

As it turned out, the United States would be the greatest beneficiary of British inventiveness. During the Civil War, a large group of northern investors financed the Union mobilization. After the war, America found itself blessed with extensive and efficient capital markets that were able to expand quickly in order to invest in British technologies. Financing flowed into banking, railway construction, and the mining and manufacturing sectors.

Toward the end of the nineteenth century, another round of innovation began that economic historians refer to as the Second Industrial Revolution. Again, energy technologies were key to the innovations that launched this revolution: first came electricity and the capacity to 'electrify' almost all mechanical things; then came oil and gas and the internal combustion engine.

Between 1870 and 1920 an important invention made its appearance every fifteen months: the typewriter, the telephone, the electric light bulb, and the phonograph in the 1870s; aluminium and vulcanized rubber in the 1880s; wireless communication in the 1890s; and the electric washing machine, the airplane, and the world's first mass-produced automobile in the first decade of the twentieth century. Most of the products that were to dominate markets for the next fifty years 'were modifications of technologies developed during this period.'[3]

In concert with these changes, by the early years of the twentieth century, economic leadership was coming to rely on systematic investment in R&D to deliberately invent new technologies.[4] The leaders in this were the Germans, whose efforts to establish their chemical industry led, at companies such as I.G. Farben, to the birth of the corporate research lab. Although a number of American corporations followed suit before the turn of the century, it would not be until after the Second World War that the United States replaced Germany as the world's leader in technology.

However, it was the United States that drove the Second Industrial Revolution and the United States that benefited the most from it. The hallmark of this new era was high-volume, standardized production for consumer markets, and it was the United States that proved best able to convert inventions into mass-market products. The country enjoyed an enormous domestic market, a highly mobile labour force, large and sophisticated capital markets, easy access to cheap energy sources, and a well-developed transportation and communication infrastructure; it was building more facilities for technological education; and it had strong entrepreneurial leaders in men like Henry Ford, Andrew Carnegie, and John Rockefeller. All of this created the necessary conditions for high-volume, standardized production for mass markets.[5]

By the second half of the nineteenth century, these factors had combined to launch the era of big companies, and the expansion of transnational or multinational enterprises (MNEs). Before 1914, there were more European than American MNEs: by the Second World War, there were thousands, and American firms dominated. These companies set the tone for the present era of global commerce.

Great Britain initially led the way. By the late 1700s, British companies were operating cotton-weaving mills across Europe; by the 1850s and 1860s British factories in Europe were producing plate glass, metals, and chemicals, and British construction firms were active on the continent. Between 1870 and 1914, 119 British MNEs, including BP,

Burmah Oil, and Rio Tinto, made foreign investments. By the eve of the First World War, fourteen of the hundred largest British manufacturing firms were MNEs, including Cadbury and Dunlop. Well-known Swiss firms with overseas investments before 1914 included CIBA, Geigy, Brown Boveri, Hoffman Laroche, and Nestle. Dutch and Swedish MNEs were also active internationally; these included Shell, Unilever, and Phillips from Holland and SKF, ASEA, LM Ericsson, and Alfa-Laval from Sweden. Siemens, the German MNE, had been active across Europe since the 1870s, and other German firms like Krupps and AEG, were active in the 1920s in iron, steel, and chemicals. IG Farben was involved in American manufacturing joint ventures between 1929 and 1934. Pirelli, an Italian firm, had factories in Britain, Spain, and Argentina, and Fiat was producing elsewhere in Europe and the United States by 1930. Major Japanese firms were active internationally well before the Second World War; they included Mitsubishi, founded in the 1870s, and Mitsui.[6]

With respect to foreign investment, the United States caught up with and passed other nations after the Second World War. By 1967 the United States accounted for 55 per cent of global foreign direct investment (FDI), with West Germany following at 34 per cent, Great Britain at 16 per cent, and Japan at 1.5 per cent. In dollar terms, the postwar growth in FDI was impressive, rising from $92 billion in 1960 to $165 billion in 1970, to $257 billion in 1978, and to $553 billion in 1996. The market dominance of MNEs was also impressive. In 1980 the activities of just 382 MNEs accounted for 28 per cent of the GNP of all Western industrialized nations. If intracorporate flows are included, they accounted for 60 per cent of world trade.[7] At a minimum, there are now more than 37,000 MNEs, networked to over 200,000 affiliated firms, which control more than 75 per cent of world trade, with about one-third of this total being intrafirm.[8]

There are powerful reasons for the emergence and growth in size of corporations, as well as for the global market dominance of MNEs. The technologies developed during the First and Second Industrial Revolutions had a profound impact on corporate size. Assembly-line production techniques were only the most visible aspect of this. Technological advance also extended new forms of infrastructure across nations and continents and around the world. The energy, transportation, and communication technologies unleashed by innovation – notably, the railways and telegraph in the first revolution, followed in the second by the automobile and telephone – helped integrate all regions within countries, pulled national economies together, and contributed to national unity. As one Italian observer noted, after the 1840s the railways 'stitched the Italian boot.'[9] Huge new utilities also had to be established to manage the infrastructure required to supply industries and consumers with electricity and fuel.

The massive investment, construction, and organizational requirements associated with these developments contributed immeasurably to the growth of large-scale private-sector enterprise across Europe and North America. Especially in Europe, governments controlled the utilities that had been established to operate much of the public infrastructure, including the railways and new communication services. At the same time, corporate enterprise emerged to develop and manufacture those technologies, to find, process, and distribute new energy supplies, minerals, and materials, and to manage the construction of new infrastructure. The large national utilities created during this period would be privatized beginning in the 1970s; this would add additional large-scale corporate structures to the ranks of the private sector.

The innovations enabled by new energy technologies gave rise to whole new industrial sectors, including steel and organic chemicals. Some of these, like the automotive sector, spawned enormous enterprises involving integrated manufacturing and service capacity on a continental scale, along with the infrastructure to make motive fuels widely available.

Other market considerations played an important role. Securing the backward linkages to supplies of raw materials and other production inputs required organizational scale, while the downstream links to consumer markets required widespread distribution, sales, and service networks. For example, as the United States began to mass-produce and mass-market cars in the early 1900s, smaller automotive manufacturing companies could not survive, and innovative companies became parts suppliers to the major automotive companies.

The corporate response to the rise in offshore competition, especially after the mid-1970s, added to the pressure for enterprises of international scale. The challenge was to cut costs, to raise productivity through the use of advanced computer and communication technologies, and to create stronger market presence through mergers and acquisitions. At the plant level, the enabling power of microprocessors and computer-aided manufacturing technologies transformed production techniques across all industrial sectors; this propelled a new round of productivity gains that forced corporations to rationalize production within industrial sectors through mergers and acquisitions and that brought about substantial innovations in associated corporate management practices. In addition, higher-volume production technologies and productivity increases led to substantial increases in production capacity. New plants could supply world demand, and this forced the globalization process even more, since large producers had to look to offshore markets as outlets for a growing range of products and services. While this was happening, service-sector firms also began to rationalize in order to build organizational capacity to deliver support to their large client firms that operated internationally. In these ways, the globalization of business was extended across the full range of industrial sectors.

The momentum of these changes accelerated in the 1980s and 1990s as advances in production and communication technologies gave companies the capacity to integrate transnational production facilities by creating electronic intracorporate networks. Companies used the enabling power of new computer and communication technologies to extend and manage their supplier networks on an international basis and to access the best suppliers at the lowest cost. In a similar fashion, they acquired more advanced technological tools for managing information flows and for global marketing activities. Also, R&D networks were established that allowed teams in several locations to work in a co-ordinated manner on joint projects. This enhanced the efficiency of innovation processes by allowing the most cost-effective mobilization of corporate resources, and it quickly evolved to include cross-border project teams.

During these transitions, the same technological innovations were being introduced into the production facilities that American, European, and Japanese companies were building in the Third World. This meant that both sides needed global or at least international market access and marketing capability. The present global economy, which is the expression of the Fifth Round of provisioning, now reflects cross-border market interdependence between the First and Third worlds: flows of primary, partial, and finished goods as well as financing, marketing efforts, and people all move in both directions between countries. First World wealth has come to rely on Third World consumption, and Third World growth on access to First World markets.[10]

The information economy has not tempered the trend toward large-scale corporate dominance. Indeed, if anything it has increased the incentive to create global business networks. The pace of the corporate mergers and acquisitions that are helping fuel this transformation shows no signs of slowing down. Cross-border mergers and acquisitions topped $540 billion in 1998, more than three times the average of $145 billion between 1990 and 1994.[11] The pressures on transportation industries are especially intense; forecasts suggest that further rounds of consolidation could halve the number of major automobile manufacturers and national airlines by 2010.

Developing and extending the new communications infrastructure across nations and around the world also requires huge corporate scale. At the national level, Information Age companies have emerged and grown with astonishing speed, and their impact on the structure of industry has been just as dramatic. In the United States, eleven of the twelve largest American companies at the beginning of the twentieth century had not survived to the beginning of the twenty-first, and '8 of America's 25 biggest firms in 1998 did not exist or were very small in 1960.'[12] And the pace of change continues to accelerate.

In most Western economies, enormous innovative energy is being generated by small, entrepreneurial start-up firms. However, these firms face formidable obstacles at the market entry stage. The cost of launching new products can be prohibitive if the ambition is to occupy a global market niche; the costs of even a regional product launch can be daunting. So the vast majority of start-up firms become suppliers to the giant computer, communications, and software firms that now dominate the global marketplace. Many small firms that choose to go after a global market niche on their own – companies that wish to become the gorillas of their market niche[13] – and especially, many firms operating in areas of rapidly changing technology (where companies must dominate their niche quickly to have any hope of succeeding), tend to seek mergers and acquisitions that will accelerate their rise.

Another compelling reason why companies must grow quickly is reflected in the failure of national governments and international organizations to curb the market dominance of MNEs. In the United States, these efforts began in the late 1800s when overproduction led to the formation of corporate cartels to control market entry and prices.

Governments responded with trust-busting legislation, including the Sherman Anti-Trust Act of 1890. Similar actions were taken in Germany and elsewhere. Paradoxically, efforts to prevent market-distorting collusion between companies led to outright mergers and the formation of giant corporations, both of which were still legal.

Later efforts by regulatory authorities to break monopoly control of market segments did not always lessen the dominance of MNEs. For example, the break-up of Standard Oil in 1911 ultimately led to the creation of six more MNEs, since corporate success in the rapidly expanding oil-and-gas sector could not be achieved without a strong market presence. Some of the companies created by this action, including Amoco, Chevron, Exxon, and Mobil, are still among the largest energy companies in the world and are at the forefront of globalization.[14]

Deregulation of the telecommunications industry led to the creation of additional major corporate players. The antitrust case against AT&T in the United States, which began in the 1950s, forced the utility to shed many of its operating arms, which then became large enterprises in their own right. (Both Lucent Technologies in the United States and Nortel, the Canadian communications industry giant, evolved from the decision to spin off AT&T's labs and manufacturing facilities.) Recently, AT&T has acquired new companies, and in 1999 it merged its international communications facilities with those of British Telcom. As a result, there is speculation that AT&T will eventually fully reconstitute itself.

Another assault on MNEs began to gain momentum in the 1960s when the dominance of American corporate giants sparked a huge backlash from newly independent Third World nations as well as a number of European ones. These nations tended to believe that market dominance by MNEs was stifling their growth prospects by restricting the development of domestic industry. The perception also grew that corporate autonomy would inevitably subvert national sovereignty.[15] Many analysts believed, for example, that the presence of MNEs would result in conflict between ideologies, values, and consumption habits, which in turn would lead to the erosion of traditional values and cultures. More radical voices argued that the very structure of international capitalism had to be destroyed, and calls multiplied for the placing of curbs on MNEs in order to restore the power of national governments to control economic and social development.[16]

The debate over the role and influence of MNEs came to a head in the early 1970s with UN efforts to create a New International Economic Order (NIEO). The NIEO was presented as an effort to 'democratize' international economic relations by placing the activities of MNEs under national control. Despite the resistance of most Western economies, the UN established the Centre on Trans-National Corporations in 1973. Its aim was to 'assist in devising of a national and international policy towards MNCs' that would minimize their 'pervasive influence on domestic political processes and decision-making' and channel their activities more effectively.'[17]

In large measure, this initiative died on the vine. It was launched at exactly the same time that many Western nations were suffering from the effects of growing Third World competition and the migration offshore of significant portions of their manufacturing and resource industries. Not surprisingly, most Western economies were dead set against it. However, when the NIEO finally died, it was not Western protests that killed it but rather the market success of the Asian Tigers and other emerging economies as well as the growing desire of many Third World countries to attract MNE investment.

A similar though less visible fate awaited efforts to create a countervailing European market able to compete in terms of scale with the United States. Like the city-states before them, which formed leagues of cities to protect their markets, European countries (and other groupings) saw their national companies losing their competitiveness and sought to protect them by forming regional trading blocks. The rationale for regional trading blocks is usually cloaked in arguments about the benefits to be gained by creating larger markets. These arrangements are intended to force the pace of regional trade and investment, liberalize regional markets, accelerate the cross-border rationalization of regional industries, and contribute to technology transfer. In large measure they tend to achieve these objectives. At the same time, all such initiatives are fundamentally transitional arrangements designed to create internationally competitive regional producers. Thus, the European Common Market was designed to provide the market scale required for regional companies to rationalize production; the end result would be European MNEs able to compete globally with the Americans and Japanese.

Regardless, by the time the Common Market came into existence, American and Japanese MNEs had already created European subsidiary corporations or entered into strategic partnerships and joint ventures with European companies. This gave them a significant presence behind the tariff walls of the 'closed' European market. The rationalization of European production and corporate organization that preceded the formation of the EU may actually have helped integrate European companies into global networks in association with American and Japanese firms. The same process occurred in North America through the negotiations for the Canada-U.S. Free Trade Agreement and the subsequent NAFTA, only this time it was MNEs from Japan, Europe, and the emerging economies of the Third World that made the cross-border investments required to gain market access. Instead of excluding 'foreign' MNEs, the creation of regional trading blocks may well have accelerated the global integration of business.

As the pace of technological advance and corporate restructuring picked up after the mid-1970s, long-standing government policy positions began to erode. In particular, earlier notions of national control over strategic industries took a savage beating. In the early 1980s there was serious concern about the potential loss of access to natural resources. Just as worrying was the loss of control over emerging technologies such as computer chips as the production of these items, and others considered vital to national security, moved offshore.

Military authorities continue to place a high priority on ensuring that strategic technologies are produced domestically; thus, in the United States, the microchip industry is still strong. But generally speaking, in most countries direct national control over strategic technologies has given way to an emphasis on ensuring access to essential flows from whatever source.[18]

Another issue relating to market autonomy is transborder data flow (TBDF) – that is, the unregulated increase in data exchange across national borders. This issue flared up in the late 1970s and early 1980s. As the new technologies of the global communications infrastructure brought about revolutionary changes in data transfer – which includes the transfer of money – fears grew that national control over strategic information was being eroded.[19] However, the international debate over this issue quickly lost momentum, largely because the free flow of information has always been vital to business success. It is said, for example, that the Rothschild fortune was given a major boost by timely investments the family was able to make on the basis of advance news received by courier pigeon of Napoleon's defeat at Waterloo. In their time, even pigeons could have a powerful effect on investment behaviour, and the same could be said about all subsequent advances in communications. Interference with data flows would erode the confidentiality of corporate information, the speed of international market transactions, and overall economic performance.

But nothing has liberated information flows and global investment more than the new digital communications infrastructure. The speed of technological advance has been remarkable, and so has been its impact on global investment flows. Exchanges of information can now take place in real time between locations anywhere in the world. The integration of facilities for currency exchange with facilities for trading bonds and equities in highly interactive and responsive networks has opened the floodgates for international markets. The result has been an explosion of international financial transactions and a significant reduction in barriers to international investment flows.

There are again rumblings of government concern about this; regulators are looking hungrily at TBDF as a potential revenue generator. For example, they could 'tax' international financial transactions as they flow across borders. One proposal, the Tobin Tax, calls for tariffs on foreign exchange transactions, which would be used to safeguard Third World countries against losses arising from excessive currency fluctuations.[20] Yet few individuals, companies, or nations believe that governments should have anything to do with controlling or 'cashing in' on global information flows. Indeed, individual Internet users are now the main opposition to policies that would interfere with the free flow of information around the world.

Cultural Change and the Peace Dividend

Whether anyone likes it or not, and in the same way that the railway and telegraph once 'stitched' nation-states together, the international IT infrastructure is 'stitching' national economies into a global marketplace, with all the benefits and cultural vulnerabilities this implies. The integration of states in the common pursuit of social provisioning is beginning to limit the ability of governments to act in several areas that have long been part of national jurisdiction. This same integration is also making cultural change an implicit part of participation in global provisioning processes.

The new global communications infrastructure has profound implications for national cultures. The transparency and permeability of

national borders that it brings about has already led to the globalization of media and information services. Through the Internet, individuals and organizations can freely communicate across borders and
easily move cultural content around the world, even in contravention
of national restrictions. In this respect, AOL's merger with Time-Warner
is perhaps the defining merger of the New Economy, insofar as it has
linked media and information delivery conduits to the content providers, including CNN, and thereby facilitated the flow of cultural content through worldwide communications networks utilizing the most
advanced technologies.

The global economy is also being driven by the growth patterns of
Western nations and technologies. Thus people can argue – and many
do – that Third World countries are sacrificing their cultural heritage
to achieve the profligate consumption patterns of high-income countries. Echoing the refrain of earlier eras, they rail against market forces
and MNEs and argue that the erosion of culture and national sovereignty is being precipitated by unrestrained capitalism.

Like Plato's rant of 2,500 years ago, these arguments miss the basic
point. It is not the commercial ambitions of MNEs that are undermining national sovereignty and culture; rather, it is the need to organize
to provision huge and growing populations. The leading national
economies are making rational choices to pursue these growth patterns in order to ensure for their own peoples the advantages and
benefits provided by economic growth as well as the high levels of per
capita consumption of natural capital that are required to support
growth and the reduction of poverty.

All countries are now being forced to reach out to global sources of
natural capital in order to provision their societies. This is now the
reality for all of the world's peoples, and it is making further cultural
integration inevitable: economic advance and cultural change cannot
be separated. As we move toward the Age of Global Provisioning, the
only safe harbour for cultural protection is in those small portions of
the world where limited numbers of people are still able to sustain
ways of life based on the exploitation of local resources. For everyone
else, the choice is simple: find an alternative to reliance on global business networks and advanced technologies to meet your provisioning
needs, or bow to the inevitability of social and cultural adjustment.

Except for their scale, the pressures for cultural integration generated by Round Five are little different from those which arose during
the previous rounds of provisioning. Cultural and linguistic diversity

has been squeezed down relentlessly ever since hunter-gatherer societies began making the transition to settled agriculture.

The processes of economic integration now underway are remarkably benign compared to the ones that proceeded them. The extensive economic integration that has taken place over the past thirty-odd years has been relatively peaceful; the world has evolved so that nation-states no longer unilaterally organize to secure inbound flows of natural capital. The hallmark of Round Five is a global economy based on two-way flows of investment, production, and trade. The resource exploitation of the colonial era and the wage competition of the 1960s and after are things of the past. Territorial empires that once set out to acquire wealth by force must now acquire that wealth by integrating economic and commercial functions across national boundaries in ways that benefit all parties. The preferred agents for organizing these flows – and perhaps the only agents capable of doing so – are the thousands of independent MNEs and the hundreds of thousands of supplier firms and service providers, all of which are linked through global production and marketing networks. It is these networks that now provision advanced economies and the economically advanced enclaves in Third World countries.

In the first four rounds of provisioning, conflicts (often armed) over access to natural capital were a constant reality among tribes, cities, kings, emperors, and nation-states. In these conflicts the issues were clear and the enemy was easy to identify. Now, in Round Five, responsibility for provisioning has devolved to many thousands of independent companies acting across national borders and independent of cultural ties, and the 'enemy' – if one chooses to see it this way – is ubiquitous and thus difficult to fight.

In sum, there is an easily understood and compelling logic to relying on private enterprise, as the evidence of five thousand years consistently demonstrates. Whether the approach was deliberate or not, transferring responsibility to market forces and letting individual entrepreneurs and companies identify market needs and organize to fill them has proven to be remarkably effective when it comes to generating access to natural capital. Allowing the private sector to respond to market signals has been the best solution to supplying inbound flows of natural capital.

Critics of globalization, of whom there are many, must provide a clear alternative to the present, long-established system if their arguments are to affect future economic activity. To put these organizational issues in sharper focus, in the next chapter I look more closely at how the global economy is organized and the enormous potential it holds for enhancing human well-being.

Chapter 8

The Organization and Potential of Round Five*

Round Five has been the outcome of two things: a shift in reliance for social provisioning from nation-states to private-sector organizations; and the steady adoption by nation-states around the world of the common policy and structural adjustments required to bring national actions into line with the new realities of international market interdependence.

The First and Third Worlds are now permanently locked together. To continue to grow, the advanced economies are going to have to help the Third World grow. This will require the transfer of technologies and investment as well as reciprocal market access. Nations are being integrated into global markets and production systems based on the two-way flow of investment, goods, materials, people, and ideas among countries. Indeed, to bring about further advances in the overall well-being of the peoples of the world, the organizational requirements that presently underpin growth are going to have to be extended to all corners of the world. This holds enormous potential for dramatically improving the lot of billions of the world's poor.

The new monoculture of development assumes that countries must find ways to meet the organizational requirements appropriate to the

---

* Because Part III deals with equity and ecological constraints to growth, the following discussion looks at the potential of the global economy in isolation from these considerations. Thus it reflects the type of optimistic analysis generally seen in many recent publications, which either ignore equity and ecological issues or argue that growth will redress them. There is considerable merit in these arguments, especially with respect to the potential of liberalized markets to create employment and wealth in Third World countries, but they are weaker for the omission and ultimately misleading.

task of building on their 'comparative advantage.' Countries derive this advantage from their unique factor endowments and from their relative place in the hierarchy of global production and consumption. It is implicit in the model that more advanced economies will steadily surrender their control of status quo production to countries having a global advantage in such production, while constantly migrating toward higher value-added forms of economic activity, for which their more sophisticated social infrastructure gives them a competitive advantage. This view is based on international experience since the advent of the Industrial Revolution; since that era, industries and entire industrial sectors have consistently migrated to lower-wage economies or to regions having other market or production advantages. Once this process has begun, it cannot be undone. When nation-states following free market principles began commandeering global flows of natural capital, other nations found themselves faced with shrinking options. They could find and exploit their niche on the ladder of ascending production sophistication, or they could be left behind.

Provisioning Societies in the Global Economy

The organization of the provisioning arrangements of the global economy can be described in very simple terms: it is fed by technological innovation and investment, it is held together by the new global communications and information technology infrastructures, its primary agents are entrepreneurial companies and MNEs, it is supported by government adherence to free-market policies, and it is facilitated and monitored by a number of international agencies.

The global economy is organized around technology. At the corporate level, companies are organized around the use of production technologies and are linked electronically to suppliers, customers, and markets. Technology also ties all the parts of the global economy together and allows it to operate: international communications networks and innovative, computer-based corporate management technologies now provide the essential infrastructure of the global economy. Of much greater significance, technological innovation both allows and drives the international migration of industry based on comparative production and market advantage. By creating new economic opportunity on the frontiers of technological advance, innovation generates both the practical means and the political willingness to allow the global migration of industry lower down on the rungs of the technology ladder. Technological advance facilitates and makes possible the integration of industry with markets. Without continued innovation on a large scale, job creation and entire national economies – indeed, the global economy itself – would collapse.

Governments, and especially the military, continue to play a key role in setting R&D investment targets and policies, educating and training scientists and technicians, and establishing other elements of national science and technology infrastructure. However, most of the technology required to produce and market products and services for global markets is developed by private-sector companies and is owned by them.

These ownership conditions and the pivotal role played by MNEs in creating and transferring technology between countries are the defining characteristics of the global economy in terms of its impact on the developing world. Most technology transfers to Third World countries are made within the framework of parent company investments in subsidiary firms or through negotiated arrangements with strategic partners. They are transfers within the MNEs themselves, or they are transfers governed by tight legal restrictions. Other technology flows accompany project initiatives underwritten by foreign direct investment (FDI) mobilized entirely by MNEs, or they are made through MNE investments linked to projects initiated by international aid donors. In recent years much of this corporate activity has involved the privatization of state-owned utilities and the upgrading of national communications and transportation infrastructures.

Technology cannot be transferred successfully unless the skills to operate, maintain, and upgrade it are transferred simultaneously. Thus, a significant portion of global investment in the training of Third World workers is made in a corporate context rather than through international aid programs. The private sector has long played a dominant role in global human resource development. For example, by the mid-1980s, 94 per cent of all international training provided by Japan was carried out by Japanese subsidiaries operating in developing countries.[1] A similar situation prevails in almost all technology transfer initiatives undertaken by private-sector firms from other countries.

The dominant role of MNEs, the importance of FDI in shaping opportunities for growth, and the strategic role of communications infrastructure are now profoundly affecting the national policies of all countries. At present, the vast bulk of FDI flows into advanced economies. The United States is still by far the largest recipient of international investment flows. Other advanced economies, including Canada and a handful of newly emerging economies, have built their industrial capacity through foreign investment. Thus, the challenges facing developing countries in their efforts to compete for FDI are significant. While low wages create some advantage, efforts to attract FDI can succeed only if overall domestic arrangements are fully consistent with the policies and investment environments of advanced economies.

The starting point for organizing national economies for participation in the global economy is to open the country to FDI and to transfers of technology through MNE production facilities. The degree to which countries adjust successfully to these key components of the global economy will determine, in large measure, their success in promoting growth. This policy framework begins with an open, transparent trading regime and independent, neutral mechanisms to police banks, market transactions, and currency flows. In this respect, predictability is vital in order to convince investors that their investments will be safe and that they will be able to repatriate their profits.

The next need is to create institutions capable of mobilizing domestic investment capital to complement and in some instances replace FDI. These institutions – including banks, pension funds, and stock markets – are necessary in order to build domestic savings and the pools of investment capital that countries need in order to move up the curve to higher value-added forms of production.[2]

Binding intellectual property laws, backed by a sound legal infrastructure to enforce them, are necessary if a country is to attract investments involving the transfer of proprietary technology or the joint development of technology. To this end, an independent judiciary must be developed, strong regulatory regimes must be established, and enforcement agencies must be instilled with professionalism.

National values also come into play, especially as they relate to local business practices, attitudes toward graft and corruption, and methods of distributing investment funds and profits. To some extent, weaknesses in these areas can be overcome through a strong commitment to freedom of information flows, open and independent media, democratic political institutions, and political stability. However, these changes may require fairly significant political and cultural adaptation and are likely to be opposed by vested interests.

Government policies for deregulation and privatization can send clear signals to potential investors regarding the openness of national governments to foreign investment. Even when privatization decisions are driven by financial necessity – as is the case with most energy and urban infrastructure projects – the government's commitment to its policy framework is critical to the ability to attract private capital.

This entire policy package needs the full backing of the national government in order to be effective. There are few half measures. Attempts by national governments to attract foreign investment through subsidies and the granting of domestic market monopolies have succeeded in buying locational investments. However, many of these initiatives have essentially diverted international investment flows into uncompetitive enterprise. The sponsoring country may derive some short-term benefit; however, in the long term, 'bought' investments tend to create structural rigidities that eventually begin to constrain growth by limiting domestic technological innovation and the spin-off benefits expected from an MNE's presence. Moreover, once created, monopolies tend to stifle further change. FDI tied to the creation of domestic monopolies does not work; nor do investment decisions bought with subsidies.[3]

Cities play a vital role in the new global economy and effective urban management is critical in attracting investment. It is in cities that all of the factors influencing investment decisions come to a head.[4] FDI does not really go to nation-states: except for resource sector investments, most FDI flows into cities. Border measures and national policies are becoming more and more harmonized around an international norm; as a result, the competition for investment is focusing increasingly on aspects of the urban environment.

The management challenges associated with operating global corporations and far-flung investments make access to international transportation, communications, and financial services infrastructure almost preconditions to investment. Thus, all of these things must shape infrastructure development priorities. City-level communications services, the cost of land, the availability and cost of local energy, water, and other municipal services, transportation infrastructure, the skills of the labour force, accessible R&D facilities, the existence of local business partners and service and supplier industries, and the overall quality of life in urban areas – including political stability and security considerations and environmental quality – are often the key factors on which investment decisions are ultimately made.

As a result of the pressures arising from global economic integration, resources and infrastructure investment are increasingly being channelled into wealthy urban enclaves. For example, airports and urban connector roads tend to take precedence over rural infrastructure and to take the lion's share of available investment funds. This is not a policy of conscious neglect of the rural poor and the needs of impoverished people living in the peri-areas of large cities, but it has the same effect. The logic, of course, is that as the enclaves grow, the benefits of economic advance will filter down to the urban poor. There is strong evidence that this can in fact happen. But as we shall see later, there is even more compelling evidence that this filtering down may not happen quickly enough to prevent massive urban problems related to distributional inequity.

Finally, in order for these domestic economic development policies to work, all nations must adopt and interpret their national policies in accordance with generally accepted international norms. This means there must be a high level of political consensus among nations regarding policy objectives, and also regarding methods for overseeing their international application and for promoting the efficient operation of free markets. There is also a compelling need for international transparency in the setting and enforcement of national trade and economic development policies.

The International Monetary Fund (IMF) and the World Trade Organization (WTO) are the two unequivocal international agents for promoting, overseeing, and – within the scope of their mandates and the agreement of their members – enforcing the rules of the new global economy.

To promote international monetary co-operation and orderly and stable currency markets, the IMF monitors the economic policies of countries and provides temporary financial assistance to help ease balance-of-payments adjustments. The IMF carries out its surveillance responsibilities mainly through annual consultations with individual countries and by producing twice-yearly global overviews in the context of its World Economic Outlook (WEO) exercise. Financial assistance is typically made available in instalments, which are linked to the borrowing country's observance of specific economic and financial policy conditions. These 'performance criteria' or 'benchmarks' must be satisfied before funds are released. The IMF does not provide financing for specific purposes or projects, and its loans can be used by the receiving country to make a wide variety of international payments.[5]

The task of the WTO, whose members are nation-states, is to move the world away from protectionist policies that constrain global economic growth. It facilitates trade between nations by removing barriers to trade over which the governments of the member nations have control.[6] The WTO emerged from earlier efforts by the General Agreement on Trade and Tariffs (GATT) to enhance the contribution of trade to the processes of economic growth through successive rounds of trade liberalization. GATT's initiatives focused mainly on reducing tariffs and other quantitative limitations on trade as they affected primary products, including agriculture, and manufactured goods.

The WTO's membership has expanded significantly to include developing countries, which now constitute the majority of members. The WTO has maintained the basic policy stance of GATT, especially with regard to eliminating agricultural subsidies; that said, its focus in the present day is new economy issues, including trade in services and the international protection of intellectual property rights. Also, initiatives are in train to enable the WTO to deal more effectively with environmental regulations and national policies respecting labour standards.

These two organizations are the main targets of groups opposed to globalization and its perceived shortcomings. Both are often accused, among other things, of being pawns of the MNEs and the developed economies to the detriment of national sovereignty, the environment, and global equity. The conditionality clauses of loan agreements have been a particular source of rancorous debate insofar as they seem to impose onerous austerity measures on borrowers – measures that can impose severe social costs, especially on the poor.

The World Bank Group includes the bank itself, the International Finance Corporation (IFC), the World Bank Institute. This group, and various other international financial institutions (IFIs) including the European Bank and the Latin American, Asian, and African development banks, are generally lumped together with the WTO and the IMF by critics of globalization.[7] On the surface, this has validity: these organizations are not specifically mandated to promote globalization, but their policies and investments are largely driven by neoclassical economic analyses and are consistent with the dominant policy requirements of the global economy. For example, the IFC's mandate is specifically to build or support private-sector investment in developing countries, and it is proud of how it uses its investment funds to leverage significantly higher private-sector FDI. Similarly, the investment strategies of all the IFIs have been dominated by support for big energy, natural resource development, large-scale, high-yield agriculture, and infrastructure projects. The IFIs tend to use their project investments to encourage privatization, the elimination of domestic subsidies, and the full-cost pricing of services.

In recent years, all of the IFIs have begun to factor environmental and sustainable development issues into their programs and to place more emphasis on capacity building. In the past year or two, poverty reduction has also gained prominence as a policy objective. In fact, some now argue that everything the World Bank does is directed toward this end. However, these changes in policy priorities do not alter the fact that the investment activities of all of the IFIs do indeed support and help shape nations' efforts to integrate their economies with the global marketplace.

It Works!

The great hope attached to globalization stems from the simple fact that it seems to work. This does much to explain why so many nation-states are reorganizing their economies and social systems in order to participate in it. Aggregated trends in trade and investment flows, economic growth rates, and national savings rates all point to rapid improvements in the competitive strength of developing countries *vis-à-vis* more advanced economies.

Overall world trade as a share of GDP has not been growing faster than in the pre-1914 era, when the full effects of the Industrial Revolution were still being felt. However, because national economies are so much larger, the total value of annual trade grew 540-fold between 1820 and 1992.[8] There has been faster trade growth recently in services than in manufacturing. This is especially true of commercial services (e.g., transport, travel, financial, communication, construction, information, professional, personal): 'Between 1980 and 1993, trade in these services grew at nearly 8% per annum, while trade in goods averaged about 5%.'[9] Foreign investment has grown rapidly and is credited with boosting global growth.[10] The international flow of short-term financial investment, including investment in stocks and bonds, has also seen spectacular growth in recent decades.[11]

These changing patterns of investment, production, and trade have had a strong impact on the economies of many developing countries. Between 1973 and 1993, the average GDP growth rate for developing countries was 3.5 per cent, compared to only 2.5 per cent for advanced economies.[12] The growth among Third World countries was not uni-

form, of course. Parts of Africa lagged badly, and many Eastern European countries lost ground as they struggled to adjust to free-market
economics. That much said, the growth of some Third World nations
has been spectacular. In the mid-nineteenth century, it took the United
States almost fifty years to double its output; China doubled its GDP
in seven years during the 1990s.[13]

Since the early 1970s, developing countries have been exporting
more and more manufactured goods relative to primary products.
Moreover, many developing countries have dramatically increased their
capacity to finance their own growth by achieving domestic savings
rates well in excess of the 5 to 15 per cent that is typical in OECD
nations. Chile's innovative pension fund, which makes mandatory de-
ductions from workers' pay, contributed to a national savings rate of
29 per cent and helped that country become one of the fastest-growing
in the world in the early 1990s.[14] Across Asia, government controls
and incentives have succeeded in mobilizing large amounts of capital.
Singapore's savings rate exceeds 50 per cent, and 'China, poor as it is,
saved 30% of its national income.'[15] This has contributed significantly
to high levels of investment in plant and equipment and to rapid rates
of growth in these countries. In recent years, many developing countries have also diversified their capital pools by creating stock exchanges and equity markets, which have accelerated the growth of
domestic investment flows.

As the currency crises of the 1990s illustrated, the effects of global
economic integration can be highly volatile. Although monetary instability persists, the relatively rapid recovery of most of the affected
economies suggests that these crises may simply be repositioning de-
tours along the relatively straight path of economic growth. It also
suggests the monitoring and control mechanisms on which the global
economic system depends are working fairly well.[16]

The World Is Poised for Continued Growth

Given all of the above, it should not surprise us that there is enormous
optimism around the world regarding the potential for global growth
to bring significant gains in human welfare. Even the conservative
analysts at the OECD believe that 'the world is on the threshold of a
tantalizing opportunity – the possibility of a sustained long boom
over the first decades of [the twenty-first Century].' They argue that 'a

confluence of forces – particularly the transition to the knowledge society, the emergence of a global economy, and the pursuit of environmental stability – could come together to propel huge improvements in wealth creating capacity and well-being world-wide.'[17]

Indeed, when we ignore ecological and equity constraints, there are solid grounds for this optimism. Much of the world is now organized to support growth. Many nation-states have adopted the open-market policies and institutional frameworks required for growth to take hold. The international institutions that support globalization are in place, and their policy frameworks seem to be working. MNEs have restructured their operations, and functional arrangements are now in place to network production and marketing arrangements across national boundaries.

Furthermore, it is easy, when looking at the dismal performance of some Third World countries, to lose sight of the impressive gains being made by many others. Clearly, not all Third World nations are benefiting equally. In the past two decades, many parts of Africa have been torn apart by war, drought, ethnic tensions, political instability, corruption, and AIDS and have basically lost growth momentum. The Soviet Union and other countries of eastern Europe are finding it very difficult to make the transition to free markets. Strong population growth across Asia is eroding the per capita gains that economic growth might otherwise have brought about.

On balance, however, the Third World is poised for rapid growth. In terms of the international economic system, there is little to prevent the further extension of the Western growth model. The potential for Third World economic development to take off and eventually become self-sustaining is comparable in every way to the impact of the Industrial Revolution on western Europe and America except in one important dimension: scale. The population base of the Third Word is roughly five times the combined population of Europe and America, and the ratio will soon be six to one. Thus, if Third World growth really does take off, the implications for increases in global commerce will be stunning.

The huge gap that has emerged between the living standards in Western countries and those of the developing world has occurred 'because, by and large most of the planet has not even begun to participate in the quality modernization that has characterized the West's history over the last 300 years, let alone become integrated with the

[Western-dominated] global economy.'[18] Developing countries comprise roughly 85 per cent of the world's population, 77 per cent of the world's land mass, and 63 per cent of global commodity production, but their economies constitute less than 22 per cent of world income and only 12 per cent of global stock market capitalization. Moreover, despite the favourable trend in FDI, the total investment in these nations from First World institutional investors has yet to reach even 2 per cent of their assets.[19]

Per capita averages distort the huge impact of even slow economic advance. To explain, the Third World's new middle class is now approaching one billion people, and it shares many values and consumer practices that transcend national boundaries. These people buy cars and television sets, take holidays, and pay home mortgages. The Asian middle class alone is expected to grow to 700 million people by 2010, by which time it will have a spending power estimated at $9 trillion.[20] The growing importance of Third World markets is illustrated by projections which suggest that Third World countries are going to account for approximately two-thirds of the increase in global imports over the next twenty years.[21] Moreover, if the Third World does nothing except replicate patterns of Western economic production and consumption, this will probably be enough to sustain global growth for many years.

Technology Futures

As discussed earlier, the ability of economies to migrate to higher levels of production sophistication, and thus to continue to fuel global growth, depends on the capacity for sustained technological innovation. Here again, optimism prevails.

Throughout the 1990s, the technologies of the New Economy – microprocessors, telecommunications, biotechnology, medicine, agro-biotechnology, the Internet, and so on – unleashed unprecedented growth in employment and global economic activity, at least within the integrated portions of the world economy. Building on this base, projections for the next rounds of technological advance, while not uniformly optimistic, tend toward the view that the new technologies have the 'dazzling potential' to address many of today's 'profound problems, such as unemployment, malnutrition, disease and global warming.'[22]

Forecasting the future directions of technological innovation is an imprecise science. When we look back over the past few decades, we find that a great many expected technological advances failed to materialize and that other, totally unexpected innovations have had a major impact on societies. For example, the world is still waiting for fusion energy to power global industry. Also, no one forecast the rise of the fax machine in the 1980s or that it would then be made almost obsolete when advanced communications software yanked the world into the Internet era.

The pace of overall technological advance is accelerating in more and more fields. Even so, history suggests that most discoveries at the level of basic science will continue to take as many as twenty-five years to achieve broad commercialization. Thus the major innovations likely to have impact over the next two decades are probably going to arise from technologies already under investigation.

Below I draw from a number of sources to indicate the broad areas of current and near-term technological innovation that can be expected to commandeer most investment funds and to fuel New Economy growth.[23]

Increased computer speed and capacity. The biggest innovation we can expect is that computers are going to get much, much faster. Microprocessors in the order of a hundred thousand times faster than today's, and perhaps as much as a million times faster, are on the way. This will produce the equivalent of a human brain in each chip (memory in the million gigabyte range is more than the human brain). There will be the potential to build supercomputers with as many as a billion superchips. New approaches to computer design may lead to a variety of computer types, from digital to analogue, neural, and quantum. Some may even use molecular arrays. By 2025, a single computer could be as powerful as all those now in Silicon Valley.

The advances in computing power achieved so far have consistently increased functionality and created new opportunities for niche-market suppliers of products and services. Some now believe that current computer capacity exceeds the needs or abilities of most computer users. However, the coming advances in computer speed, when combined with advanced communications linkages, artificial intelligence, and advanced multimedia capability, may remove these blockages. The key technological advance required is for existing communications networks to extend high-speed connectivity widely throughout society. It is the challenge of 'going the last mile.'

Communications infrastructure and Internet functionality. Advances in computing power, together with developments in fibre optics, satellites, wireless networks, and related interface technologies are already revolutionizing global communications. Higher speeds and unlimited volume capacity will remove bottlenecks in the present communications infrastructure. This will probably lower transmission costs and create enormous opportunities in the field of multimedia.

More and more people are using the Internet, and this trend will continue. New communication technologies could soon result in 75 per cent of the world's people being linked to the Internet. Africa will soon be ringed with broadband fibre-optic cables able to provide high-speed Internet access for the entire continent.[24] By 2005 there will be more than 300 million Internet users worldwide. By 2010, 95 per cent of people in the industrialized world and 50 per cent of people in the developing world could be online. The project of wiring the world and providing localized Internet service for all these new users will create an enormous demand for technicians.

Software, artificial intelligence, and smart machines. As computers become more powerful, software that 'thinks' will be developed. Even now, software is being developed to help write computer programs and – more prosaically – to speak and to write musical scores. How far can this process go? We don't know yet, but advances in computer power will eventually lead to software of almost unimaginable capabilities.

The applications for this sort of technology are vast. They include robotics, speech recognition, machine vision, and virtual reality simulation. These may seem esoteric when discussed separately, but when integrated into expert systems they will provide intriguing opportunities in many fields, from manufacturing to law enforcement to medicine. Advances in computing power, miniaturization, software functionality, and sensing devices will result in a broad range of new 'smart machines,' including voice-activated robots. These machines will expand the potential for custom manufacturing, allow the automation of production and management functions, and lead to the automation of many jobs in the service industries. In some countries, there may eventually be more robots than humans. Robot 'brains,' based on computers that execute 100 trillion instructions per second, will start rivalling human intelligence.

All of this could have powerful effects on the new media and cultural industries. The United States is often accused of dominating global culture. It is less likely to do so once greater bandwidth and communications speed, and reduced costs of multimedia creation, begin opening doors for more diversified cultural offerings.

These innovations will create dozens of significant new business and employment opportunities. In particular, they will create a huge demand for engineers, scientists, and technicians. The world will not likely be able to meet it.

Medical technologies. In the medical field, knowledge is doubling every eight years, and vast opportunities are emerging for the creation of new health care products.

Innovations in health care took off in the mid-1800s after the discovery of germs. This has led, in the present day, to institutionalized medical care, phenomenal growth in medical knowledge, and the development of medical instruments and diagnostic and treatment technologies, many of which rely on advanced computer technology. Over the next decades, the development of medical technologies will continue. However, the biggest changes are expected to flow from the complete mapping of the human genome – again, something that depends on advanced computer applications – and from the knowledge this will generate regarding the genetic basis of disease and human disorders. How far medical biotech and genetic engineering will go is going to depend on social attitudes to issues such as the production of 'customized' children. Also, advances in medical prosthetics could lead to the widespread use of artificial eyes, ears, and other manufactured parts for the more than 95 per cent of the human body that could be replaced by synthetic alternatives.

The potential for improved health care is so great that unanticipated population pressures could result. Some contend that everyone born today in North America is going to live to 120. The consequences of this would be profound; for example, the population of some regions could be 25 per cent higher than presently forecast.

Chemicals, aerospace, new materials, and engineering. The priority attached to ongoing investment in the big areas of innovation that have driven

Western economies since the end of the Second World War will continue to account for a high percentage of industrial research effort. Key research priorities include chemicals and aerospace, new materials, and military applications of an enormous range of technologies. In the process, innovations arising from practical engineering applications and breakthroughs can be expected. While these areas of innovation imply 'more of the same,' their impact on employment and economic growth can be substantial.

Basic science. With respect to basic science, significant gains are expected in progressing toward deciphering the code of life and establishing the genetic basis for plant and animal growth and diversity, creating a unified physics and exploring the universe. The emerging field of nanotechnology – the control and manipulation of matter on a molecular scale – could eventually have the same transformational power as the microchip, with applications ranging from supercomputers (mentioned above) to manufacturing, solar energy, medicine, and pollution control.

Clean energy technologies. In the 'green energy' field, the focus of effort will be on alternatives to carbon fuels, with a particular emphasis on power generation and transportation. Fuel cells will be one option, whether fuelled by hydrogen or by derivatives of natural gas or biomass. Over the next ten years, however, the most progress will probably be made in the area of ultra-clean cars, which could emit as little as one pint of gasoline vapour for every 100,000 miles of driving.

On balance, it is hard not to be enthusiastic about the potential for technology-led growth to move the entire world toward far higher levels of social and economic well-being. The organizational capacity to sustain the pace of technological advance is stronger today than at any other time in human history. This potential ultimately resides in the global pool of human resources, the phenomenal knowledge base on which the world now sits, and the capacity to expand not only knowledge but also its applications across the full spectrum of human interests. There were hundreds of thousands of technicians and scientists at the turn of the last century; now there are hundreds of millions, and they are networked together in ways that allow the sharing of new knowledge in real time. There is, then, no potential shortfall in human ingenuity. We can be reasonably confident that the momentum being generated by current technological innovations will continue for the next several decades.

Yet, as will be discussed in Part III, growth may be doomed if we don't find ways to provision it, and doing so is going to be a formidable challenge. The impact of accumulated ecological and equity constraints on the ability to provision continued growth is going to be powerful, and technological innovation is the only weapon available to societies to peacefully address these constraints. There is much talk in international circles of the need to address ecological decline, but so far it has not been translated into significant technology development efforts. Moreover, much of the investment that has been made – for example, recently announced fuel cell initiatives in Canada and the United States – involves government programs designed to stimulate private-sector commitment to directed technological advance. All in all, there is a serious imbalance in the global innovation agenda.

Obviously, New Economy innovation and the technological requirements of ecological sustainability are not closed boxes. Most New Economy technologies have important implications for the efficient use of energy and materials. These same technologies also underpin most of the analytical and management capacity required to evaluate and control human impacts on the environment. Without these technologies, it would be impossible, for example, to assemble global data to generate climate change models, or to assess the viability of regional fisheries. There is potential synergy between the directions of New Economy invention and the global community's ability to address issues of ecological scarcity. Nevertheless, the overwhelming majority of global innovation effort is focused on New Economy opportunity. Action must be taken to redress this imbalance if the world is to develop the capacity to provision continued growth and reduce global poverty. The scale and requirements of this challenge are discussed in Part IV.

Competing for Space on the Rungs of the Technology Ladder

Policy conformity among countries does not mean that all nations – or even groups within nations – can follow the same development path. No single national approach or monolithic industrial system offers universal hope for economic progress. There are too many countries for this, and they are too diverse in their geography, natural resources, human endowments, and stages of development. There cannot be other than great variations in industrial structure among nations.

The one constant is that all of the world's countries are competing in technology. Furthermore, they are all seizing every growth opportunity that presents itself. This is leading to dramatic changes in economic and political power relationships between nations, and there is no certainty which countries will win. The global economy is based on endless competition and on the rise and fall of new ideas, products, companies, and even nations. The only thing that is clear is that countries that do not compete will fall behind.

To maintain their high living standards and market position, advanced economies will have to keep their technological edge. Yet competition is going to be getting tougher at all rungs on the technology ladder. There is no guarantee that specific countries will be competitive on any rung even if they do all the right things. Other countries, including emerging economies, can do the same things, and perhaps do them better: competitive advantage can now be manufactured.

At the highest rungs, the Americans' overall leadership in technological innovation is unlikely to be seriously challenged. However, other wealthy countries such as Canada are building advanced technology industry foundations at a rapid rate, and a number of emerging economies are showing New Economy strengths. Some, like Singapore and Hong Kong, now actually surpass America in key indicators of technological sophistication such as education and savings rates. Recent statistics on computer literacy place Singapore, Hong Kong, and Taiwan in the top ten, and Chile now ranks ahead of Germany and the United Kingdom.[25] India has developed a significant, world-competitive software industry to go along with its recent entry into the ranks of nations with nuclear weapons. Malaysia is committed to transforming its entire economy to become a leader in the development and production of information technology products for world markets, and Brazil is beginning to flex its potentially mighty industrial capacity.

Moreover, the talent pool that is spearheading technological advance is becoming increasingly spread out. This reality is often hidden by the use of per capita statistics that hide the growth in absolute numbers of the scientific and technical personnel available in high-population countries. Even in areas of basic science, the numbers of technical workers with advanced degrees in countries such as India, China, Brazil, and Mexico make their participation in extending technological frontiers a virtual certainty.

Nor is it obvious that First World countries will necessarily lose their position in relatively low-skilled fields. As productivity-enhancing technologies evolve, the relative importance of labour costs as a determinant of industrial location is being eroded. In advanced technology manufacturing, for example, labour costs are consistently declining relative to the costs of technology and overheads (including marketing). The typical labour component of advanced manufacturing plants is less than 10 per cent of the total costs. Thus, competitive pressures and market considerations rather than wage differentials are soon going to dominate investment decisions, if they are not already doing so.

Within the framework of this competition for market position, dramatic changes are unfolding in economic power structures and in the relative positions of nation-states. The United States' trade imbalance with China is already close in size to its trade gap with Japan, and if China's growth rate continues at recent levels it could replace the United States as the world's leading economy within two or three decades. Moreover, the terms of the technology and FDI agreements that China is negotiating with private-sector firms seem to transfer full intellectual property rights to China over the period of the agreements. Thus, China is becoming a key player in efforts to stabilize global economic performance, and in the long term its role in global affairs could come to rival that of the United States. In a similar fashion, by 2025, India could drop Germany from fourth to fifth position in the ranks of leading economies, and Canada, which ranked seventh in 1997, could find itself out of the top fifteen. Indeed, by that time nine of the top fifteen economies could be countries now regarded as developing.[26]

So the race is on. The goal is to stay ahead. There is no certainty, nor are there guarantees of success. And there is no finish line. The implication is that all national effort must be devoted to the task of shaping competitive strength, but without any clear idea of where it will lead in terms of social utility. If the idea of competition without end does not seem to be a great social objective, it is worth remembering that it was like this through all five rounds in the globalization of human activity that brought us to our current situation. There is always an element of uncertainty in technological competition, and the gains from previous redistributions of economic and political power in the transitions between rounds have always been accompanied by undesirable volatility, human conflict, and suffering.

We also know that growth offers a huge reservoir of hope for the poor of the world and that stopping innovation – even if it were possible to turn off human creativity – is not a practical, desirable, or even feasible policy choice. The world has little option but to sustain the growth dynamic. We are fated to live with the certainty that economic growth depends on technological advance and with the equal certainty that the constant migration to higher levels of randomly generated technological employment is an uncertain basis on which to predicate the future economic and social well-being of individual nations or the world.

The road ahead is strewn with obstacles over and above the tensions and conflicts of commercial competition. The great looming issue, the profoundly unnerving challenge, is going to be this: How are we to provision the enormous incremental needs of growth and poverty reduction in the face of existing signs of serious ecological overshoot? Using existing technologies, the world is already drawing down natural capital at unsustainable rates, and it must reduce its total draw from ecological systems below current levels. Moreover, nations are continuing to focus on the opportunistic pursuit of economic growth, and the unpredictable patterns of technological advance this leads to are unlikely to produce solutions to the challenge of equitably provisioning human societies from rapidly deteriorating ecological systems. The implications of this situation are profound. If the world is indeed faced with growing competition for access to diminishing sources of essential natural capital, conflict over access must be expected. Equity issues and their nationalistic and cultural overlays can all be expected to play a part in the drawing of battle lines. Without radical change, we face the spectre of devastating conflict over access to declining sources of natural capital, as well as widespread human suffering arising from ecological collapse.

Nation-states have rushed to embrace the global economy with an almost wilful disregard for these equity and ecological issues, which will erupt with a vengeful fury within the same time frame that the growth dynamic of Round Five brings about a major realignment in global economic and military power and a drawing out of cultural tensions. This potentially lethal combination could derail growth and plunge the world into social and political chaos. In Part III I investigate these equity and ecological issues and assess their potential to cripple optimism regarding the peaceful advance of human societies and to drive the global community into a downward spiral of wretched despair and futile conflict. This is a disturbing story.

PART III

The Twenty-Five-Year Challenge to Growth and Social Stability

How global competition for provisioning in conditions of ecological scarcity and inequity can bring growth to a halt, precipitate social chaos, and unleash conflict between tribal, cultural, and religious groups and nation states.

Chapter 9

From Egalitarian Tribes to Global Inequity

On the surface, the biggest threat to economic security is social instability. Because societies rely on flows of natural capital for provisioning, the biggest underlying threat to social stability, and thus to growth, is ecological disruption.

So what lies down the road? Is growth resolving the problem of inequitable distribution? How do issues of equity cross-link to ecology and what does this portend for social stability? Is the world approaching, or even exceeding in some respects, its ecological limits? Can we expect growth-ending ecological failures? Where does the truth lie? Indeed, is it possible to even talk about 'truth,' or does the world have to make far-reaching decisions on the basis of less than perfect information and analysis?

The assessment in the following sections indicates there is a very high probability of major social and ecological failures in the next twenty-five years. If these occur, they will bring economic growth to a grinding halt and unleash the fury of human competition for basic survival.

Feedback Loops and 'Flips'

Before we proceed to the evidence, it is necessary to note that ecological and equity issues have always been sources of tension within and among human societies and that gloomy projections such as these have been heard many times before. There is a long history of Cassandra-like predictions that disaster is about to strike as a result of human population growth and rising per capita consumption overwhelming the natural world. The warnings of Malthus in the mid-

1700s, the theories propounded in the 1970s about 'limits to growth' and 'the population time bomb,' and the current debates over environment and development – in particular, over climate change, the water crisis, the assaults on biodiversity, and the loss of arable land – all suggest that the world should have already arrived at or is fast approaching some miserable denouement. Yet this has not happened. The dire predictions have not come true. Economic growth has never been more robust or brought more benefits to more people in such a short period of time.

The inaccuracy of these forecasts does not mean there are no legitimate grounds for concern. Rather, when these forecasts fail, it is because feedback loops are operating that help ecological and social systems accommodate external pressures.[1] Most feedback loops are beneficial as they mute the effects of ecological erosion or lead to technological, economic, and social innovation and adjustment. However, when pressures reach the point where they overwhelm these mechanisms, they produce sudden 'flips' in ecological and social systems. When flips occur, the consequences can be disastrous. Fisheries are lost, or famine strikes, or national economies collapse, or war and civil unrest break out.

By way of illustration, in the environmental domain, aquatic systems have an innate capacity to absorb external pressures through their own feedback mechanisms. These include the capacity of all life forms – including fish, seaweed, and micro-organisms – to tolerate varying degrees of pollutants.

But at a certain point, elements in ecological systems reach saturation levels so that the next increment of pollution causes the system to 'flip.' This happens with the growth of algae: nitrogen and phosphate pollution from agricultural runoff can be absorbed by aquatic systems up to a critical threshold beyond which the entire system 'flips,' algae blooms occur, and the affected area is suddenly oxygen starved.[2] To the extent that a flip kills off or contaminates key components of a food chain, it will likely have consequences for all organisms above those components in the chain, including humans. This happens, for example, when toxins in fish accumulate in the humans who eat them. When those toxins reach critical levels of concentration in humans, cancer, birth defects, and premature death are the result. Catastrophic declines in fish stocks can also be caused by overfishing or by inappropriate uses of fishing technology; both can drive fish populations below minimum reproduction levels. They can also be caused by habitat destruction that eliminates essential food sources or by human-induced global warming, which alters sea temperatures and reproductive processes.

Feedback mechanisms and flips are found in all ecosystems. In the case of land-based systems, an individual species may be decimated by logging. Remnants of that species survive until the loss of a last, critical tree triggers its final demise. In a similar manner, the loss of a critical wetland can destroy a population of migrating birds.

Climate change – the ultimate deadly flip for humans – is mitigated by a variety of feedback loops, including the capacity of the oceans to absorb CO_2 and the same beneficial effects of reforestation. However, as discussed later, if feedback mechanisms are overwhelmed on a global scale, the result can be flips of almost unimaginable severity in terms of the impact on human life.

Social feedback mechanisms can also help insulate societies from the effects of ecological decline. Political and organizational change, technological advance, economic adjustment, human migrations, and war have over the years mitigated some of the worst effects of human pressures on natural capital. These feedback loops have enabled human societies to increase their access to flows of natural capital, find substitutes for scarce materials, utilize resources more efficiently, and reduce environmental damage through pollution control measures. They have also led some societies to meet their provisioning requirements at the expense of others.

These feedback loops – in particular those relating to technological advance – have reduced fears of resource scarcity, dramatically increased the global food supply, and enhanced human health and longevity. They also hold out the promise that humanity will be able to offset the effects of future ecological stress.

All five rounds of provisioning can tell us something about how social feedback loops work. In our current context, rural/urban migration and the present-day global migration of people have been responses to changing economic and ecological conditions. Indeed, the Western economic growth model itself is a comprehensive societal feedback mechanism, insofar as it involves successive rounds of technological advance and utilization of the experience gained from taking different approaches to promoting economic development.

So it is not surprising that predictions of looming disaster are generally debunked in the popular press and in scholarly works (the latter written mainly by economists). There is plenty of evidence from many sources that humans are adept at augmenting natural capital flows. Indeed, the positive record of these feedback mechanisms has fed enthusiasm for the view discussed earlier that continued growth is essential if nations are to succeed in fighting poverty and environmental decline.

Perhaps then, it is ecology and not economics that is the real 'dismal science.' Perhaps, also, the concerns of forecasters have been misplaced. Or were the timelines of these earlier predictions of disaster simply wrong and it is too soon to judge?

Malthus Revisited?

The truth is probably somewhere toward the centre of the continuum of these opposing views. Growth clearly works and the power of human creativity should not be underestimated. On the other hand, even Malthus was probably more right than wrong if we limit our assessment of him to local or regional environmental effects. And on a global scale, his predictions have become more compelling over time.

Rees, who came up with the term 'ecological footprint,' declares that 'no ecosystem can support large concentrations of humans.' All economic activity, he points out, begins with the use of things produced in nature, and human enterprise accesses this natural capital by displacing other species and eliminating competition.[3]

We certainly encounter this pattern in a quick review of the five rounds of provisioning. Ecological and social feedback loops have not prevented calamitous failures from occurring. Perhaps these loops have disguised the underlying reality, but the pattern has been consistent: throughout history, human societies have depleted or fully utilized nearby sources of natural capital and then reached out to more distant ones.

Furthermore, the premises of ecological overshoot remain valid. Our knowledge of what is happening in the natural world has increased dramatically. We now know beyond any doubt that the dramatic increase in demand for 'inbound' flows of natural capital (minerals, fossil fuels, agricultural output, etc.), which preoccupied earlier prophets of doom, is now being exacerbated by an assault on global ecological systems and on the services required to absorb human waste associated with the production and use of inbound flows (air, water, land, biodiversity, the atmosphere, etc.). The provisioning challenge facing the world is now vastly more complicated, intractable, and potentially unforgiving than when Malthus wrote his treatise.

We have learned a lot about the environment since the late 1960s, when concerns crystallized over the population–growth–resources–environment paradigm. We have learned much more about how natural systems work and about the interactions and feedback loops that come into play within these systems. And scientists have developed an impressive track record for accurately predicting ecological overload. For example, they have generally been right about the effects of acid rain, the loss of biodiversity, the depletion of natural fish stocks, the destruction of the ozone layer, the effects of toxic and cancer-causing chemicals, and climate change.

We also know that advanced economies are much more pollution-intensive than the simple assessment of air and water quality within their borders suggest as the total, global chain of cause and effect relations related to their consumption of natural capital must be taken into account. It is their global ecological footprint that is important. The spread effects of the pollution loadings of advanced economies together with all of the myriad forms of ecological disruption that take place in other countries in order to sustain the inbound flows of natural capital on which the economic success of advanced economies depends must be built in to the equation: this must include the global ecological consequences of the rapid pace of industrial growth in the Third World that now supports the Western growth dynamic.

The big environmental issues of today involve complex interactions of positive and negative feedback mechanisms, and there can be significant lag times between cause and effect in the accumulation of pressures that trigger changes affecting the health of people, the productivity of renewable resources, and the viability of societies. We know that once an ecological trend is clear, as in the cases of ozone depletion and climate change, the pace of change may be slow, but the momentum behind these changes can be almost unstoppable and continue, literally, for hundreds of years. As the pressure on ecosystems builds, so does the potential for catastrophic flips. And we know that human substitutes will never be able to replace core ecological services, from the role of micro-organisms (which support soil productivity and food chains) to the operation of atmospheric ecosystems (which screen out dangerous solar radiation and maintain the heat balance that humanity depends on for survival).

We also know that the links between wealth and natural capital are binding. Flows of natural capital underpin wealth creation; it follows that they are also at the root of issues relating to poverty and inequitable distribution. The gap between the world's wealthy and the world's poor reflects the relative capacity of these groups to access flows of natural capital. In turn, this capacity is based on access to technology and to more efficient forms of social organization for provisioning societies. Those with the technology and organizational capacity secure preferential access; everyone else loses.

We have seen how ecological scarcity has often been a spark that ignites human conflict. There is little to suggest that today's nation-states will react any differently than earlier societies to conditions of ecological scarcity. Human ingenuity has allowed societies to substitute human-managed production systems for naturally occurring ones, and this has implications both for the ability to sustain such systems and for the ability of the poor to participate. These advances have perhaps bought time for more fundamental solutions to emerge to the task of provisioning societies. But they have not changed the trend itself: the world is now on the verge of massive ecological decline, and the implications for continued growth are likely to be catastrophic. The danger is clear: societies are going to seek to maximize their own welfare by whatever means available, including war.

If we do not find ways to intercede on a global basis to mitigate the effects of ecological decline and the growing competition for scarce natural capital, the world will begin to experience its worst Malthusian nightmares well before 2025. Is the world about to descend into chaos? This will depend partly, but not entirely (for some things are beyond human capacity to influence) on how the world's societies develop and apply new feedback mechanisms and responses to the challenge of provisioning the world's peoples in conditions of global ecological scarcity.

A Brief History of Income Inequity and Natural Capital Flows

The debate over income distribution and global poverty is preoccupied with statistical measures and with trends in per capita income – in short, with money. This fixation obscures the fact that access to natural capital is as much a measure of distributional equity as it is of relative financial wealth.

Notions of wealth and poverty vary between societies, and they certainly varied widely throughout the five rounds of provisioning. That said, the one constant has always been that the wealthy have had better access than the poor to flows of natural capital.

It is not simply a matter of the wealthy eating better, living in larger homes, and being able to consume more things. The assessment of natural capital flows must be conducted on a complete systems basis. As discussed in Part I, the lifestyles of the wealthy rely on sophisticated infrastructure and on a broad range of related services and employment, and these things dramatically increase the need for flows of natural capital. Also, the wealthy have always lived with less pollution in their lives. Wealth enables outreach – generally through infrastructure, trade, and diversion – to ever larger and more distant ecological goods and services. For example, a sewer pipe creates a cleaner living environment by dispersing household waste throughout a wider water system than can be accessed by a house that must dump its refuse in a ditch in the backyard. Other outreach mechanisms spread the pollution related to provisioning wealthy societies throughout global ecosystems.

Given the relationship between income and the consumption of natural capital, it should not be surprising that relative wealth in today's world reflects how groups within societies are organized and how they use technology to provision themselves. Each of the five rounds of provisioning was led by societies that adopted new technologies and forms of social organization in response to the need – created by population growth – to augment flows of natural capital. Income inequalities within and between societies persistently accompanied all five rounds of the human journey and were most pronounced as individual societies, or groups within societies, made the transition from one round to the next and thus moved ahead of others. In the process, the world has moved away from small, egalitarian social units (when technology consisted of spears and local knowledge and all societies and everyone in them were on a more or less equal footing) toward increasingly stratified social structures and divisions of wealth as technologies and organizational approaches to provisioning ever larger populations became more complex.

It is quite possible that hunter-gatherers defined the concepts of wealth and income distribution – if they thought about them at all – in terms of the variable beneficence of nature. Within clan and tribal units, everyone shared nature's produce more or less equally. Significant differences probably existed between tribes or clans: those living in regions well stocked with biological resources may have had an easier time than groups occupying marginal lands, and there may have been year-to-year fluctuations. But regardless of local circumstances, when population growth or other factors stretched the limits of regional capacity, new 'wealth' could only be accessed by taking it from neighbouring tribes or by having a portion of the population migrate to unoccupied lands.

During Round Two, when agricultural societies began to take root around the world, basic social wealth continued to revolve around land – on how much and how bountiful. Only now the land's wealth was measured in terms of the crops that could be grown or the number of animals that could be grazed. This direct dependence on the land, which was often managed in a communal manner, meant that pure agricultural societies were still relatively egalitarian. This pattern continues today in some areas of the world, such as parts of Nepal, where villagers still work family plots, share water resources, and harvest crops communally.

Later on, different forms of social organization became necessary in order to co-ordinate production, manage the distribution of output, and address the management challenges associated with denser populations. These requirements led to the establishment of chiefdoms, kingdoms, and eventually empires. Flows of tribute then followed to recognize the power and privilege of the new ruling classes; this is how hierarchies of status, social prerogatives, and relative wealth came into being. This pattern arose in all agricultural societies around the world, from Egypt under the pharaohs to nomadic herdsmen under Genghis Khan, to China and Japan under regional warlords, to the emerging agricultural civilizations that spread across Africa and, later, Meso-America.

Agricultural surpluses led to the founding of cities, which quickly evolved into nodes of wealth and privilege. Cities became the centres of political and religious power, and cities that launched the processes leading to technological advance and eventually to sustained economic growth.

The growing economic and political power of cities created an imbalance. Rural areas were quickly reduced to the subservient role of providing urban populations with natural capital. One result of this was a slow unravelling of rural social structures under the unrelenting pressure to raise agricultural output to meet urban needs. Another was the emergence of an enduring and apparently universal gap between rural and urban incomes. The pressures exerted by cities on rural ways of life continue today, and it is unlikely that small agricultural holdings and family farms will survive much longer.

Economic growth and wealth accumulation resulted in differential access to natural capital flows and thus to differences in the quality of life. The slow but steady accumulation of wealth began to take hold in Egypt around five thousand years ago, when per capita incomes began to rise. This first surge eventually peaked in Imperial Rome around AD 350, shortly before the Roman Empire collapsed.[4]

Within this same time frame, the Athenian ideal of citizen rule led to a concentration of wealth and power in the Greek city-states. Nevertheless, the quality of life in these city-states was still largely determined by inbound flows of natural capital from surrounding regions and by the 'wealth of the world' acquired through trade. However, these flows were not certain, and most cities were plagued by inadequate water supplies and difficulties in disposing of wastes. The result, if Athens is any guide, was that despite all the urban wealth, most city dwellers lived hard, poor lives in squalid conditions. Life was even harder for the slaves, who accounted for one-quarter of the population. (Poverty has many dimensions.) Wealth remained largely in civic hands and was invested in huge civic institutions and buildings. According to Aristotle, Athens was a city of public opulence surrounded by private squalor.[5] The same situation prevailed in Roman times, although levels of general well-being and societal wealth rose considerably as a result of the spread of Roman towns and cities. Rome, where the tribute of the empire was concentrated, was especially wealthy.

The urban infrastructures built during these times became the models for all later approaches to urban planning; however, while potentially available to all, the benefits of these infrastructures accrued disproportionately to the wealthy. Street paving, which was known in even earlier times, was laid down for the first time in Rome in order to meet the needs of the concentrated urban masses. Patrician houses were equipped with bathrooms and water closets and heated in winter by hot air carried through chambers in the floor.[6] Aqueducts piped water from distant springs. The Cloaca Maxima, the massive sewer built in 600 BC and still in use 2,600 years later, carried waste to the Tiber and thence to the Mediterranean.[7] Similar technologies were used in Londinium (now London) and elsewhere throughout the empire.

Rome's patrician classes enjoyed the city's institutions, arts, and cultural activities from their vantage point of well-appointed homes and country villas, and they made philanthropic contributions to pay for the gory spectacles that entertained the general populace. But the great majority of the capital's citizens lived in fetid slums. Water closets were only installed on first floors and not at all in tenement quarters. The Romans used human excrement as fertilizer on the region's fields, but as the city grew, the volume of it outstripped local farmers' needs.[8] The same thing happened with animals and wheeled traffic: the noise of wheels on cobblestones at night drove the poet Juvenal into insomnia. Eventually, Julius Caesar banned carts during the day; about 150 years later, the emperor Hadrian placed restrictions on the number of teams and carts permitted to enter the city.[9] Rome was designed for a smaller world, and the sheer scale of its needs finally overwhelmed its infrastructure and provisioning capabilities. As these collapsed, the culture of Rome died with it.

This early experience set a pattern that has been repeated in every subsequent urban area undergoing rapid expansion. Despite huge public investments in environmental infrastructure, the means for delivering and extending these services eventually fail to keep pace with the demands of growth.

The collapse of the Roman Empire plunged most of Europe into a long and deep trough of generalized poverty and stagnation. It would take almost 1,300 years for Europeans to reach again the levels of public wealth and infrastructure services enjoyed during Roman times.[10] There was little economic growth again anywhere until the late Middle Ages. Most of the world was relying on subsistence agriculture, and few people accumulated wealth. Crude estimates by *The Economist* suggest that between the collapse of the Roman Empire and 1800, western European GDP rose by only 0.1 to 0.2 per cent per year. 'At that pace, living standards barely changed in one's lifetime, with real incomes taking some 500 years to double.'[11]

However, wealth did accumulate in spectacular ways among the propertied classes with the evolution of the manorial system of agriculture, whereby serfs worked their lord's land. The gaps between rich and poor in those times was easily as broad as it is now. Serfs were little more than slaves, while the assets of the landed 'gentry' were vast. The richest man in British history, if one puts a modern value on his holdings, was William of Warenne, a medieval baron who was killed by an arrow in 1088. His wealth is estimated at $139 billion based on the estates awarded to him in return for his loyalty to William the Conqueror. 'The top of Britain's historic rich list is still dominated by the family wealth generated in Norman times.'[12]

This hierarchy of relative wealth and poverty peaked during medieval times. It began to break down in reaction to population surges attributable to innovations in agricultural technologies and the rise of cities. As we have seen, cities altered the nature of global outreach to new sources of natural capital by adding trade to the pre-existing processes of migration and conquest. By the mid-1400s, commercial activity was beginning to compete with land ownership as the primary source of wealth.

As the small business era took hold, and as the trade and banking houses of Venice, Florence, and other city-states in northern Italy began to prosper, wealth and power began to concentrate in the hands of a new group of aristocratic households. A unique census of Tuscan properties in 1427 provides insight into this altered distribution of wealth, in terms of urban versus rural holdings and also in terms of the concentration of urban wealth in the hands of a small elite: 14 per cent of Florentine households 'had 67% of the money wealth and 78% of the moveable property in Tuscany,' while within Florence 'the richest 100 households, less than one percent of the total, had 27% of the wealth.'[13]

The fortunes amassed by these families contributed heavily to technological advance, the economic reawakening of Italian city-states, and the new humanist philosophy of the Renaissance, which broke the formal structures of European feudalism. Although poverty was still endemic across Europe, and although improvements in living conditions advanced only around the margins, the dynamic energy and innovative forces unleashed by the Renaissance eventually propelled Europe toward colonial conquest, more extensive global trading arrangements, and the era of industrial innovation.

While these changes were taking place across Europe, other parts of the world remained dependent on nature's bounty. The emerging Western nations began to leave the rest of the world behind in terms of generalized wealth. However, right through until the early 1800s, the gap between European nations and the rest of the world broadened only slowly; the vast majority of Europeans remained mired in poverty. For urban dwellers in particular, the gap in wealth and quality of life between rich and poor remained stark.

With respect to pollution, Venice was endowed with unique natural advantages. It was able to dump its waste (most of which was organic) directly into the sea and to rely on tidal flushing for its removal.[14] Elsewhere in Europe, however, urban conditions were a source of growing concern. Like Athens and Rome, London accumulated a set of serious environmental problems that eroded its quality of life. These included tainted water, poor air quality, and the accumulation of refuse. Dung and excrement were carted away once a week. However, the volume of waste eventually contaminated the local countryside, and the accumulation of dung in the streets got so bad that the first urban sanitary law in England was passed in 1388. It prohibited the throwing of filth and garbage into municipal ditches and rivers.[15]

By the sixteenth century, there were similar laws across Europe. The first public sewage plant was established in Bunzlau, in Silesia, in 1543, and in 1596 the British reinvented the flush toilet.[16] Yet population growth quickly rendered new water mains obsolete, and the citizens of London actually had less water per person in the eighteenth century. Not until the nineteenth century did the bathroom become part of middle-class homes.

When the commercial era finally reached England (1570–1620), London vaulted ahead of Amsterdam and other contenders to become the world's great commercial centre. By the mid-1700s, as a result of the global exploitation of resources through conquest and colonization, the merchant classes were again becoming wealthier. Most Londoners, however, remained poor.

Then came the Industrial Revolution, which changed patterns of income distribution on an unprecedented scale. The first-level effects were on population growth and the pace of urbanization. There were roughly 200 million Europeans at the time of the Napoleonic Wars; by the First World War there were 600 million. In a little over a century, the population of Europe had grown from about one-sixteenth of the global total to about one-third.[17] At the same time, European and American societies were making the transition from rural to urban life. The growth of urban populations during this era had profound social and environmental consequences. Again using London as a yardstick, the growth of employment opportunity lagged the rate of urban growth; the rural poor were flooding the city and often ending up in the streets. The result was high levels of urban poverty. In 1831 'close to 10% of the entire population of the country was receiving poor relief.'[18] Workhouses were established, and after 1840 housing for the poor was made available. Poverty led to crime, which led to a significant expansion of the police force while overcrowded jails led to prison reforms.

The volume and composition of urban waste began to create formidable problems. Until now, most waste had been from humans and animals. It was organic and thus decomposed relatively easily. During the Industrial Revolution, urban wastes became more toxic. Coal was now the main form of energy, and industrial water effluents and air emissions began to contain chemical residues. Volumes of solid waste also increased as populations surged.

As had happened during Roman times, technological solutions were found to these problems, but those solutions were quickly rendered obsolete by the pressures of population and industrial growth. For all the gains in wealth made by the merchants, the industrialists, and the landed gentry, most urban dwellers continued to live in squalid conditions.

In London, there were repeated outbreaks of cholera and other diseases throughout the 1800s. Right into the early years of the twentieth century, most infant deaths were a result of summer diarrhoea spread by flies feeding on horse dung.[19] Water and sanitation services remained inadequate despite costly upgrades and extensions.

Paris during these years was a place of unspeakable poverty. As in London, poor laws were introduced in the mid-1800s. Then, between 1852 and 1869, under the direction of Haussmann, the centre of Paris was completely redesigned and rebuilt, including its infrastructure. This was 'arguable the biggest urban renewal project the world has ever seen,' and it was undertaken in the midst of oppressive urban squalor.[20]

Similar challenges were encountered all across Europe. Bathrooms were still unknown in Vienna in 1900, and the suburbs lacked piped water.[21] Huge urban migrations and population flows were also taking place across North America. New York was struggling to deal with a doubling of its population and the challenges of accommodating low-paid workers. The latter were met in part by the building of mass-transit lines beginning in 1863. The systems expanded rapidly in the early twentieth century to cater to housing estates for workers, which were being built on cheap land at the end of railway lines.[22]

Around this time, some individuals were accumulating enormous wealth. John D. Rockefeller (1839-1937) founded Standard Oil and eventually made a fortune of C\$300 billion in present dollars. Bill Gates, currently the richest man in the world, is worth one-third to one-sixth of that amount.[23]

The technology-driven growth of the first decades of the twentieth century, which was supported by broad public participation in equity markets, ended with the market crash of October 1929, which was followed by the Great Depression of the 1930s. This growth was then reignited by war production and by postwar conditions that spawned the Golden Age of growth and prosperity in America and Europe – an era that continues today and is reaching all corners of the world.

Land continues to be a significant source of wealth, and many great 'old money' fortunes are still based on it.[24] That said, the face of wealth is changing as technological advance and social change provide new sources of wealth creation. In advanced economies, the entertainment and sports industries are making some people enormously rich. Meanwhile, corporate executives, high-tech entrepreneurs, and holders of employee stock options are swelling the ranks of millionaires. In the New Economy, sources of wealth generation have shifted from land and inheritance to knowledge, skill, and personal drive.

The Global Economy and Income Distribution

The gap between the world's richest and poorest countries is now enormous, and it is growing.

There was very little movement in average incomes around the world until well into the nineteenth century. Even so, by 1820, incomes in Europe had increased to two or three times those of the rest of the world. Estimates for that year suggest that 'roughly three quarters of the world's people lived on less than \$1 per day,'[25] and that average incomes ranged from about \$500 in China and South Asia to \$1000 to \$1,500 in the richest countries of Europe.

From that point on, the race for economic gain was no contest. Most of the world essentially remained stagnant from the early 1800s until after the Second World War; however, North America, western Europe, and Japan saw economic growth raise per capita incomes by ten to twenty times. The outposts and enclaves of the colonial powers were also gaining in wealth; however, their presence had little positive impact on the relative wealth of the vast majority of people in the colonies. Indeed, some have argued that in many regions, colonial occupation *reduced* average per capita income.[26]

As a result, the wealth gaps were already huge when the development decades began after the Second World War and the Third World began trying hard to catch up. Despite impressive Third World growth, the gaps are still widening. Since 1960 the gap between the richest fifth and the poorest fifth of nations has more than doubled. 'In 1960 per capita GDP in the richest 20 countries was 18 times that in the poorest 20 countries. By 1995 this gap had widened to 37 times.'[27] In absolute terms, the wealthiest one-fifth of nations account for 86 per cent of global GDP, export 82 per cent of all goods and services, attract 68 per cent of all FDI, and have 78 per cent of all telephone lines and over 93 per cent of all Internet users. The comparable figures for the poorest 20 per cent of countries range from 1 to 1.5 per cent.[28]

Gaps are also widening *among* the developing nations: emerging economies that have attracted high levels of FDI and created successful export industries are forging ahead of others.[29] Regardless, only a handful of Third World economies have been able to actually narrow the income gap that separates them from advanced economies.

Trends in income distribution *within* countries can be difficult to determine, since appearances can be strongly influenced by the time frames on which statistics are based. Nevertheless, there is an emerging consensus that income gaps within most countries – and certainly those containing the vast majority of the world's people – are also widening. Wage gaps have fallen in several Southeast Asian economies where economic growth has been rapid; however, the recent experience of economies with large populations is less positive. China, India, Indonesia, and Russia, for example – four countries accounting for half the world's people – have all recorded widening income gaps.

In recent years, the gaps within most advanced economies have also been growing. In the United States, the rich are leaving the middle class and poor behind: in the decade ending in 1998, the poorest 20 per cent of Americans saw their incomes increase by only 1 per cent, middle-income earners gained only 2 per cent and the incomes of the richest 20 per cent increased by 15 per cent.[30] This was despite the lowest unemployment rate on record (4 per cent), massive infusions of FDI, and New Economy innovations that fuelled almost two decades of strong economic growth. A study in Canada between 1984 and 1999 found the wealth of the top 20 per cent of families increased by 39 per cent while the average wealth of the bottom 20 per cent actually shrank.[31] Similar trends are evident across Europe and in Australia.

Thus, the long historical tendency for income distribution to be highly skewed in favour of the wealthy seems to be continuing today. Again, while the cause is unclear, it is hard to avoid thinking that 'free and unmanaged globalization can cause economic and social hardship by exacerbating poverty and income inequalities.'[32]

A second area of consensus is that income distribution patterns in Third World countries are tilted more sharply in favour of the rich than they are in advanced economies. The GINI index measures income distribution. Its scale ranges from 0 (all citizens have the same income) to 100. A GINI of more than 40 is generally assumed to be in a socially dangerous zone. The World Bank's application of this index indicates that the OECD countries, which have an average per capita income (PCI) of $24,329, have an average GINI of around 30, with a distribution ranging from 40 down to 23 (skewed up by the United States at 40). In contrast, ten Asian economies, with an average PCI of $1,168, have an average GINI of 34.7 and a distribution range from 29.7 to 48.4. Also, twelve countries from Latin and Central America, with an average PCI of $2,521, have an average GINI of 50.2, with a range from 41.1 to 60.1.[33]

Thus, the growth statistics for many Southern economies suggest that progress is being made in human well-being. But these statistics hide a disturbing trend: income inequities are increasing and the scale of absolute poverty persists in the Third World.

Differences in national policies seem to be at least partly responsible for the differential effects of growth and globalization on patterns of national income distribution. Countries emerging from communist rule tend to still have flatter income-distribution profiles than free-market economies. Wage differentials are increasing in these countries, and this may be an inevitable adjustment they have to make as they evolve into free-market economies. China, for example, now has a GINI above 40. The sharp divergence between the GINI averages for Asia and those for LAC may also be partly a result of the tendency for urban incomes to be higher than rural; in LAC, in percentage terms, significantly more people now live in urban areas. Also, the social security programs of advanced economies tend to raise the incomes of the poor and thus 'flatten' GINI.

The steady integration of national economies into global production and marketing networks is creating global labour markets that will continue to exert pressures to increase existing income differentials in Third World countries. The demand for skilled workers is placing nations in competition not only for investment but also for people, and this is helping drive up wages all around the world. In many developing countries, a premium must now be paid for skilled workers and even for some not so skilled. In Romania, for example, a typical pension based on thirty years of contributions is around US$27 per month. Workers in a newly opened McDonald's franchise might earn $80 per month, while Romanians working for international firms, IFIs, and UN agencies may be paid at international rates.[34] Similarly, in India, where the per capita income is around $440 per year, international competition for software skills in the rapidly growing software industry had pushed wages up over $7,000 per year for skilled workers by 1998.[35] Presumably, these wages will continue to increase as long as there are global supply shortfalls and better international employment and lifestyle opportunities for mobile labour.

There is a widely held perception that because income gaps are widening, the well-being of the poorest groups in society must be declining. Yet a growing body of opinion suggests that growth is *good* for the poor, even if the benefits flowing down to them are not on the same scale as those flowing to the rich.

A study by the World Bank on the economic performance of eighty countries over four decades concluded that the incomes of the poor rise 'one-for-one' with overall growth and that they benefit from growth even when income gaps are increasing. The report also argued there is no systematic relationship between growth and changes in income distribution patterns. The effects of macro-economic policies such as stable monetary regimes, openness to trade, and smaller government 'raise the incomes of the poor as much as average incomes'; thus, 'all income groups benefit equally from reforms.'[36]

Some of the wording in this report seems to overstate the significance of the findings. It does not mean to imply that the poor are out of the woods. Rather, it is simply saying that that if the benefit of growth to someone earning $7,000 per year is 5 per cent (i.e., $350 or about $1 per day), then someone earning $1 per day will also benefit by 5 per cent (i.e., $0.05 per day).

A WTO study of the impact of trade on the poor makes much the same case, but in more muted terms. It says that increasing trade between countries causes per capita incomes in the poorer nation to approach those of the richer one and that rising incomes 'lift' the poor as well as the wealthy. It points out that the risks of increasing income gaps are likely to be small and generally short term, if they arise from such things as falling prices for products from previously protected sectors. On the other hand, it also notes that it is hard to measure the benefits, as they are diffuse.[37]

To some extent, these observations are supported by evidence from advanced economies. For example, despite the growth of distributional inequity in the United States, falling unemployment rates have been putting new money into the pockets of the poor, including the unskilled, and giving people the opportunity to gain work experience and new skills. Unemployment insurance for people with less than a high school education declined in the five years of high growth ending in 1999 from 10.8 to 6.8 per cent, and the unemployment rate for black teens dropped from 36 to 22 per cent, while the overall rate fell from 6 to 4.3 per cent.[38]

Yet dropping unemployment roles in the booming, integrated American economy cannot be used to compare progress in the 'bipolar' economies of most Third World nations, which are split between those in the formal economy, where most of the gains from growth occur, and those in the informal economies, where poverty is endemic.

These arguments, especially those of the World Bank study, are also hard to reconcile with other data. For example, they conclude that the effects of growth have not altered income distribution patterns and that there are no differences in the effects of growth between advanced and emerging economies. This simply does not jibe with the evidence presented above regarding growing income gaps.

Nor is it clear whether gains at the bottom end of the income scale are meaningful as long as increasing wealth gaps keep raising the poverty bar. It may be possible to have growing income gaps and still reduce poverty, but poverty reduction would be more certain if the gaps were closing or at least not growing. Increasing income gaps constantly reimpoverish the lowest ranks as price escalations at the top flow down to the bottom. Thus, those stuck in poverty may have higher incomes than before, but they are stuck nonetheless, and their circumstances are no less desperate.

The tendency for poverty to reappear in conditions of rising income inequality is dramatically revealed by a Canadian study showing that, for the first time since the Great Depression, a growing number of people working full time – perhaps as many as one in six – are not earning enough to support a family. This is turning back the policy agenda almost fifty years to the time when the right of the working poor to a 'living wage' sparked a wave of social reforms. And it raises a fundamental policy issue: Should employers carry the burden of ensuring that work pays enough to keep people above the poverty threshold? Or should this be up to governments and taxpayers?[39]

Regardless, the most telling concern about poverty relates to how little change there has been in the absolute numbers of people mired at the low end of the income scale. Aggregate measures of global poverty continue to reveal a discouraging situation. The World Bank uses $1 per day as the income threshold below which people in the developing world are living in extreme poverty. The percentage of Third World populations living on less than $1 per day fell from 28 to 24 per cent between 1987 and 1998. However, because of population growth, the absolute numbers remained constant – around 1.2 billion people. There were regional differences in performance. Some regions were able to substantially reduce extreme poverty (East Asia, the Middle East, and North Africa), while the numbers mired at the lowest levels increased by 10 per cent in South Asia, 20 per cent in Latin America and the Caribbean, and 34 per cent in Sub-Saharan Africa. In Eastern Europe and Central Asia, the numbers increased from 1.1 million to 24 million.[40]

When we apply a relative or consumption-based poverty measurement (e.g., the minimum level of resources required to enjoy living standards widely accepted in each society) instead of the $1 per day measure of extreme poverty, the absolute number of impoverished people in the world rises to around 2.5 billion. This suggests that the consumption-based poverty threshold is actually just under $2 per day. When we use a daily income of $2 as the baseline, we find that half the world's people – over 3 billion of them – are now living in poverty.[41]

Clearly – and this is what the World Bank report is really saying – in conditions of rapid population growth, a significant number of people must move up the income curve for the percentage living on less than $1 per day to drop by a few percentage points. Indeed, the numbers able to escape the $1 per day threshold of extreme poverty over the past decade have been impressive, amounting to several hundred million people. Gains have been especially noteworthy in China, where the economy as a whole actually doubled in size in the space of seven years during the 1990s, and where the incomes of as many as 160 million people rose above this threshold. The problem is that these gains have been eroded by the almost equally large numbers of people falling into poverty or born poor. From this we have to conclude that growth has not helped many of the world's poor – that one in five or six, and perhaps as many as half, have not benefited from it. In already densely populated countries where poverty is rampant and where population increases continue to be rapid, some move up a bit, but others flow in behind to take their place on the lowest rungs. Poverty is persistent.

The Coming Challenge of Global Poverty

In advanced economies, growth has not eliminated distributional inequities but it *has* enabled the poor to lead better lives. However, these gains have been achieved under the most favourable possible conditions.

The Western economies have benefited from low initial populations, slower population growth, and almost limitless access to natural and human capital (the latter through flexible immigration policies). From a job creation point of view, and also from a financial perspective, they have the important ability to expand job-creating infrastructure more or less in tandem with population growth. In terms of recent performance, the American economy (see Part II), is also uniquely organized to attract and benefit from global flows of investment – flows that have unleashed the job-creating power of the knowledge-based, globally networked economy of Round Five.

In the future, the Western economies are going to benefit disproportionately from demographics. The challenge facing most developed countries is not how to create employment opportunities but rather where to find the skilled people that their expanding, technology-led economies will require. Recent estimates are that total population growth in the industrialized countries will be hard pressed to average more than 1 million per year between now and 2050.[42] The United States is the only advanced economy that still has a fertility rate at or above the population replacement level; Japan and most western European countries will actually be facing significant natural population declines over the next several decades. Thus, virtually all population growth in the advanced economies will have to come from immigration – a source that can pretty much be turned on or off as circumstances warrant.

The challenges facing Third World countries in coping with poverty and population growth are truly formidable. Compared with what the industrialized world went through, the numbers are daunting. In 1955, when the global population was approaching 3 billion, there were roughly twice as many people in the developing world as in the advanced economies. By the end of the 1990s there were over 6 billion people worldwide, with most of the increase occurring in Third World countries.[43] This explosion of humanity is what created the present, intimidating scale of global poverty. Population growth has simply run ahead of national economies, which now lack the capacity to expand infrastructure and services fast enough to create formal-sector jobs.

Third World cities have been especially hard hit as they have had to absorb roughly two-thirds of this increase. Since 1950 the population of cities has grown from 700 million to over 3 billion. The result in most Third World nations has been a relentless increase in the numbers of people who must eke out a living in the urban segments of informal economies. Poverty is becoming a primarily urban phenomenon.

There are an estimated 5 million 'poor' in Bombay, and 30 to 60 per cent of residents in most large cities in the developing world live in informal settlements or shantytowns (e.g., Sao Paulo, 32 per cent; Mexico City, 40 per cent; Manila, 47 per cent; Bogota, 59 per cent).[44] As many as 100 million unemployed people are roaming the streets of Chinese cities. The population of Third World cities will likely expand by another 2.5 billion people by 2025, and by 2050 there will be six people living in the Third World for every one living in the advanced economies. And Third World countries will have to absorb these people in circumstances that are already at a crisis point. They already face high base populations, high levels of poverty, growing levels of crime and violence, sharp income-distribution curves, global stress on ecological systems, inadequate levels of national and municipal service capacity, and serious financial constraints that are already limiting the capacity to maintain (let alone extend) infrastructure and social services.

Provisioning Bipolar Cities

Given this starting line, it seems likely that most new urban residents will end up living in shantytowns with no electricity, sanitation, or running water and with little or no hope of improving their lot. If the wealthiest countries of the world, with all their inherent advantages, are still having trouble with resource distribution and with meeting the investment requirements of urban and rural infrastructure, imagine what the Third World is facing!

Nor should it be at all surprising that nation-states are having a hard time adapting to the organizational requirements of Round Five and that the results of trade liberalization and poverty reduction programs have been mixed. The entire approach to growth and poverty reduction is based on 'trickledownism' – that is, on spreading the benefits of economic growth by expanding the infrastructure and creating more job opportunities in modern enclaves. This approach worked well for advanced economies that benefited from a host of highly favourable conditions. It is not working in countries already saturated with poor people and facing further population surges. The evidence strongly suggests that heavy reliance on globalization and the expansion of wealthy enclaves to alleviate global poverty is simply not going to work, at least not in the next twenty-five years.

A better approach to reducing world poverty was suggested in the discussion of provisioning societies in Parts I and II. It is especially important to design urban infrastructure so that it meets the needs of the urban poor; doing so will generate informal-sector wealth, create employment opportunities, and enhance access to the flows of natural capital that are necessary to eradicate poverty.

As discussed in Part II, it may not be valid to talk about how countries are integrating themselves with the global economy: it is really the advanced, largely urban-based portions of economies that are doing this. As the Italian futurologist Riccardo Petrella explains it, power is coming to lie 'with a league of traders and city governments acting on a world scale, whose main concern will be to promote the competitiveness of the global firms that they accommodate.'

The cities now leading world economic growth are increasingly 'global' in the sense that they are interconnected and in competition with one another to attract investment, corporate presence, people and skills, industrial production units, and so on, and they are constantly reinventing themselves to be more attractive to mobile capital and mobile people. For example, Shanghai is vying with New York and Tokyo to become the international business and financial centre around which the economies of the Western Pacific will be organized; by 1996, 40 of the top 100 MNEs in the world had opened offices there.

The wealth generated by socially and technologically advanced urban areas is what stimulates most of the growth that occurs elsewhere in national economies. There is nothing new in this. Concentrated enclaves of power and wealth have always been part of all human societies, except perhaps for hunter-gatherer clans and tribes and early agricultural societies. But scale is now the obstacle, and there is no guarantee – as the experience of LAC indicates – that rapid urban growth will lead to rapid gains in per capita incomes. Population growth can easily overwhelm the gains brought about by growth in wealthy urban enclaves.

Urban growth will not help the poor as long as approaches to poverty reduction continue to focus on 'trickledownism' and as long as the benefits of growth go mainly to wealthy enclaves. As things stand now, the world is heading toward a future of divided mega-cities, with the wealthy living and working in armed compounds,[45] surrounded by vast, increasingly dangerous, poverty-saturated peri-areas separated from the enclaves by income levels and growing cultural differences.[46]

The world's poor must anticipate a continuation of the abject conditions that are the consequence of living without access to appropriate infrastructure. Roughly 2 billion, poverty-embedded people lack access to modern fuels or electricity. They can't afford energy-driven amenities such as refrigeration. They don't have access to potable water, and they can't afford the energy it takes to purify water before use. The result is high rates of infection and disease. The poor have limited access to schools and health services. They don't own their land or houses, so can't access legal or financial services. Police do not patrol the areas where they live. Informal sanitation services only partially remove the filth that surrounds them. And they lack political clout and the capacity to change their circumstances. They survive only through their own tenacious efforts. On top of this, the urban poor are being denied the job-creating power of infrastructure and the conduits that would give them access to greater sources of the natural capital that are essential for wealth creation.

There can be no economic growth without cities, and it is only in cities that mass employment can be created. As the idea of 'trickledownism' suggests, the key to creating more jobs, and different jobs, is to tie in to the technologies and infrastructure services of global provisioning networks. Only in this way can societies provision full urban employment. Without an expansion of hard and soft infrastructure tailored to the needs and capacities of the urban poor, there can be little progress in terms of addressing basic issues such as personal development, property ownership, increasing the value of the assets of the poor, and diversifying employment opportunity during the transition from informal- to formal-sector economic activity.

Wealth, Poverty, and the Five Rounds of Provisioning

It should now be clear that distributional inequity has been a constant throughout all five rounds in the provisioning of human activity. Through this long history, distributional patterns have been linked to the manner in which societies have organized the task of provisioning, and greater wealth has accrued to the societies or subgroups within them that led the transitions between rounds. Recent trends toward growing inequality in income distribution have been following this same path.

Significant progress has been made; even so, the global reality is that wealth gaps between countries and also within countries are getting wider. The benefits of growth are now accruing to nation-states, and to groups within nations, in accordance with the degree to which they have passed through the five rounds and are thus able to participate in the newer organizational structures through which the most significant provisioning processes now take place. Those fighting a rearguard action to sustain their status as hunter-gatherer societies are often among the poorest groups. Just up from the bottom rungs on the hierarchy are those countries, or groups within countries, that rely mainly on domestic stocks of natural resources and on local sources of capital for investment, and where most people are employed in producing goods destined exclusively for local consumption.

The poorest nations are those still in the early stages of the transition to urban life. In such countries, income gaps emerge between those in rural areas producing for essentially local consumption and those limited to the process of provisioning urban areas and international markets. The wealthiest countries are highly urbanized and are the ones leading technological advance. These nations rely on international flows of resources and their own production functions and provisioning arrangements are integrated across national boundaries. In all countries, and especially in Third World cities, wealth accrues to networked enclaves that have access to the technologies and organizational capacities of Round Five provisioning processes. Those not able to participate in these enclaves – that are stuck in the informal economies of rural areas or in the peri-areas of large cities – remain mired in poverty.

The evidence is fairly conclusive that wealth – if there is enough of it, and if social morality so dictates – can enable societies to address questions of poverty. Yet historical experience suggests that most societies have a high tolerance for gaps in relative wealth and are reluctant to make concerted efforts to reduce distributional inequities. Some go further and argue that a hierarchy of wealth is necessary to economic growth – that there are not winners and losers in this process so much as leaders and followers. Indeed, as the long ideological conflict of the Cold War and the demise of centrally planned economies shows, a strong case can be made that distributional inequity is a motivating force.

It would seem then, that the big distributional and poverty issues are between rural and urban areas and, in both areas, between those linked to the processes of provisioning associated with Round Five and those tied to the technologies and forms of provisioning associated with earlier rounds.

Cities play a key role in creating these divides and must play a key role in eventually eliminating them. This is because the linking of cities – or enclaves within them – is what drives the global economy and because the way cities are provisioned is what drives patterns of rural land use and thus the shape of rural poverty. Similarly, only cities have the capacity to reduce global poverty by creating mass employment.

Looking ahead, the next overhaul of the world's cities will have to be at least as dramatic as the transformations that have occurred over the past fifty years. But the adjustments will have to be accomplished in half the time and will have to start from a poverty-saturated base and at a time when growing tribal and cultural strains are already testing the strength of community and national cohesion. It is in cities that leading-edge growth and wealth-generating processes occur and where social tensions between rich and poor will have to be resolved. If these social and cultural divisions are not addressed, they may ultimately strangle the growth process.

Reducing global poverty will have to involve improving poor people's access to natural capital. Western cities already have their provisioning supply lines in place; new urban populations will have to find ways to compete if they are to increase their access to natural capital. To this end, they will have to organize their outreach to new sources of ecological goods and services around the use of technology, with all that implies for social reorganization and cultural change. Clearly, Third World cities are going to have a difficult time competing if ecological scarcity constrains global provisioning capacity.

In the following chapter I look at the rapidly growing potential for ecological surprises to constrain provisioning functions between now and 2025.

Chapter 10

Ecological Roadblocks to Growth and Poverty Reduction

The Signs of Ecological Overshoot

The evidence of ecological decline is well documented. For example, *People and Ecosystems: The Fraying Web of Life*, a collaborative report by the WRI, UNEP, the UNDP, and the World Bank, concludes that there are many signs pointing to the declining capacity of the world's major agricultural, coastal, forest, freshwater, and grasslands ecosystems. It suggests that all of these systems are suffering from the effects of human activity, and it concludes: 'The current rate of decline in the long-term productive capacity of ecosystems could have devastating implications for human development and the welfare of all species.'[1]

The one apparent bright spot seems to be that forest cover in North America is regenerating.[2] However, it is difficult to see this as a success story in environmental conservation brought about by conscious human actions: most of the gains are simply the result of natural regrowth on abandoned farmland. These 'gains' are also being more than offset by alarming reports that the world's forests may face extinction as a result of the continuing encroachment of farmland and escalating rates of global logging.[3]

Other reports are definitive regarding the human assault on biological diversity: the effects of pollution, habitat loss, and other forms of human encroachment into wilderness spaces are destroying the world's biodiversity at rates one hundred to one thousand times faster than natural evolution.[4]

The 'Global Environmental Outlook' (GEO), UNEP's millennium report on the environment, reaches similar conclusions. This report, the result of five years of data collection and assessment by a huge number of individuals and organizations from around the world, provides a uniquely comprehensive look at the state of the global environment.[5] It confirms the decline of land, forest, freshwater, marine, and coastal ecosystems and notes the assault on biodiversity. It then documents the ongoing struggle to enhance urban environments (especially regarding sanitation and air and water quality) and the growing health and environmental problems associated with chemical use (including the use of chemicals for agriculture). The GEO report also summarizes the consequences of human actions on the atmosphere and the continuing need to be concerned about the ozone layer.

Each of these forms of ecological decline has important consequences. However, as the GEO report makes clear, the most potentially devastating environmental issue in terms of its implications for human life and societal well-being is global warming. The effects of most forms of ecological disruption tend to be felt, initially at least, at local or regional levels. Climate change effects are global and are doubly dangerous because they exacerbate the effects of all other localized forms of ecological stress. The atmospheric accumulation of greenhouse gases, which block the release of heat that would otherwise escape into space, is already altering the planet's climate. Moreover, as discussed below, it seems inevitable that atmospheric greenhouse gas concentrations are going to double before remedial measures can be established to slow down their accumulation. Thus, we can expect climate change to do increasing harm, and that its effects will be felt by the world for hundreds of years.

Pollution and ecological decline are no longer merely local problems; they are global in scope, and they affect all societies, even those that have not contributed directly. Recently, for example, Canada launched into space (on a NASA satellite) a remote-sensing device called MOPITT. MOPITT detects the long-range spread of air pollution, especially carbon monoxide, which serves as a 'tracer' of other pollutants associated with burning fossil fuels, forests, and grasslands. The first images beamed down by MOPITT provided the most complete picture ever assembled of the patterns of air pollution around the world.[6] They showed vast clouds of otherwise invisible pollution from the burning of forests and grasslands in Africa and South America reaching as far as Australia, and they showed dust – possibly containing microbes – being carried all the way to North America. Other studies show huge, noxious clouds of pollution enveloping large parts of Southeast Asia and portions of this pollution crossing the Pacific

Ocean to North America in surprisingly strong concentrations.[7] It can no longer be disputed that human provisioning efforts are exceeding supply limits and eroding the viability of the world's ecological systems.

In the following sections I give substance to these observations by considering three environmental issues that will challenge the world in the coming quarter-century: climate change, the global water crisis, and the human food supply. In doing so I hope to illustrate how everything is interconnected now that the life-support mechanisms of all ecosystems are being tapped to the full by efforts at human provisioning.

After these three sections, I will examine the problems afflicting the global fishery in order to show how ecological cause-and-effect relationships spread the impact of environmental stress. These spread effects make it seem as if many societies – especially the wealthier ones – are not experiencing ecological overshoot or serious constraints on their ability to meet their provisioning needs. As the demands for natural capital mount over the next couple of decades, this interconnectedness will increase the likelihood of severe ecological flips. There is no longer much flexibility in ecological systems. They are much like an inflated balloon: if they are squeezed in one place, pressure is felt everywhere else.

I will also show that this interconnectedness makes market prices and mechanisms unreliable tools when it comes to deciding how to provision societies in conditions of ecological scarcity. Thus, there is an urgent need to look more to technology and management solutions to address the huge challenge of provisioning growth and poverty reduction.

The scope of this challenge, and the limited time frame available to deal with it, defies comparison with anything the world has faced before. These are no longer local or regional or even national issues. They are global, and they must engage all of humanity in the common cause of finding solutions.

The Compounding Effects of Climate Change

The world's climate is heating up. We *know* this. We are less certain about why it is happening and we are at odds about what to do about it and the costs and benefits of different responses. As will be seen in the following discussion, the only certainty is that we will have to

adjust to the formidable and in many respects unpredictable consequences of continued global warming.

Since 1860, when worldwide temperatures were first recorded, the
global mean temperature has increased over 0.6°C, or over 1°F. The
pace of warming has been accelerating, with the change after 1980
accounting for over half the increase. Since composite global record
keeping began in 1867, 2002 was the second-warmest year on record,
exceeded only by 1998. Furthermore, six of the ten hottest years occurred in the 1990s, with the remainder occurring after 1983. Regional
variations around this average temperature rise are quite striking and
strongly indicate fundamental changes in the global weather system.
For example, summer temperatures in the High Arctic (including northern Russia, Canada, and Finland) have increased between 6 and 8
degrees in the past two decades.[8] Although the increase in mean temperature seems small, the consequences of this warming trend are
already significant. Above the 45th parallel, spring is coming about
eight days earlier than a decade ago. The height at which the air
temperature reaches the freezing point has been rising since 1970 at
the rate of nearly fifteen feet a year; plants are moving up the mountains. Glaciers around the world are in retreat, and this is placing
critical sources of summer water flows in danger. The polar icecaps
are melting, and polar bears are losing weight as thinning ice makes
access to their food sources more difficult.[9] The level of the world's
oceans has risen between 10 and 25 centimetres because of thermal
expansion and the accelerated melting of polar icecaps.[10] Low-lying
Pacific Islands are experiencing water surges; indigenous peoples in
Canada's Far North are beginning to build moats to keep rising waters from eroding the low-lying lands on which their settlements are
built.

In the past two decades, considerable evidence has been gathered to
suggest that the warming trend is leading to more violent fluctuations
in global weather patterns. Warming is accentuating the global water
cycle. As a result, the planet is 'breathing deeper,' and this is bringing
severe drought to dry areas and more intense rainfall in others, often
accompanied by stronger winds. Since 1900 in the United States, total
winter precipitation has increased 10 per cent, dry areas are dryer as
higher temperatures cause more evaporation, and 'extreme precipitation events' have increased by 20 per cent.[11] Worldwide, between 1963
and 1992, the incidence of droughts increased five to seven times,
floods were up between eight and twelve times, and tropical storms

increased four-fold. In 1998, fifty-six countries were affected by severe floods and at least forty-five by drought. These events have been accompanied by a dramatic rise in weather-related insurance claims in the past decade.[12]

Climate change is the most complicated and pressing issue facing humankind, not so much because of what has already occurred, but because of what may happen next. In 1988, the World Meteorological Organization (WMO) and the United Nations Environment Program (UNEP) formed the Intergovernmental Panel on Climate Change (IPCC) to assess climate change trends and causes and to forecast consequences. Since then, the IPCC has published three major assessment reports.[13] The most significant conclusion emerging from the third IPCC Report, issued in 2001, is that the rate of global warming is accelerating and that its consequences for human societies are increasingly bleak. The 1990 report forecast global mean temperature increases in the order of 0.8 to 4.5°C by the end of the present millennium. The best central estimate at that time was for an increase of 2.5°C. Sea levels were forecast to rise between 13 and 94 centimetres by 2100, with a central estimate of 49 centimetres. The 2001 report increased these forecast temperature increases to between 1.4 and a truly devastating 5.8°C, with sea-level increases over 25 per cent higher than earlier estimates.

Future temperature changes of this order of magnitude are going to have a devastating impact on human societies. The most seriously affected are likely to be those living in low-lying coastal areas, and the great majority of the world's people live within 100 kilometres of a coastline. A 21 centimetre increase in ocean levels could flood the homes of more than 78 million people. At 100 centimetres, almost 20 per cent of Bangladesh would disappear beneath the rising seas. So too would a large part of New York City and other coastal towns and cities around the world. Massive public works projects will be required to protect international ports and to slow the inland migration of hundreds of millions of coastal dwellers. Saltwater surges and intrusions into aquifers in coastal areas will affect both the availability of water and agricultural output in vast areas of productive, low-lying coastal land, especially in Southeast Asia. The effects of higher temperatures and less predictable weather patterns on agricultural production are difficult to quantify, but there will surely be severe problems of adaptation. In terms of human health, global warming is expected to increase the migration rates of infectious diseases. The implications for biodiversity are certain: vast populations of plants will be affected, and many forms of animal life will be stressed or lost as a result of habitat changes. A significant increase in economic and political tension and human conflict is expected to accompany these changes.

Climate change is an enormously complicated issue because of human complicity in the processes of change. Scientists studying global warming have focused mainly on trying to separate human or anthropogenic influences from naturally occurring fluctuations. The idea that human actions can alter global climate by increasing the atmospheric concentrations of greenhouse gases (GHGs) has been around for a long time. In 1896, a Swedish chemist, Svente Arrhenius, was the first to predict that the accumulation in the upper atmosphere of CO_2 emissions from the burning of coal might lead to global warming by trapping infrared radiation received from the sun that would otherwise have escaped back into space. However, it took another ninety years for the world to begin taking the threat seriously, and for a broad scientific consensus to coalesce around the view that this greenhouse effect – caused by atmospheric CO_2 and other GHGs – is the principal driver behind the recent warming trend. Roughly 1 per cent of the upper atmosphere consists of GHGs, the most important of which are carbon dioxide (CO_2), methane (CH_4), nitrous oxide (N_2O), and halocarbons (fluorine and chlorine-based compounds that also erode the ozone layer).

The turning point occurred with the publication of the IPCC's first report in 1990. This report called for an international agreement to mitigate global warming and led to the negotiation of the Framework Convention on Climate Change (FCCC), which came out of the Rio Conference of 1992. By the time the second assessment report was published in 1995, it was generally acknowledged that human causes, rather than normal climate fluctuations, were the main driver of global warming, or at least a major contributing factor. The consensus view of the IPCC, supported by some two thousand scientists from around the world, was that 'the evidence points to a discernible human influence on global climate due to the build-up of GHGs since pre-industrial times.' In the 2001 report, the consensus view had hardened: 'Most of the observed warming over the last 50 years is likely to have been due to the increase in green house gas concentrations.'

For roughly two centuries, corresponding with the period of rapid industrialization that was triggered by the steam engine and the large-scale burning of fossil fuels (which release large quantities of CO_2), there have been continuous increases in the atmospheric build-up of GHGs. Other human activities accompanying technological and economic advance – such as the mechanization of agriculture, the massive clearing of land, and the diversification of industrial production – have added enormously to the release of other GHGs including methane, halocarbons, and nitrous oxide. The consensus view is that atmospheric concentrations of these GHGs have been rising at approximately the same rate as human societies have been creating them.

In terms of relative importance, well over half the problem arises from the burning of fossil fuels. Roughly another quarter arises from soil erosion as a result of poor grazing, farming, and ranching practices, as well as logging (which results in a net loss of the carbon filtering or sequestering capacity of plants and soils). The balance comes from the release of ozone-depleting chemicals such as chlorine, benzene, and methane. These chemicals, including agricultural sources of methane, are the focus of efforts under the Montreal Protocol to find effective substitutes and containment practices.[14]

The accumulation of GHGs from human activity is accelerating. By 1960, they had increased 20 per cent over preindustrial levels; by 1999, they had increased 30 per cent; and they are forecast to double again before 2030.[15] The warming that has taken place over the past century, the rise in sea levels, and the fluctuations in climatic patterns that have occurred so far are entirely consistent with the theory that the greenhouse effect is a result of the release of growing volumes of human-produced GHGs.

Among the counter-arguments advanced by sceptics of this theory, the most intriguing is made by those who point to the fluctuating levels of solar radiation and the effects of this on cloud cover. These theories challenge the broadly-based scientific consensus on which the FCCC is based by suggesting that CO_2 and other GHGs have little impact on the earth's temperature compared to natural processes.

It has long been known that variations in the brightness of the sun caused by changes in its speed of rotation, the incidence of solar flares, the gravitational effects of other planets, and so on, have significant effects on the earth's climate and that the brightening of the sun throughout the twentieth century has played a role in the warming process. These effects are amplified, it seems, by changes in cloud cover associated with changes in the sun's brightness. Overall, cloud cover – especially that of lower clouds – tends to cool the earth by reflecting sunlight back into space. It is argued that increases in solar activity tend to decrease cloud cover, which means that the overall warming effect is greater than that of direct heating from the sun's rays alone. At least part of the explanation for the link between increased solar activity and a reduction in cloud cover is that an increase in solar activity results in more intense solar winds, which attenuate or reduce the volume of galactic cosmic flux reaching the earth. This flux, or high-energy particles that originate in outer space, helps aerosols in the atmosphere pick up water particles and form low-lying clouds, and lower volumes of flux mean less cloud cover. The result – according to one study that found a correlation between long, repeating cycles of global warming (i.e., cycles of increasing and decreasing temperatures that have taken place every 135 million years) and changing levels of cosmic energy particles (CEFs) reaching the earth caused by interference associated with the periodic passage of our solar system through an arm of the Milky Way – is that most of the climate variation in the past half-billion years, as well as in the past century, can be explained by these changes in cosmic rays.[16]

It is important to emphasize that no one is arguing that the world's climate is not warming. The debate is over why this is happening, what we can expect in the future, and what if anything we can do about it. Also, it is not surprising that different theories of cause give rise to differences of view with respect to forecasting the pace and consequences of the present warming trend. Thus, for example, the authors of the study just referenced conclude that the climate-warming effects of another doubling of today's atmospheric CO_2 levels will only lead to a further global temperature rise of about 0.75°C. This is considerably below IPCC estimates and raises questions about the need to incur the economic costs of reducing GHG emissions.

At the same time, there are good reasons to believe that global warming may happen even more rapidly than suggested by the IPCC projections. These are averaged over a 100-year time frame, and the need for aggressive response measures may become desperate in its immediacy well before then.

It is difficult to forecast the future of global warming. It is even more difficult to decide what can be done about it, not only because of differences of opinion regarding human complicity, but also because of the need to make assumptions about population and economic growth, the choice of policies to address the problem (i.e., reducing reliance on fossil fuels), and the likely success of measures to curb

GHG emissions. Nonetheless, climate change models are now sophisticated enough that their 'predictions' accord very closely with past experience and we can speak of near-term effects with growing confidence. Even so, the best we can presently do is estimate which areas will become dryer or wetter, warmer or cooler; also, how quickly sea levels will rise and weather patterns will grow more violent. From these projections, we can estimate in turn the implications for agricultural and food production, for human migrations out of coastal areas, and for various other likely happenings.

But models, of course, cannot predict with absolute certainty, and debate rages over their reliability. For example, in light of the debate over solar activity being a causal factor, it is noteworthy that the models are weak in predicting the effects of changes in cloud cover. But this does not mean, as some speculate, that the models are wrong regarding the effects of warming on the density of cloud cover as a result of higher evaporation rates from surface waters and various forms of pollution. Depending on the type of cloud cover this creates, it could either slow or accelerate the rate of warming by either reducing incoming or trapping more outgoing solar radiation.[17] How might these effects interact with continued high levels of solar activity? We don't know.

The ultimate shortcoming of present forecasts is that no one knows what the comprehensive effects of another one- or two- degree rise in global temperature will actually be. Moreover, no one knows at what point the consequences of global warming will become irreversible and thus precipitate unstoppable changes in global climate that will, with implacable certainty, dictate the human future. This is especially worrisome as the climate change models do not adequately take into account the effects of all possible feedback mechanisms.

Naturally occurring climate stabilizing mechanisms seem to exist. There are several favourable feedback loops that could possibly temper the pace of warming. For example, the world's forests and agricultural lands could conceivably act as vast carbon sinks. Also, the warming of the oceans could increase their capacity to absorb carbon.

But there is also growing evidence that the rate of global warming is going to accelerate as a result of other feedback mechanisms, which together could produce rapid changes in climate, with catastrophic consequences for life on earth as we now know it. A number of these potentially destructive mechanisms are summarized below:

- Warmer temperatures could cause tropical forests to die and could turn grasslands into deserts. This could lead to the release of 10 billion *tons* of CO_2 – the equivalent of adding as much as one-third to present levels of atmospheric concentrations.[18] A similar effect is already evident in northern latitudes: the Arctic tundra has warmed so much that it now gives off more CO_2 than it absorbs. These changes could be dramatically augmented by the effects of global warming on the life cycles of phytoplankton in the world's oceans. These microscopic creatures serve as a huge carbon sink in that they remove as much CO_2 as all land plants. A reduction in phytoplankton, which could be precipitated by a slowing of ocean currents due to global warming, could have a strong impact on the rate of accumulation of CO_2 in the upper atmosphere.[19]

- 'The ocean is the flywheel of the global climate system,' and it has been warming in the past fifty years at a rate that is 'way out of the bounds of internal variability' and at rates that are highly consistent with the theory of anthropogenic climate warming.[20] This has profound implications for the potential of global warming to destabilize weather patterns by affecting the strength of the world's ocean currents. Huge ocean currents flow north past Labrador and Iceland, carrying warm, tropical water that delivers heat to the northern half of the Atlantic and moderates the temperature in Europe and adjacent lands. Colder, heavier water currents dip below the northerly surface flow of warm water from the tropics and flow southward to complete the 'conveyor belt.' There is strong evidence that this conveyor belt has repeatedly slackened and at times even shut off in the past 100,000 years. This has produced dramatic climate shifts across the Northern Hemisphere, including one ten-degree temperature swing that took place in the space of just a few years. Some researchers now believe that the moister air associated with global warming could, ironically, shut down the northerly flow of the conveyer belt current and plunge much of Europe into a deep chill, with vast social consequences, especially for farm production. The increased cloud cover and precipitation could even trigger a new European Ice Age. Already there is evidence of a significant slowing in the volume of the southward current.[21] Similar changes in the intensity of ocean currents are also evident in the Pacific Ocean.

- Global warming could trigger the release of vast quantities of methane from methane hydrate deposits frozen beneath the Arctic permafrost and trapped in ocean mud at depth. The deep-ocean methane hydrate deposits have the potential to be an enormous source of carbon-based fuel (they represent more than twice the carbon reserves of all other fossil fuels combined). On the other hand, these deposits, formed through the microbial decomposition of organic matter, could trigger catastrophic global warming as a result of the fragility of these deposits and their potential to release astonishing quantities of methane. Researchers have found evidence of at least three past climate impacts due to releases from these sources. One of these – a possible explosive release of methane from a single large site, likely the floor of the Barents Sea off Norway's coast – 'could have triggered the notable increase in temperature that occurred over just a few decades during the earth's last ice age some 15,000 years ago.' The reasons for these releases are unclear. Possibly, they can be triggered by a change of pressure due to melting ice or a rise in temperature.[22]

On balance, the evidence seems to indicate that 'warmer begets warmer still.'[23] Higher global temperatures are already happening, and even higher ones may soon arrive even faster than IPCC estimates suggest. At least one highly qualified scientist believes that the 'degree of change will become dramatic by the middle of the 21st century, exceeding anything seen in nature during the past 10,000 years.'[24] The likelihood of rapid change in as little as ten years seems to be increasing.

It is against this confusing background that we must judge the adequacy of the world's response to climate warming. In this respect, the single most important point to make is that some economies may succeed in decreasing their 'carbon intensity,' but almost no countries are presently in a position to reduce their growth in total GHG emissions, and no overall reduction in global anthropogenic emissions is achievable between now and 2025. Indeed, it is likely that the presence of these gases in the upper atmosphere will more than double by then.

As the dialogue over how to respond has unfolded over the past several decades, the world's nations have divided into three camps: the United States; the thirty-odd countries of the OECD and eastern Europe, which are still pursuing the Kyoto Accord (the implementation plan for the FCCC); and the rest of the world, including all developing countries, which have not assumed any obligations for dealing with the problem.

The Kyoto Protocol was negotiated in 1997 and set as a target an average 5 per cent reduction of GHG emissions from 1990 levels for advanced economies. This was to be achieved between 2008 and 2012, with more aggressive reductions to be achieved after that date.[25] The key player in global climate change talks and the source of approximately one-third of global emissions, the United States, withdrew from the Kyoto negotiations in early 2001, largely because of its growing concern about the costs of compliance and the economic disruption that might ensue. The United States was also frustrated by the protocol's failure to place any kind of ceiling on emissions from Third World countries. In February 2002, the United States released its own plans for combating climate change – plans that would effectively tie the reduction of emissions to the rate of economic growth on about a three-for-one basis. That is, if the economy grew by 3 per cent, GHG emissions would be reduced by 1 per cent. It is estimated that in ten years, this new approach will reduce total emissions by about 18 per cent below what they would have been without any controls. This plan, which relies entirely on voluntary efforts by industry, will result in reductions that are less than 20 per cent of those set for the United States in the Kyoto Protocol. Moreover, an appraisal of this plan conducted by the PEW Centre on Global Climate Change suggests that voluntary efforts alone will not prevent overall American emissions from growing between 15 per cent and 50 per cent by 2035.[26] The Kyoto Protocol did not set any control targets for developing countries. Because roughly 75 per cent of present emissions still come from the industrialized nations, it was argued that advanced economies should bear the main burden for rectifying the problem. This position was adopted even though developing country emissions are growing rapidly and will match or exceed the volume of emissions from the industrialized world within two or three decades.

The result of the Americans' withdrawal and the failure to set control targets for Third World nations means that, when ratified, the terms of the Kyoto Protocol will apply to only countries, which between them will soon account for less than one-third of global GHG emissions. Whether or not the protocol will actually come into effect is still in doubt. Before Kyoto becomes legally binding, a minimum of fifty-five parties to the convention will have to sign on, including Annex 1 countries (the developed economies) that between them accounted for at least 55 per cent of that group's CO_2 emissions in 1990. At the time of writing, some one hundred countries had signed on. However, with the withdrawal of the United States, the only hope of meeting the Annex 1 emissions threshold is if Russia signs.

An innovative range of 'carbon-trading' mechanisms were included as part of the Kyoto framework to help channel investment to the lowest-cost containment options, thus maximizing the reduction in GHGs from money spent. One of these trading options, the clean development mechanism (CDM), was specifically set up to address the issue of Third World emissions. The CDM allows advanced economies to receive credits against their Kyoto targets for GHG reductions that are a result of projects they finance in Third World countries that join the protocol. However, these investments will not reduce net global emissions beyond the commitment levels of the handful of developed economies that have accepted the Kyoto targets.

The constraints to progress are more complex than the failure to get the global community to agree to a unified approach for reducing GHG emissions. They are also technical, and they are tied to the enormous inertia of present growth patterns, especially in the Third World.

On the technology front, a delay in reducing emissions is inevitable. Innovation across many areas of economic activity is unlikely to have much impact on emission levels over the next twenty-five years. In the transportation field, for example, much is made of the potential for hydrogen fuel cells and 'hyper-cars' (light-weight vehicles powered by hybrid gas/electric systems) to dramatically enhance fuel efficiency while reducing emissions by impressive orders of magnitude. Yet it looks as if it will take until 2004 or 2005 before these vehicles are introduced into the marketplace, and only then in areas such as California, where legislation dictates the pace of progress toward the use of zero-emission vehicles. It will then take at least several decades before these vehicles come to dominate the marketplace and existing stocks of old-style fossil-fuel motors are phased out.

This transition could take even longer if it is not driven by regulation or by aggressive industrial leadership. This is especially true in the United States, where consumers, encouraged by years of cheap energy, have begun to embrace larger, less fuel-efficient cars, notably SUVs. The result is that overall automotive fuel efficiency is being pushed back toward the levels that existed in the early 1970s, when concerns over the exhaustion of oil and gas reserves and OPEC-induced fuel price hikes led to the introduction of progressively tougher targets for fuel economy.

But if the advanced economies are having difficulty meeting the schedule for reducing GHG emissions, it is nothing compared to what is taking place in the rest of the world. Increasingly, Third World growth is threatening to perpetuate the problem. Emissions from developing countries will grow much more quickly than in the developed economies because of the nature and pace of Third World economic growth.

The Chinese economy is expanding rapidly, and that country's limited options for meeting its growing energy requirements illustrate the dimensions of the coming challenges. Having started from a low base in terms of per capita emissions, China is now the world's second-leading producer of GHGs, and it could triple its emissions by 2020.[27]

China has only recently emerged as a leading producer of GHGs. For thousands of years, human muscle power was China's main source of mechanical energy, supplemented by sophisticated hydrological systems to irrigate fields and by the burning of wood, straw, and organic wastes.[28] Many features of these early energy systems are still present in today's China. It is estimated that as late as 1978 between 1,500 and 1,800 days of labour, including irrigation work, were still invested in farming each hectare of rice, and ancient irrigation methods are still in operation. For example, the irrigation system that today waters the vast Chengdu Plain in Sichuan province is still largely the same as when it was first completed around 230 BC. Fossil fuel use (charcoal and coal) began to be widespread before AD 1000, partly because China lacked wood. Today, forests cover only 8 to 10 per cent of Chinese territory.

Looking forward, China's domestic energy requirements are expected to double before 2025.[29] In terms of domestic sources to meet this growing demand, there is apparently only limited potential to develop the Tarim Basin oil reserves, and the Three Gorges Project has already tapped China's largest source of hydro power. This leaves coal (of which China has significant reserves) and nuclear power as the large-scale domestic options for meeting China's energy requirements. Thus, 'without significantly altering its energy structure, the bulk of China's 2025 primary energy supply will be coal (68%) and oil (25%).'[30]

The formidable challenges China faces in reducing its GHG emissions are encountered across most of the Third World. India, Brazil, and most African countries, still rely on biomass for cooking and on their own muscle power for transportation.[31] In fact, this can be said of over half the world. The tropical climates of most of these countries provide greater incentives to use renewable energy forms. However, the efforts of these countries to promote economic growth look as if they will be based mainly on fossil fuel use, and the Third World is driving global energy markets in the direction of continued reliance on fossil fuels.[32] Carbon-based fuels account for roughly 75 per cent of all energy use worldwide and up to 90 per cent in most industrialized counties.[33] Yet demand is growing most rapidly in developing countries, and approximately 80 per cent of new energy investments are now being made in these countries. In terms of the composition of these investments, oil accounts for 30 per cent, natural gas for 23 per cent, coal for 22 per cent, renewables for a respectable 19 per cent (which is higher than in most advanced economies), and nuclear for 6 per cent.[34]

It will be very difficult for the developing world to move away from these patterns of energy consumption. Within the next several decades the total number of cars in Southeast Asia is expected to exceed the combined total of all cars in Europe and North America. The Kyoto-exempt nations will account for up to four-fifths of the projected increase in CO_2 emissions between 1990 and 2010 and for half the world's energy use by 2020.[35] By then, the total GHG emissions of Third World countries could exceed those of advanced economies. Clearly, the success of climate change policies rests as much on the Third World as it does on the advanced economies.

The unhappy reality is that dramatic climate changes are already in train as a result of the existing 30 per cent increase in atmospheric concentrations of GHGs above preindustrial levels and possible natural causes. Based on present national commitments, there is little prospect of curbing overall increases in the release of GHGs over the next several decades, and it is likely that atmospheric concentrations will double again to at least 60 per cent over preindustrial levels. Given this outlook, some scientists believe that climate change is already unstoppable, which makes the only 'smart' option trying to 'avoid the worst consequences.'[36] The grave risks to all human societies that are inherent in this trend are highlighted by the growing possibility that the world is about to surpass those threshold levels of change at which catastrophic flips in global weather patterns might occur. Indeed, the world may already be on an irreversible downslope toward climate-induced disaster.

Finally, it is worth pointing out that there are powerful reasons for considering alternatives to continued fossil fuel use that have nothing to do with climate change. The enormous extent of air and water pollution arising from the production and use of fossil fuels has been documented for many years now, and there is growing evidence of the serious consequences this has for human health and the operation of natural systems. However, by themselves these concerns are unlikely to precipitate much change in present patterns of energy consumption. Without the synergistic pull of a strong international commitment to reduce anthropogenic GHG emissions, it is doubtful that much progress will be made in reducing these other threats to human health and that of ecosystems.

Regardless, all societies must now learn to live with the consequences of increasingly unpredictable weather patterns. Two of the critical areas where these effects will be most pronounced are in relation to the availability of water to meet the diversity of human needs and the effects of global warming on the ability to feed the world's people.

The Global Water Crisis

Human societies have always been challenged by the need to secure water supplies. The first known wars between city-states were fought over access to water. That was around 3000 BC. Access to adequate water supplies constrained the growth of Athens and contributed to the squalid living conditions of its citizens. Rome built aqueducts to bring it water from as far away as the Appenines, but eventually could not bring enough of it. Most cities throughout history have had difficulty providing sufficient water and sanitation services to sustain growth. Even today, in the world's richest countries, cities are hard pressed to maintain their water infrastructures and to guarantee water quality.

A brief look at the water challenges facing Turkey provides insight into the nature of the present global water crisis.[37] Turkey is a fast-growing middle-income country about to enter the European Union. It is also relatively well endowed with water resources. For these reasons, it would seem well positioned to meet its water management challenges. Yet those challenges are proving to be quite intractable. To begin with, the sources of water tend to be far from the urban areas that need that water. Also, after years of neglect and the unregulated disposal of industrial, agricultural, and municipal waste, Turkey's water resources have been severely degraded in just those areas where they are needed most. Many of the country's important watersheds, especially the ones near its seacoasts, are now heavily polluted. The aquifers serving urban areas are slowly being emptied; the draw on them now exceeds replenishment rates, and some of the water that is returned to them is increasingly polluted by seepage from human activities. There are very few treatment plants to clean up industrial and urban water effluents before they are released into water systems.

In Turkish cities, the water infrastructure is inadequate; around half the people in major urban areas are on municipal water distribution systems, and only half the water entering these systems reaches customers. As well, little of the water that does get through some urban systems is fit to drink. The availability of water supply and sanitation services is even more limited in rural areas.

The present draws of water are already placing pressure on Turkey's wetlands, which are the largest among European OECD countries and of strategic importance for maintaining biodiversity. Yet the country faces significant new, growth-related demands that could require a doubling of water withdrawals by 2010.

In addressing these issues, the government is focusing mainly on increasing water supplies. In urban areas, priority is being given to the building of water-purification plants and the extension of distribution infrastructure. Tourist centres, especially those in coastal regions, are also being targeted for this upgrading. But upgrading can only be done by extending the draw to more distant sources. In rural Turkey, the main priority is the completion of the $30 billion South East Anatolia project, which has involved the construction of power dams and the creation of an estimated 200,000 jobs on 1.7 million hectares of newly irrigated land.

To address funding and management constraints that are impeding the ability to implement these plans, the government is hoping to increase private-sector investment and management involvement through build-own/operate-transfer (BOT) or more permanent forms of private-sector management in concert with concessionary lending from international organizations. To ensure predictable revenue streams that will justify private-sector investment, the country has been moving toward full-cost pricing of water services, although it was still stumbling in the late 1990s over political resistance to forcing people to pay their water bills.

Finally, with respect to industrial and municipal pollution, Turkey is moving toward implementing EU-compatible environmental regulations. There are signs that the enforcement of these regulations with respect to industrial effluents will eventually become more rigorous. Progress on cleaning up municipal effluents before they are released into waterways and coastal zones seems to be slower.

It is difficult to judge whether these plans will succeed. However, it does seem that the focus on supply is designed to meet urgent, short-term human needs rather than enduring, long-term ones. And even in relation to short-term needs, it seems as if the investments being made will be far from enough. Thus, the country may do all that it can and still end up falling farther behind.

Meanwhile, pollution continues, groundwater problems are worsening, and time is running out to limit the damage. At a certain point the depletion of aquifers will cause structural damage and constrain replenishment. Once polluted, groundwater can take hundreds of years to return to pristine conditions.

At the same time, Turkey is *exporting* water problems to its neighbours. The Anatolia project is interfering with the flow of the Tigris and Euphrates rivers into Syria and Iraq. These flows are regulated by agreement; that being said, Turkey holds the whip hand because the headwaters of these rivers are in Turkey and the country is militarily strong. These transborder issues are complex and potentially volatile. They also form part of a broader water management issue, in that farther south, water is one of the issues on the table in peace talks between Syria and Israel.

Turkey's water management problems and their regional spillover effects are a microcosm of the 'global water crisis.' What you find in Turkey is representative of what most countries in the world must now deal with, and Turkey's responses are fairly typical of the ones being taken by most countries. The task of ensuring access to adequate water resources is now outstripping the capacity of at least eighty other countries. According to the UN, water shortages now affect over 40 per cent of the world's people and could cripple industrial and agricultural growth in scores of nations. Already as many as 1.2 billion people lack access to clean drinking water, nearly 3 billion live without proper sanitation facilities, and more than 5 million die each year from easily preventable water-borne diseases.[38]

Groundwater is now the primary source of drinking water for more than 1.5 billion people. Yet all around the world, aquifers are being depleted and degraded by pollution. Serious depletion is occurring as a result of the draws made by megacities. For example, the aquifer underlying Mexico City is being emptied, and as a result, the ground is collapsing – up to 7.5 metres over the past century in some areas –

ending for all time the ability to regenerate the aquifer to previous levels. The city now has barely enough water to flush its sewers, which don't reach all the people anyway. Manila's Guadalupe aquifer has dropped between 50 and 80 metres. This has allowed saltwater to intrude up to 5 miles into the aquifer. The same thing seems to be happening to the aquifers supplying Jakarta, Madras, parts of Florida, and a number of island nations.[39]

Agricultural production, which accounts for roughly 70 per cent of all human water use, is also at risk from the depletion of aquifers. Groundwater is a critical source of irrigation in many important agricultural regions, accounting for some 10 per cent of the world's total food production.[40] In the United States, agricultural output has already declined in several regions where highly productive irrigated land can no longer access water from shrinking aquifers: 100 million hectares – 20 per cent of the land that used to be supported by the Ogallala aquifer – have been taken out of production because of lack of water. The aquifers supporting massive agriculture production on the great northern plains of China and in significant agricultural areas of India, Pakistan, and Europe are also being drawn down at rates far in excess of their rates of replenishment.[41]

Elsewhere, human draws are causing rivers to run dry. This has consequences for downstream water use and is also destroying river and estuary habitat and biodiversity. In China, for example, the Yangtze River now runs dry every year. In 2000, for the first time ever, water in the Rio Grande failed to cross the American border with Mexico.

With respect to the pollution of aquifers, what you see on the land is what you probably eventually get in the water. Moreover, it is not just emerging or middle economies such as Turkey that face problems – this is happening worldwide. In the United States, one-quarter of landfill sites in the state of Maine have contaminated groundwater. Every industrial zone in India has made the groundwater unfit for drinking, and the same thing seems to be happening in China. Rural aquifers are also being affected by pollution from agricultural sources. In the United States, fully two-thirds of the aquifers tested in a national survey were found to contain pesticide and nitrogen fertilizer residues. The same situation prevails in western Europe, and excessive levels of agricultural chemicals are being found in groundwater in China, Mexico, Sri Lanka, and eastern Europe.[42]

Aquifers, of course, are only part of the water systems being polluted by human wastes. According to the U.S. Environmental Protection Agency, 40 per cent of the nation's surface waters are too polluted to meet the goals of the Clean Water Act. Indeed, there are few pristine rivers and lakes left anywhere in the world outside of inhospitable areas that are unfit for human habitation and are also devoid of exploitable resource wealth. As a result of pollution and excessive draws on water sources, 'more than 20 per cent of the world's known freshwater species have become extinct, been threatened or endangered in recent decades.'[43]

The effects of agricultural runoff on river systems and coastal zones give further cause for concern. Almost all river systems in or near urban centres or areas of intensive agriculture are polluted, and enormous algae blooms caused by agricultural pollution are having serious effects on the productivity of vast areas of the world's coastal waters – for example, the Gulf of Mexico.[44]

The implications of water pollution are profound and go far beyond the effects on the impoverished. Even in Canada, which has more fresh water per person than any other country in the world, seven people died in 2000 in the town of Walkerton from inadequate purification of water infected with E. coli caused by agricultural runoff. Other incidents across the country suggest that water-borne diseases may require more stringent purification processes than previously thought adequate.[45] All land-based contaminants eventually find their way into coastal zones, oceans, and ocean food chains, which eventually lead back to humans. Levels of mercury found in keystone ocean fish species now sold in Canadian stores – including shark, tuna, and swordfish – significantly exceed levels considered dangerous to human health if consumed on a regular basis.[46]

Finally, water availability can be strongly affected by climate change as patterns of rainfall become more uncertain, as rising sea levels add to the risks of salination, and as water from more violent weather systems becomes destructive or unusable.

Water Wars and Equity Issues

With respect to the consequences of global water shortages and thus the design of policy solutions, it is best to make clear distinctions between rural and urban issues, especially as they affect the rich and the poor in both locations.

Rural versus urban (and industry) consumption. Half the world's people now live in urban areas, and about 80 per cent of industrial production is located in those areas. By 2025, almost 65 per cent of the world's people will be urban dwellers. Most of this increase will be taking place in cities in developing countries – cities that already face severe infrastructural problems. The challenge of supplying as many as 6 billion people with water and meeting the needs of vastly expanded city-based industrial activities will place urban needs in ever greater competition with rural ones. Yet irrigation will be essential in order to open new agricultural lands to feed growing urban populations.

As competition for water access increases, and especially if market mechanisms are chosen to sort out this competition and countries move to full-cost pricing, agriculture will lose out. Industry and urban consumers will be better able to pay for their water. Thus, the greater burden of adjustment will be placed on those who provision urban societies with food. Choosing the right policy instruments to manage this circular flow of needs and cause-and-effect relationships will require a deft hand.

The moral struggle: conflict between rich and poor. When cities and their industries begin competing with rural areas for water, the rural poor are likely to lose access to what is now for them a free commodity. Attempts to impose 'full cost' pricing on rural areas can only worsen the plight of the rural poor, since without water or the ability to pay for it, they will lose their land.

In contrast, the shift to full-cost pricing has potential benefits for the urban poor, who presently pay far higher prices for water than the wealthy living in their enclaves, which are hooked up to municipal water infrastructure. In a growing number of districts in the slums of large cities, water pipes provide single points of water access (i.e., the 'community spigot'). However, most of the urban poor draw their water from heavily polluted sources and must incur high energy costs to boil and purify it for use, or they buy it in portable containers at inflated prices from informal-sector water resellers. As a result, the urban poor in developing countries often pay five to ten times more for water than they would from a well-run municipal system.[47] Unfortunately, most cities now lack the resources to extend municipal water and sanitation infrastructure to meet the needs of the urban poor. Moreover, using current approaches, there is little prospect that they will be able to catch up, let alone meet the needs of the urban population surge expected over the next twenty-five years. Nor will having the urban rich pay more for water automatically lead to the more rapid extension of water infrastructure for the poor. Water revenues tend to disappear into general government revenues and to then be doled out across the spectrum of government programs, many of which, like education, the military, and roads, have no revenue streams associated with them. In the case of privately operated water facilities, the reinvestment of funds is generally based on expected returns. Thus, to hasten the extension of infrastructure in the peri-areas of large urban centres, lower-cost, decentralized, technological options must be found.

Conflict between countries. The desire to acquire resources has been an important cause of wars throughout history. As natural capital becomes scarcer, the potential for conflict over access to that capital increases. Analysts suggest that future wars are likely to be caused by efforts at communal survival in the face of environmental scarcity, and no scarcity is more serious than a shortfall of water. As the discussion of Turkey's water management challenges illustrated, it is a small step from taking actions to address national concerns over water management to the need for international dialogue and negotiation over water sharing between nations. There are some two hundred shared river basins around the world, and many of them could become triggers for conflict between nations.

Whether or not competition over water access leads to water wars, the potential for water shortages to precipitate social chaos and human suffering is enormous. All the nations of the world will have to deal with the moral and practical dimensions of potentially massive human catastrophes brought on by drought, the exhaustion or pollution of groundwater, the loss of agricultural output arising from water shortages, and the fallout from competition between the rich and poor for access to and control of water resources. Water is a necessity. It is not something to be allocated according to wealth. Around 95 per cent of the world's population growth will be taking place in developing countries, much of this in the poorest, most resource- and water-stressed areas. Thus, pricing issues will always pose a dilemma for political decision makers. All governments will find themselves having to deal either with questions of equitable access or, more indirectly, with the moral and practical consequences of a failure to balance need with the capacity to pay or the right of access.

Toward a New, Global Water Agenda

There is a pressing need to get a clear focus on the framework within which solutions to the global water crisis must be found. Once this new 'global water agenda' is defined, the approaches required to implement it can be considered. In this respect, it is premature to start from the assumption that pricing and market mechanisms are the answer. More fundamentally, what types of solutions should we be seeking? And how can we ensure fair access to water in the short time available to find and implement those solutions?

The two most critical dimensions of the new water agenda are the need to meet urban (and industrial) water needs by redesigning urban water infrastructures and the need to change rural water and land management practices so that decisions are made on a watershed or bio-region basis. Once agreement has been reached on these objectives, the selective use of pricing mechanisms could prove helpful in terms of moving forward at least portions of the new agenda. Despite the near perfect consensus of experts on these objectives, political leaders around the world are still fixated on outdated and inappropriate solutions. In this regard, the ministerial declaration coming out of the Third World Water Forum held in early 2003 in Japan seemed to look to massive, centralized infrastructure projects to address water-supply issues and contained no concrete recommendations for the common management of transborder water resources. Until there is strong political will for change, little real progress is likely.

When we look at comprehensive solutions to the problem of managing rural water resources, it is clear that the biggest impact of water scarcity will eventually be on the world's food supply. The availability of water, and especially the manner in which it is used to support agricultural activities, has placed a big question mark over the world's future capacity to feed itself. Moreover, as will be seen in the following section, the management of water resources is only one of the broader land-management challenges the world must come to grips with if it is to feed the 30 per cent increase in global population expected in the next twenty-five years.

Feeding the World

The huge gains in the productivity of agricultural lands brought about by the Green Revolution enabled the world to feed an additional 2 billion people within fifty years. Incremental gains in food production are still being made, and agricultural prices remain low. This suggests that there are global food surpluses. Thus, even though at specific points in time millions are starving, it is argued that this is because of problems in the distribution of food and the challenge of paying for its production rather than fundamental limitations on supply. This mindset underestimates the coming challenge. While distribution may now be a contributing factor, the issues associated with feeding the world's people are much more complicated than simply getting existing food to those in need.

The Constraints to Agricultural Production

Almost all of the world's agricultural lands are now in production, most areas able to support Green Revolution technologies are now using them, productivity gains are levelling off, the demand for additional food to feed burgeoning populations is accelerating, and there are no new innovations on the horizon that hold out hope for matching the kind of productivity gains achieved over the past fifty years. Moreover, a number of ecological and social pressures are combining with the potential to erode the future productivity of agricultural lands and practices. Food production is already being constrained by soil degradation, water shortages, and the effects of climate change. A variety of social pressures – notably the desire to create rural employment opportunities and the need to curtail agricultural pollution – could also hinder further productivity gains. So it is not surprising that some contend the world is facing a rapidly worsening food shortage that will soon force the poorest among us to fight for survival.[48]

There are abundant signs of an impending food crisis. The following paragraphs summarize the constraints that must be overcome if the world is to have any hope of meeting the rapid growth in food provisioning requirements that will arise between now and 2025.

The availability and quality of land. There is precious little untapped agricultural land left to be put into production. By one estimate made by the Wildlife Conservation Society and the International Earth Science Information Network at Columbia University, fully 98 per cent of the land that can be farmed for rice, wheat, and corn is now in production. The implications of this are indicated by an FAO estimate that almost all of the '25% increase in global food production that occurred between 1983 and 1993 took place from within the existing area of cultivation.'[49] Thus, if the expansion of land is felt to be the answer to world food needs, this will have to involve the conversion and upgrading of marginal lands, including the conversion of tropical rainforests and the extension of irrigated land in areas where water availability allows this to be done.

There is a lot of imprecision in estimates of the availability of agricultural land on a regional or even national basis. Nevertheless, it can be said that there are few places in Africa where new agricultural land can be brought into production. Furthermore, soil erosion in Africa has increased three-fold over the past three decades, desertification has affected one-quarter of sub-Saharan nations and pressure from huge numbers of subsistence farmers can be expected to deplete the continent's productivity still further. Per capita food production across Africa has actually declined over the past several decades, and the future does not look promising.[50] Africa has the highest population growth rate in the world. Many of its nations are suffering from political instability and war, and its peoples are being weakened by the scourge of AIDS. All of this means that progress toward food self-sufficiency is unlikely. In Asia, even less new land is available. China is having to feed 20 per cent of the world's population from 7 per cent of the world's cultivable land. It has managed to do this over the past fifty years or so by raising output per hectare by an impressive 25 per cent. However, the potential for further gains, at least from Green Revolution technologies, is limited, since most areas are already using them: over 80 per cent of all rice growing areas, for example, are now using high-yield varieties.[51] Recently, for the first time in over forty years, China has begun to import food; it may soon be absorbing all of the world's surplus grains.[52] A similar situation exists in India and Pakistan and elsewhere throughout Asia, although more new land has been brought into production than in China through the use of irrigation.

Paradoxically, the greatest potential for increasing global agricultural output may well reside in the advanced economies, but gearing this up may prove difficult over the next twenty-five years, especially if it requires the use of additional farm labour with high-yield production skills. Also, governments would likely have to intervene to create market certainty and minimum price stability.

Soil and land degradation. If existing agricultural regions are to produce more food, then the world must be concerned about what is happening to the quality of these lands. An estimated 40 per cent of the world's agricultural land is 'seriously degraded,' so much so that output on 16 per cent of the world's cropland is falling.[53] Up to 10 per cent of irrigated land is now affected by salination. (When irrigated land dries out, the minerals in the water are deposited on the land. In some areas, 'a hectare can accumulate two to five tons of salt annually, and eventually plants won't grow.'[54]) Also, soils around the world are losing their organic richness; pesticides, fertilizers, and one-crop agricultural practices are leaching out and destroy the organic systems that naturally fix carbon and nitrogen, help retain water, and support the growth of plants. Poor agricultural practices make soils vulnerable to erosion. In many developing countries, for example, the practice of burning corn stalks for fuel is widespread: about 60 per cent of crop residues in China and 90 per cent in Bangladesh are removed and burned. This destabilizes the soil. The result is that when planting season begins and fields are ploughed, dry soils simply blow away.

Access to water. Global water demand has been doubling every twenty years, and agriculture is a major contributing factor to this. Almost all of the world's rain-supported agricultural lands have been under cultivation for some time. Thus, more than half the increase in world food production from the mid-1960s to the present has taken place on newly irrigated land. Around 70 per cent of all the water drawn from the world's rivers, lakes, and aquifers is now being used to irrigate land that produces 40 per cent of the world's food.[55] If new land must be brought into production to feed growing populations, food increases are going to rely even more heavily than in the past on irrigation. Yet, as discussed earlier, the aquifers that support major agricultural areas in China, India, Europe, and America are already being depleted, and human draws are already overtaxing a number of important river systems.

The loss of agricultural biodiversity. As noted earlier, as many as half of all the world's plant and animal species are now threatened with extinction. Agriculture has played a key role in this phenomenon. The destructive effects on biodiversity of present-day approaches to agriculture arise in two ways. First, the extension of agricultural land is one of the biggest causes of the loss of the habitat that is essential to preserve biodiversity; second, mono-cropping and the heavy use of synthetic fertilizer is making soils barren and weakening natural mechanisms for drawing nutrition from the soil.

   In addition, the relentless shift to mono-cropping is increasing the likelihood that the world will lose a great deal of the plant diversity that is essential for long-term agricultural survival. The transition from highly diversified production for local consumption to reliance on a small number of high-yield crops and agricultural techniques in order to feed the urban masses has increased human vulnerability to the consequences of biodiversity loss.

Wheat provides a good illustration. Over the millennia, about two thousand varieties of wheat have emerged through natural processes. The world now relies on a small core of 'manufactured,' high-yield seeds – perhaps only four or five at any one time – to produce almost the entire annual wheat harvest. The problem arises from wheat rust, the deadliest enemy of wheat crops. Wheat rust mutates. Thus, wheat breeders are constantly struggling to identify emerging mutations and to build genetic resistance into the next round of seed varieties. The only source for finding this resistance is in the two thousand original strains. Since these strains are no longer grown – at least not in commercial quantities – their loss or limited availability has placed the future of wheat production at risk. And what goes for wheat goes as well for all other food sectors. In sum, the present response to demands for greater agricultural productivity to provision ever growing populations is placing at risk the very biological basis of agricultural viability.

Climate change and agricultural output. Agriculture and climate change are tightly linked in cause-and-effect relationships. Agriculture, as it is currently practised is the source of around one-quarter of anthropogenic GHG emissions. At the same time, agricultural output is extremely vulnerable to changing climatic conditions.

Agriculture is contributing to climate change in several ways. Rice paddies release heavy emissions of methane, as do cows and other ruminants.

Inappropriate land management practices are also contributing significantly to methane and CO_2 emissions. Plants, including trees and crops, are natural 'carbon sinks' as they absorb CO_2 from the air. When they die and decay, as occurs when they are harvested by humans, they release that carbon back into the environment. When the overall mass of vegetation is growing faster than it is being lost, this contributes to the goal of reducing the release of GHGs. Conversely, a net loss of vegetation contributes to global warming. In this regard, agricultural land has considerable biomass below the surface. In the case of temperate farmland, for example, the below-ground biomass can be twenty to thirty times the volume found above ground.[56] This biomass, in the form of organic matter – soil bacteria, fungi, and other biota – often stores upwards of 44 tons of carbon per acre. On a global basis, 'the world's cultivated soils contain about twice as much carbon as the atmosphere.'[57]

Agricultural systems that rely heavily on energy inputs strip the soil of this biomass. The dead biota oxidize or rot, releasing their carbon into the air. Similarly, excessive tillage opens the soil to biological action and physical erosion, and this furthers the leaching out of organic constituents. These then decay into methane, which eventually finds its way into the upper atmosphere. Similarly, overgrazing, which contributes to desertification, and the expansion of agricultural lands into woodland zones – especially rainforest zones – add to emissions while reducing the carbon-absorbing capacities of the world's flora. Thus, both ends of the agricultural continuum – the high- energy, high-yield practices of most farmers in the North, and the destructive practices of the poorest farmers in the South – are adding to agriculture's contribution to global warming.

At the same time, agriculture is highly sensitive to changing weather patterns. Leaving aside the nightmare scenarios associated with climate change, even moderate fluctuations in normal patterns of rainfall or temperature can take a serious toll on annual agricultural output: systemic change over several years can have devastating impacts. Water surges and severe storms are a serious threat to low-lying delta agriculture, especially in the highly productive food-growing areas of Southeast Asia, which are vulnerable to coastal erosion and saltwater intrusions into groundwater. As global warming advances, its destructive impact on food production will likely be severe.

Recent modelling of the effects of climate change on agricultural output indicates the potential scale of disruptions. One study suggests that an increase in temperature of 1.5 degrees would reduce wheat output in India by 10 per cent. Egypt's entire agricultural output depends on irrigation waters from the Nile. If we go by the IPCC's first, lower projections of the rate of global warming, that country is likely to lose around 5 per cent of its arable land as a result of rising sea levels, and its people are likely to suffer an overall 10 per cent decline in their economic welfare by 2060.[58] This study did not look at the effects this might have on the already strained relations between Egypt and the Sudan over the latter country's plans to increase its draw of water from the upper reaches of the Nile for irrigation purposes. A number of modelling exercises suggest similar effects across North America, although negative agricultural effects might be reduced through adaptation. On the other hand, optimism regarding adaptation seems to assume that farmers will have a fairly long time to make appropriate adjustments (up to one hundred years in one American study) in conditions where change is steady and predictable.[59] From the earlier discussion, it seems that considerable change of an unpredictable sort could occur in the next twenty-five years.

Rural employment as a constraint on agricultural productivity. Future productivity gains could be seriously constrained by social pressures to utilize agriculture as a means for absorbing increasing numbers of workers. A reversion to higher levels of rural, farm-based employment of necessity implies greater reliance on small-scale agriculture. There are indications that small-scale agriculture can be almost as productive as large-scale farming.[60] However, even if this proves to be the case, it also implies a return to older forms of agriculture, with a higher percentage of production destined for local provisioning. Clearly, if this process is carried too far, it will create problems for the provisioning of urban areas. Small-scale production also creates a need for different forms of rural infrastructure – smaller veins, if you like – in order to channel excess rural production to urban consumers. This sort of infrastructure does not currently exist in many areas, so there will have to be considerable new investment if the push to smaller plots is to be effective. Smaller-scale agriculture will also add to the management and technological challenges that are inherent in efforts to increase agricultural productivity while simultaneously addressing climate change and pollution issues.

Pollution control and agricultural productivity. Gains in agricultural productivity are levelling off, and agricultural pollution is increasing, in part because we are now reaching the limits of the benefits that can be achieved through the use of fertilizers and pesticides. Once plants have absorbed all the chemicals they can, the 'overage' is leached out by rain and irrigation and flows into the surrounding water systems. In many regions, the limits of practical chemical use to increase output per acre have already been overstepped. To illustrate, 'in 1948 the US used 50 million pounds of insecticide a year and lost 7 percent of the pre-harvest crop to insects. Today, with a 20-fold greater insecticide use – almost a billion pounds a year ... the insects get 13 percent, and total US crop losses are 20% higher than they were before we got on the pesticide treadmill.'[61]

Similar effects in terms of agricultural pollution are arising from feedlots and large-scale animal husbandry operations, with serious consequences for water contamination.[62] Moreover, these same practices – which are at present the preferred and possibly the only option for increasing the production of animal protein – are now being extended into Third World countries, with predictable consequences for the environment.

Agricultural pollution, as discussed earlier, is now a major source of groundwater contamination, a major cause of the eutrophication of freshwater systems, and a major cause of algae blooms in lakes, river estuaries, and coastal zones. Nitrogen loading has recently become an especially worrisome phenomenon. Human activities have now added as much nitrogen to the environment as is found naturally. Indeed, there is evidence that excess agricultural applications are now being transported through the air and affecting plant growth.[63]

The Technology Challenge

The technology development challenge facing the agricultural sector is diverse. The current focus of innovation is not.

At present, most innovation efforts target increasing supply through initiatives in different areas of agro-biotechnology, including dry-land crop production, saltwater irrigation, and the genetic modification of plants and animals to increase growth rates and resistance to spoilage, disease, and insects. All of these areas hold promise, although there has been a persistent social backlash against genetically modified foods.

On the other hand, only small test plots are being used to develop non-mainstream innovations. As a result, there is a pressing need for a co-ordinated approach to agricultural innovation that will lead to integrated agricultural technologies and practices that are capable of addressing the full range of problems constraining increased output. These problems include the following:

• Water shortages.
• Carbon retention – specifically, the need to find ways to balance this with the careful reprocessing of agricultural 'waste' into bio-fuels.

- Agricultural pollution from the intensive use of chemically enhanced production.
- The need to rebuild natural soil organisms and soil productivity.
- The need to maintain essential biodiversity as well as biological systems required to support agricultural production over the long term.
- The loss of forests, and the need to 'reforest.'
- Increasing the productivity of agricultural lands in the face of huge social pressures to look to small-scale agriculture to create rural employment opportunities.

The good news is that there is growing, although still limited evidence that most of these issues can be addressed without compromising production. It seems, for example, that precision agricultural practices, including the use of drip irrigation techniques, can significantly reduce water use. This could significantly reduce the wastage associated with the excessive use of chemicals, since lower water use together with lower levels of chemicals and higher uptake translate into less run-off and less pollution. Evidence also suggests that healthy, naturally occurring soil biota can yield the same uptake of nutrients, thus requiring the application of far less fertilizer. This is especially the case with organic, multispecies farming which involves fuller use of soils' natural biota and less reliance on the chemicals that have long been part of large-scale, mono-cropping agricultural practices. Very high yields have been recorded using this approach in small farming operations. There is also growing interest in combining these approaches with the techniques of integrated pest management to help reduce reliance on chemical pesticides.[64]

There also seems to be considerable scope not only for reducing agriculture's contribution to global warming, but also for converting agriculture into an important global solution. Relatively simple changes in tilling and other practices can restore and augment the volume of carbon stored in agricultural lands. By one estimate, 'increasing degraded soil's carbon content at plausible rates could absorb about as much carbon as all human activity emits.'[65] Changes in agricultural practices would also reduce methane and NO_2 emissions from agriculture.

Another approach involves moving to closed-loop farming practices – that is, using farm wastes in downstream industries such as converting straw residuals into paper.[66] There is also great scope for converting these wastes into bio-fuels. 'Altogether, the diverse streams of farm and forestry wastes can probably provide enough sustainably grown liquid fuels to run an efficient US transportation sector, without any further reliance on special fuel crops or fossil fuels. Across the United States today, more than 85 million tons of bio-based products and materials, valued at about $22–45 billion, are produced annually, yet now most of these farm and forest residues are wasted, benefiting neither the economy nor the soil.'[67]

On the downside, alternative approaches, including precision agriculture and organic farming, may be able to sustain current yields, but there is no evidence that they can lead to higher levels of output. Choices must also be made between sequestering carbon in agricultural soils and culling out plant and animal residuals for conversion into bio-fuels.

As well, the complexities of these interactions can only be sorted out at local levels. This is a management issue. It will require a strong political commitment to bring about a co-ordinated approach to overhauling agricultural practices. As with water use, this will only be possible in the context of integrated land management. Only in this context can trade-offs between all of these objectives be harmonized.

According to one leading authority, the uncertain potential for emerging agricultural technologies to meet the future needs of growing populations means we will require 'a gigantic, multi-year, multi-billion dollar scientific effort.' This kind of agricultural 'person on the moon project' might still turn productivity trends around, but it looks as if the process will be 'incremental, tortuous and slow.'[68] And he was only talking about productivity gains!

The Story of the Global Fishery

There is a dichotomy between evidence of ecological decline and market responses to what should be compelling signs of immediate or impending limits on the ability of societies to adequately provision themselves. Markets seem somehow disconnected from these signs of impending disaster. In fact, with the exception of energy prices, which rise and fall in relation to short-term fluctuations in supply, commodity prices are falling. Farmers can't get enough for their produce to justify planting, and in most of the developed world, agricultural production is subsidized to keep farmers employed. If ecological resources are so fundamentally important to economic growth, and if they really are under assault, as argued here and elsewhere, then why are these constraints not reflected in the marketplace?

To some extent, the answer is that many forms of ecological decline simply have no immediate market relevance. Many forms of biodiversity, such as an insect species in the tropical rainforest, are not traded, and thus their existence or loss makes no immediate difference to production systems or to people's ability to consume.

A more reasoned response would point out that there are, in fact, a growing number of market indicators of the consequences of ecological decline. The costs to industry and municipalities of compliance with environmental regulations are one example. More obvious indicators might include the withdrawal of land from production as a result of water shortages, as is now happening in several areas of the world, including the United States. The effects of climate change are also now beginning to be seen in rising insurance claims for property losses due to increasingly violent weather. However, these costs are internalized in corporate and municipal budgets and thus are invisible to consumers and taxpayers. There is also a marked tendency for these costs to dissipate with time as organizations build them into their pricing structures, find ways of turning pollutants into products, or offset the costs through productivity gains.[69]

But these and other market signals seem inconsequential when set against the evidence of massive ecological stress. So, why is there such an apparent disconnect? Looking at why fish prices have not increased to reflect the erosion of the global fishery can provide the answer.

It is now common knowledge that most of the world's two hundred fisheries are being exploited beyond sustainable limits. 'An estimated 73 percent of the world's major fishing areas and 70 percent of the world's major fish species are at peak production or in decline.'[70] This has thrown thousands out of work and eroded the viability of entire fishing communities. It has led to serious conflicts between the United Kingdom and Iceland and between Canada and Portugal. In 1994, thirty conflicts over fishing grounds were reported, including several in which force was used. All of this has serious implications for future production levels. The FAO's optimistic forecast for the global catch from the wild is slightly below the catch in 2000, and it could be over 20 per cent less.[71] Yet there are fish in abundance in the stores in all Western countries, and prices have not risen as one would expect in the face of growing scarcity. So, what has happened and why should we be concerned about this?

As the following sequence illustrates, the story of the fishery is part of a much larger set of cause-and-effect relationships that threaten the stability and future of human societies. The effects are being felt, but not always in expected ways or locations. They are spread over other ecosystems and dumped on the poor, and they are not priced because their dispersion makes it virtually impossible. The sequence also shows in a compelling manner how pressures are building that will result in serious ecological flips as feedback mechanisms are overwhelmed. At that point, and not before, price increases will occur.

Technology and the intensification of extraction. The first and most obvious response to ecological scarcity is to look elsewhere for new supplies or to use new technology to increase extraction rates. In this respect, fishers the world over have done what societies have always done when faced with exploitable opportunity: they have intensified their efforts by increasing the number of fishers or by augmenting quotas. Then, when faced with declining catches, they have competed more aggressively for a share of the dwindling stocks. At the same time, they have changed their technologies the better to screen the oceans for fish not accessible using simpler fishing techniques. Fishing lines up to seventy miles long are now being used, as well as small mesh nets that catch young fish before they can grow and reproduce. The ocean floors are being dragged for shellfish and bottom feeders, and in the process marine habitat is being destroyed. In addition, the fishing industry has moved from small-boat, inshore fishing to big-ship ocean fleets that process and package the catch at sea. Inshore fishermen and workers in fish processing plants have absorbed the costs of this transition.

Fishers have also begun reaching out to more distant or novel sources of supply. Krill, for example, small, low-value crustaceans with little market appeal, is now being commercially harvested in the waters off Antarctica. Long-range fishing fleets from wealthy fishing communities have begun squeezing into long-established fishing grounds around the world and diverting a growing share of the catch from local to international markets. Big Dutch trawlers, for example, began scouring the oceans off the West Coast of Africa in the 1990s, with predictable consequences for traditional inshore fisheries.

The shift from natural to man-made production systems. The stagnation in the volume of fish caught in naturally producing ocean and freshwater environments has provided a major boost to the aquaculture industry, which more than tripled output from 7 million tons in 1984 to 23 million tons in 1996. Overall output continues to grow at impressive rates, averaging over 11 per cent for most of the 1990s. Fish, shrimp, and shellfish grown in man-made environments now account for almost 20 per cent of global production.[72]

The consequences of this shift from natural to man-made production systems have yet to be sorted out. However, substantial concerns exist regarding the pollution being generated by growing pens located in coastal areas and the effects these operations may have on natural habitat and the viability of natural production systems.

There is also great potential for aquaculture to decimate natural stocks should fish grown in pens be accidentally released into the wild. This is especially critical in the case of migratory species such as salmon, since the result could be an erosion in the ability of wild stocks to return to their natural breeding grounds. These fears are compounded by the industry's use of the tools of biotechnology to genetically alter fish to induce faster growth.[73]

There are also practical limitations to the continued growth of the aquaculture industry. In most ocean operations, the 'planted' species are carnivores and must be fed fish meal – in fact, a *lot* of fish meal. It takes two pounds of fish meal to produce one pound of growth. Something approaching one-third of the volume of the global fish catch is now being diverted to feeding animals, of which around 17 per cent now goes into feeding farmed fish. By 2010, all of this fish meal could be required for this purpose.[74] Thus, if the fish catch from the wild is in decline, there are serious constraints on the growth capacity of the ocean-based aquaculture industry. Aquaculturists are now beginning to flavour grains to make them palatable to fish, which raises a whole new set of issues.

The shift from ocean to land-based production. Most of the growth of the aquaculture industry is going to have to take place on land or draw on land-based agricultural systems for feedstock. As this begins to happen, fishing is going to compete with other uses for land and water resources and with other consumers of feed grains, including farm animals and humans.

Analysts optimistically argue that aquaculture output could double again by 2010, but it is far from clear how much a gain of this magnitude would actually contribute to global food availability. Wild fish production systems are dwindling. The land is full. Thus on both fronts, increases in aquaculture output may soon only be made at the expense of other, lower-value food commodities. In some areas a shift from low- to higher-value production is occurring. In Thailand, for example, 'nearly half the land now used for shrimp ponds was formerly used for rice paddies.'[75] Elsewhere, progress is slower. In China, which accounts for almost 60 per cent of total aquaculture production, 'concern over loss of arable land has led to restrictions on the further conversion of farmland to aquaculture ponds in some parts of the country.'[76]

This raises an interesting dilemma for future food-production strategies. On average, it takes a 1,000 pounds of water to produce a bushel of grain. Cattle in a feedlot then require up to seven pounds of feed to produce one pound of meat. The conversion rate is much better for hogs (nearly four pounds) and better again for poultry (just over two pounds) and fish (just under two pounds). Thus, fish and poultry represent a far more efficient way of converting grains into other forms of protein for human consumption than beef and pigs.[77] In a food-constrained world in which fish are competing with chickens, pigs, and cattle for access to feedstock, the fish should win. Thus, fish farming does hold out enormous promise, since it may be a more efficient use of land, water, and protein resources than other animal husbandry options.

However, while market forces are pushing for the production of cheaper poultry and fish, other vested interests and consumer preferences are pushing back. Around one-third of the world's cereals are now being used to feed livestock,[78] and both of these industries (i.e., cereals and livestock) are heavily subsidized in most advanced economies. Shifting these entrenched production systems will not be easy.

Spreading the effects across ecosystems and societies. John Alroy, an evolutionary biologist, argues that the spectacular extinction of large mammals across North America, which took place within two thousand years of the arrival of hunter-gatherer societies, was 'too gradual to be perceived by the people who unleashed it.'[79]

In a somewhat similar but vastly more complicated and rapid manner, the consequences of poor management practices and the collusive effects of human pressures on the global fishery have produced a succession of impacts on other ecological systems and societies in many parts of the world. However, the nature of these effects makes it very difficult to evaluate them and to control the consequences of human action. The transfer of the costs of adjustment from consumers to widely dispersed inshore fishermen, and the linking of the global fishing industry with agriculture in the use of productive land resources, have diffused stress on the wild fishery between ecosystems and societies in ways that are hard to see and very difficult to quantify.

In addition, the spread effects of thousands of other independent production decisions in economic sectors around the world are also affecting the fishery. The release of GHGs in Germany, overfishing in Canadian waters, the loss of essential irrigation water in China, the release of toxins in small quantities in many parts of the world, and any one of hundreds of other impacts, are now all combining to contaminate and decrease ocean fish stocks and to produce an amorphous intermingling of other forms of ecological stress and social adaptation around the world.

Shifting the burden of adjustment from the rich to the poor. The burdens of adapting to stress on the world's fisheries fall disproportionately on the poor. This happens when pollution limits the safe catch; when poaching by foreign fleets shrinks the size of the inshore fishery; when technological innovation squeezes the poor out of the fishery because they can't afford the new equipment; when the fish catch is diverted from local consumption to better-paying international markets; and when agricultural production and resources are shifted from lower-cost staples of local consumption such as rice to higher-cost foods for export and urban consumption, such as shrimp. This translates into fewer jobs for the rural poor, less low-cost food for local consumption, and an increase in the rate of drift of ill-equipped rural peoples to urban areas. The populations most at risk from the approach of ecological limits are the poor.

And the story of the fishery is not unique. As we have seen, agriculture is following the same pattern. The first response to the need for increased production was to expand into new lands. New technologies were then introduced that allowed more intensive production. In the present context, these highly energy-intensive technologies are based on the use of chemical supplements in large-scale operations that increasingly remove production systems away from natural processes, that shift the burden of adaptation onto the poor, who end up farming small plots of often marginal land, and that spread the effects into other ecosystems through pollution, deforestation, and the release of increased volumes of GHGs. And these effects are never visible to consumers of agricultural products. Like the fouled 'ethers' that in medieval times were believed to carry the plague between villages, ecological stress in one system infiltrates and tarnishes other systems while contaminating and incrementally reshaping the social fabric of communities around the world.

Why Market Mechanisms Do Not Prevent Ecological Decline

One of the defining traits of free markets is the mysterious means (the 'unseen hand') by which supply, demand, and technological and other market factors interact to set prices for everything that consumers and organizations buy.

For at least the past fifty years, environmentalists have been arguing that harnessing the power of these mechanisms by incorporating ecological and social externalities into market prices would create compelling pressure to resolve environmental challenges. Indeed, if market forces could be marshalled in this way, they might well be the only policy tools needed to dramatically shift patterns of consumption and investment. It is this ambition that is driving the emerging discipline of ecological economics. Tools such as the genuine progress indicator (GPI) are being designed to restructure normal investment and GNP accounting so as to adequately reflect the full costs of environmental and social externalities.[80]

But this siren call has produced remarkably little progress. The most significant result has been that the costs of environmental protection measures have been incorporated into investment projects based on environmental impact assessments. These actions are certainly helpful and have reduced the negative environmental impacts of specific projects. However, as discussed earlier, the challenge the world now faces is to address the cumulative effects of the residual impacts of hundreds of thousands of individual investment decisions being made around the world. Cause-and-effect relationships now arise on a global level. The resulting diversity of interactions and consequences blurs responsibility. Ecological and social feedback loops defer, diffuse, and obscure the realities of environmental depletion. Present policy tools may be extending the time frames within which we can take remedial action, but they are not changing the world's course toward ecological overshoot.

In these circumstances, markets are simply incapable of identifying, quantifying, and pricing all environmental and social externalities. Prices are determined in competitive markets by reference to immediately quantifiable data and more or less in real time; in contrast, the full costs of environmental stress can take generations to emerge and can be spread across vast distances, communities, and ecosystems.

In the case of the decline of the wild ocean fishery, for example, full-cost pricing would have to reflect not only the cost of lost jobs in local fishing communities, but also all the other incremental costs that arise as the consequences of depletion ripple around the world. These would include the loss of jobs in all inshore fisheries, the increased burden placed on the poor, the uncertain effects of the shift in reliance from natural to human production systems, the effects of growing competition for land-based resources, and the downstream consequences for the output of grains and meats; and all of these costs would have to be calculated and apportioned on a global scale.

Also, for this approach to work, prices would have to be readjusted constantly to reflect the changing state of relevant environmental and social systems. Presumably, prices would go up as new evidence of ecological decline was presented. However, because this is such a complicated and controversial process, even if consensus *were* to be reached on the extent of ecological stress, and even if there *were* agreement on the cause, price increases would only take effect a long time after the fact. The same is true of other forms of ecological stress, including climate change. By the time market signals induce a change in behaviour, it may be much too late to do anything except adapt to the consequences of global warming.

For these reasons, the objective of building full ecological costs into pricing decisions is not realistic: these efforts are unlikely to help the world address the challenges it faces in the next twenty-five years. Nor can the world rely on market mechanisms to halt ecological decline. As long as buyers buy and producers can sell at a profit, markets will play brinkmanship with ecology.

This does not negate the use of market prices as an effective tool for environmental management. But it does impose limitations on how decisions regarding the use of market mechanisms are made. The best that can be hoped for is that decision makers might arbitrarily set prices that will achieve ecological protection goals. However, to do this in ways that would pre-emptively curb ecological decline, pricing mechanisms would have to constantly overestimate the immediately quantifiable costs of environmental damage.

In the end, sound environmental management is just that! Pricing mechanisms can be used to assist, but the world needs to look to management, technology, and organizational solutions if the challenges of global provisioning are to be met. Simply stated, it is necessary to change the interface between human societies and natural systems, and this cannot be done without changing technologies and management practices. This means the world must find technology and management approaches that can alter the way agriculture is performed, the way fishing is done, the way water is used, the way energy is produced and consumed, the way we manage waste streams, and so on across all fields of economic activity.

In Part IV I will outline a plan for fighting the war on ecological decline. However, it remains, in the following chapter, to more fully define the ecological enemy lurking at humanity's gate by looking at how ecological decline can exacerbate equity issues, halt growth, and increase the potential for devastating human conflict.

Chapter 11

The Catalysts of Calamity

In the previous sections I looked independently at trends in global equity and ecological instability. In this section I look at how they can interact to precipitate social conflict.

The apparent rise in violent human conflict around the world has led to a growing debate among analysts over how ethnic, cultural, and religious differences, together with poverty and to a lesser extent ecological scarcity, are contributing to global tensions and diminishing the prospects for economic and human security.

In this chapter I draw on this analytical work. However, I argue that the notion of provisioning societies provides clearer explanations for much of past human conflict as well as insights into the kinds of wars that are likely to erupt in future years if solutions to the challenges of global provisioning are not found and if global ecological scarcity is allowed to run its course.

Competition for access to scarce ecological goods and services decimated societies and cultures in the past, and did so on an especially terrifying scale during the transitions between rounds in the organization of provisioning processes. Differences in how societies are organized to provision themselves are now at the root of global inequities, and the world's peoples are all now competing to meet their provisioning requirements from a shrinking pool of ecological sources. This is going to shape the coming lines of confrontation both within and between nations.

Globalization, Tribes, Cities, Nations, and Civilizations

A number of economists and authors now believe that cross-border flows of investment, people, technology, and resources and the development of integrated production and marketing networks between countries are together reducing tensions between nations.[1]

In earlier times, wealth was derived from land or through the direct control of natural resources. In contrast, nowadays national wealth and power are attained through economic growth. As a result, national well-being is now based on access to international markets and flows of offshore resources, rather than on the ownership of resources and access to domestic markets. It is argued that this growing interdependence constrains hostile actions by nation-states. Assuming that economic growth is the objective of national policy, wars to acquire land and resources are no longer useful: growth can be achieved with greater certainty through economic integration based on investment, trade, and reciprocal market access.

Others believe that the negative aspects of globalization are heightening international tensions. Globalization has become the whipping boy for those who resist external pressures on national cultures. Such pressures arise, for example, when economic integration places limits on the exercise of national sovereignty in the fields of trade and investment policy. Globalization is also affecting national cultures. It is argued that economic integration based on the operation of free, transparent market transactions is leading to the global spread of essentially American values such as individualism, materialism, and liberty – in aggregate, 'democratic capitalism.'[2] We seem to be tracking toward the 'global homogenization of culture, lifestyle and levels of technological immersion with a corresponding deterioration of local traditions and economies. Soon every place will look and feel like every place else, with the same restaurants and hotels, the same clothes, the same malls and superstores, and the same streets crowded with cars.'[3]

Still others argue that the greatest threats to peace, cultural integrity, and national cohesion are not external to nations; rather, they arise from *within* nations. As international tensions are reduced and as wars between countries become less frequent, localized conflicts and the reassertion of tribal bonds may be on the rise. Certainly in the Third World and in parts of eastern Europe and the Middle East, globalization seems to be contributing to clashes between cultures, ethnic and language groups, and religions. Those left behind in the race for economic advance seem to be relying again on tribal bonds for support and protection. Tribalism is gaining strength and in many regions threatens to slide into violent nationalism.[4]

It may well soon happen that wars between nations will become less frequent, only to be replaced by tribal and other forms of conflict within nations. According to Martin van Creveld, 'future wars will be those of communal survival' and will take the form of low-intensity, subnational conflicts, possibly based on terrorist tactics, that coalesce 'along racial, religious, social and political lines.'[5] This tendency toward 'tribal' conflict seems more pronounced in rural than in urban settings.[6]

The prevalence of rural violence – or the relative peacefulness of urban areas – may be partly due to the fact that cities can be powerful cultural integrators, especially when their employment-generating engines succeed in providing jobs for most urban dwellers. Yet, cities can also be the locus of social tensions when these integrating capacities are weakened, as is happening across much of the Third World. Urban poverty is socially destabilizing, and the peri-areas of cities, which offer the urban poor only squalid living conditions and the precarious prospects of informal-sector work, are experiencing growing levels of violence and crime. Homer-Dixon is deeply concerned about the implications of growing urban tensions and clashes in Third World cities, arguing that urban violence, be it political, communal, ethnic, or criminal, is likely to keep growing as a result of continued large-scale migration from poor rural areas.[7]

Obviously, not all countries or cities are alike. A continuum exists between the melting pots of North America and the cultural uniformity of Japan and Korea. Thus, different levels of political and social stability are found in the cities and nations of the world. That being said, the pace of urban growth in most Third World nations is simply overwhelming the capacity of cities to play their traditional role as cultural integrators. Furthermore, the most difficult adjustments may be in cities that draw their immigrant populations from ethnically diverse tribal communities. Many first- and second-generation migrants to cities continue to maintain links with rural areas, and as a result, new migrants tend to rely on the ties of family, clan, and tribe for help in restarting their lives. The result is that the tight bonds of rural areas are maintained in the peri-areas of many Third World cities. These bonds may even reach into the advanced enclaves, with the well off facing pressure to favour their tribal brethren in the allocation of employment opportunities.[8]

Some Third World squatter communities are now surprisingly old, with many generations of residents. The stability and endurance of these settlements can lead to social tension, with the first settlers perceiving the later arrivals as interlopers and discouraging them from building shelters or competing for scarce jobs. In Kenya, I was speaking several years ago to a third-generation resident who was raising her three children in a shack in Mathare Valley, one of the largest informal settlements in the city. As we were talking, the city was bringing bulldozers in to level some of the new cardboard-and-stick shelters that were becoming an eyesore for passing motorists and adjoining communities. Her attitude to the bulldozers tearing down her neighbours' houses was surprisingly ambivalent, but her sense of place was absolute. 'I am Mathare,' she told me. In effect, she was saying that Mathare Valley was her 'city,' that she was prepared to defend her interest in it, and that she and her family had first rights to the opportunities it provided.

Even in countries where urban growth is fuelled by the migration of peoples with common cultural backgrounds, enormous divides are developing between the favoured participants in wealthy enclaves and the impoverished masses living in the slums of peri-areas. Cities in advanced economies eventually integrate people into a single, dominant urban culture; in contrast, most Third World cities seem to be tracking toward sharply differentiated, bipolar civic cultures.

At the poor end, the notion of urban culture is now highly confusing because it has become synonymous with life in the informal sectors. The great uprooting and mixing of people in urban poverty is no longer rural in nature. Rather, it is something being shaped by the huge numbers of unemployed youth who roam the streets, by the reassertion of tribal allegiances, by the pervasiveness of violence and criminal anarchy, by the breakdown of traditional family structures, by high birthrates, by the grind of persistent poverty, and by the corrosive effects of a future without hope.[9]

This undefined culture of poverty is radically different in form and content from the urban cultures taking root at the other end of the social continuum, in the formal economy sectors. In these advanced enclaves the idea of cultural homogenization applies. These enclaves are linked to international business, communication, and consumer networks. They are organized around different forms of technology and they are subject to greater international, largely Western influence. The cultures of the enclaves are increasingly global, underpinned by materialism, by shared consumer interests, and even by linguistic uniformity as English solidifies its position as the international language of commerce.

Cities break down cultural barriers and integrate people into civic cultures; sooner or later they come to reflect the values and standards of the people and groups they contain. As the cultural gaps between formal and informal economies widen and the educational, technological, and infrastructure obstacles to upward mobility become more entrenched, the tensions between the two cultures increase and questions arise over which culture will come to control political decision making.

The basic reason for political power to exist is to shape collective action. However, no consensus can emerge as long as the gap between the urban rich and poor is extreme and continues to grow. It should be obvious that as the wealthy come to reside in walled enclaves surrounded by armed guards, democratic processes will be challenged by the existence of deep social divides. Either control and influence will come to reflect the values of the people of the shantytowns, or the well-off enclaves will come to rule through oppression.

This clash of urban cultures can also spread to the sense of nation. Internal consensus around a national as opposed to a tribal identity can take a long time to develop, and it must then be continuously stoked if a coherent sense of national culture is to endure. In this context, the growing cultural and economic divides within countries have great potential to erode state power and control. Urban culture is an important element in defining national culture, especially in societies where the great majority of people live in cities. It is not surprising, then, to find that tribal and cultural divisions within cities are being recreated on the tableaux of national unity. Reassertions of tribal allegiance are placing increasing stress on the bonds of national allegiance and the idea of a national culture. They are creating tribe- or religion-based competition for control of national political processes. As a result, the pressure to partition nation-states may become uncontrollable.[10]

Competition for political control is also growing between municipal, state, and national levels of government. It is especially intense in relation to the powers of city administrations. Cities are the engines of national economic growth, the places where most citizens now live, and the places where most social and equity issues must be addressed. Yet in the chain of political power, cities are at the low end of the political scale. Their limited political responsibilities were determined in a simpler age. Municipalities are beginning to flex the political muscle provided by their concentrations of people; as a result, the pressure to reorganize nations on the basis of regions and city-states is adding to the global wave of resentment against centralized control.

The backlash against cultural globalization, the sense that nation-states can do nothing about it, and the internal stresses on the bonds of nationhood, are all contributing to the erosion of loyalty to states and pushing many to achieve their goals through affiliations that extend beyond the national domain. This is especially evident in alliances under the banner of religion, notably Islam. Some analysts believe that attacks on cultural and personal values are creating opportunities for the spread of Muslim fundamentalism. 'Islam will be attractive to the oppressed because of its militancy. This religion, the fastest growing in the world, is the only one geared up for struggle.'[11]

On top of this, global communications infrastructure – obviously including the Internet – is creating cross-border networks of like-minded people. Business links between immigrant peoples and global, ethnically based trading networks are beginning to obliterate the practical meaning of borders as well as concepts of national allegiance.

A further threat to peaceful progress and the integrity of nation-states may be the potential for conflict between civilizations. Huntington contends that much of the tension in international politics can be explained by the relations between civilizations, which are the broadest cultural entities to which people can belong.[12] The differences among civilizations are real, with language, history, and religion playing key roles. He suggests that the present world can be divided into nine broad civilizations: Western (which encompasses western Europe, Scandinavia, Canada, the United States, Australia, and New Zealand); Latin American (including Mexico and the Caribbean); African (all of Africa south of the Sahara); Islamic (North Africa and east to the border of India); Sinic (China and Vietnam); Hindu (India and Bangladesh); Orthodox (Russia and several eastern European and Central Asian countries); Buddhist (Thailand, Laos, Cambodia), and Japanese. Huntington contends that interactions through migrations of people between civilizations are adding to social tensions in the stable states of Europe and that the United States will be weakened by cultural disputes. Thus, he believes that 'clashes of civilizations are the greatest threat to world peace, and an international order based on civilizations is the surest safeguard against world war.'[13]

In aggregate, these analysts tend to envision a world in which those living in 'zones of peace' will benefit enormously from the pursuit of economic growth while those left out – both countries and those within who lag behind – will be subject to tribal conflict, with all the pain that entails. Everyone, however, will be vulnerable to the 'clash of civilizations.'

Ecological Scarcity and Social Violence

For anyone who has comparison-shopped in North America, Europe, Japan, and most of the capital cities of the world, or who has travelled extensively in the Third World, all of these observations ring true. But they are more like snapshots of what *is* as opposed to explanations of *why*.

To get a handle on the underlying cause-and-effect relationships that are creating these conditions, it is helpful to return again to the notion of provisioning societies. This will provide a slightly different perspective on the unfolding nature of social conflict and, ultimately, what we can do about it.

In simple terms, societies are organized around provisioning processes, and social stratification reflects differences in the ways particular societies – or groups with societies – are organized to meet their provisioning needs. At the same time, competition for access to and/ or control of natural capital flows have always been at the heart of human conflict. When societies, using available technologies, can no longer adequately provision themselves from local sources or established flows of natural capital, they have always reached out to new sources though trade or migration, or they have seized that capital through force of arms. As well, when possible, societies have reorganized themselves around new sets of technologies capable of extracting the required incremental flows. Aside from a blending of these responses, there are no other options.

It seems that hunter-gatherer tribes learned to kill members of other tribes on contact and were constantly warring over land. The destruction of these clans and tribes by more powerful agricultural societies did not lead to peace; instead, ecological scarcity caused by drought, pestilence, or population growth led to further migrations and war. The first Sumerian city-states fought over water rights. The long succession of Hun and Mongol invasions of China, India, and Europe may have been precipitated by crop failures. Empires fought to expand and protect trade routes and borders. Colonial wars were wars of natural capital accretion, and afterwards, agricultural communities and colonies were kept subservient through military force. The world wars of the last century were basically wars over resource control.

The same thing is occurring today, although it is far more difficult to separate the effects of resource scarcity from the complicating role played by political, economic, and social factors. Nevertheless, Homer-Dixon, in an analysis of the relationship between environmental scarcity and violence, concludes that 'environmental scarcity contributes to diffuse, persistent, sub-national violence such as ethnic clashes and insurgencies.'[14]

In a similar vein, Yahya Sadowski contends that the clash of cultures and other political dimensions of globalization have not led to an increase in internal conflicts within nations, and they have definitely not led to an increase in conflicts between nations. He dismisses the argument raised by some that the ultimate effect of globalization is 'the clash of civilizations.' He suggests that the apparent cultural and ethnic conflicts of the 1990s – the ethnic cleansing in Bosnia, the genocide in Rwanda, the clashes between Christians and Muslims in Indonesia, and so on – are largely continuations of tensions and rivalries that long preceded globalization. He concludes by suggesting that 'all the culture wars of the 1990s were triggered primarily by cold-blooded contests for the control of land, water and power.' They were 'rational quarrels over the distribution of resources,' and none of them were mere continuations of 'ancient tribal hatreds.'[15] Sadowski also notes that culture wars are markedly less lethal in prosperous societies than in poor ones, since it is easier for cultures to share power when they aren't competing for basic resources.

Homer-Dixon is even more precise. Violence, he argues, is mainly rural 'because environmental scarcity has its most profound effects on people's lives in rural areas.'[16] He notes that 'about half the world's population remains directly tied to local natural resources.' That means some 3 to 4 billion people, and 60 to 70 per cent of the world's poor. For this reason, he cautions sceptics who underestimate the extent to which 'much of humankind still depends on its natural environment and therefore underestimate the social stress that environmental scarcity can cause.'[17]

The thrust of the case advanced by these analysts seems to be that wars are fought between culturally differentiated tribal, racial, linguistic, or religious groups, and that in most cases it is inequitable access to flows of natural capital – or perceptions that others may be gaining preferential advantage to these flows – that serves as the catalyst for conflict. It is easy to see how this occurs when the issue that sparks conflict is access to land or to the economic opportunities associated with the control of natural resources. But, the realities of ecological scarcity are far more complicated and pernicious than this, for their effects can be pervasive yet unseen and the original causes can be far removed from the events that eventually unleash human passions. For this reason, the contribution that ecological scarcity makes to present and prospective human conflict may be far more prevalent than these assessments suggest.

However – and this is where the argument advanced here begins to diverge – it is not rural people who depend most on ecological goods and services but urban dwellers. In fact, urban dwellers are vastly more dependent. The wealthiest urban dwellers consume over twenty times more natural capital than people in the poorest countries, and their impact on the absorptive capacity of global ecosystems is proportionately large. The differences are especially stark in the energy domain: 'A Chinese household, for example, spends 36 times less energy than an American household.'[18] Thus, if anyone is threatened by ecological scarcity it should be the wealthy nations of the world and in particular their urban dwellers. Yet these are the groups least prone to violent confrontations over access to natural capital.

Thus, it is not dependence on natural capital that underlies the relative proclivity to violence. Rather, the explanation lies in the great differences in the complexity of provisioning processes that exist between and within societies. The simpler the provisioning arrangements, and the more societies rely on local resources, the more vulnerable people are to disruptions of supply and thus to conflicts over access. As societies engage in the diversified and global reach of the provisioning mechanisms of Round Five, the tendency toward violence declines. Economic stratification mirrors where people and nations stand in relation to the organizational characteristics of the five rounds of provisioning. Social tensions and most of our wars are also a reflection of these differences in provisioning mechanisms. They are 'hangovers' of the types of conflicts prevalent during earlier rounds of provisioning that continue within and between hunter-gatherer clans and tribes and agricultural societies, between rural and urban societies, within urban informal sectors, to some extent between informal and formal economic sectors and between subnational entities and nation-states.

The surviving groups of ancient hunter-gatherer societies that are now squeezed into tiny land areas are no longer in continuous conflict with neighbouring tribes over hunting and fishing rights, but they are in constant conflict with the vast surrounding populations over land rights. These confrontations are likely to become more violent in the coming years as the pressures of global provisioning continue to increase.

A similar situation prevails among the rural poor in agricultural communities, who have only limited connections to important urban and international markets. In terms of the five rounds of provisioning, many rural conflicts are really continuations of old-style agricultural wars of the sort that have persisted since the advent of agricultural settlements some 12,000 years ago. Provisioning needs, using available technologies, are met from very limited sources. Wealth is still in the land. People engaged in subsistence agriculture live close to the edge. They have little flexibility to accommodate shortfalls, and they have few feedback mechanisms to offset or mediate the effects of competition for access to land, water, and other forms of natural capital. In these circumstances, cultural glue strengthens at the first signs of eroding capacity to access land or other forms of natural capital and economic opportunity. When faced with threats to their capacity to provision their societies, they are likely to get embroiled quickly in conflict and perhaps even war.

In contrast, the technologies and forms of social organization in use in the portions of society that are linked to the global provisioning networks of Round Five tend to create a buffer against shortfalls in flows from any one source. These technologies include urban environmental infrastructure, which provides enhanced and more far-reaching access to the absorptive capacities of ecological systems.

Provisioning processes add to rural tensions as large-scale agricultural enterprise that targets urban and international markets competes with small land holders for production rights. In cities, the areas outside the wealthy urban enclaves – that is, the peri-areas which contain most of the urban poor – have far less effective and diversified provisioning mechanisms. Again, because of the limitations of the technologies available and the inadequacies of the urban infrastructure, provisioning pipelines are short in these areas, sources of supply are immediate, and limited access to ecological waste disposal services creates undesirable feedback in terms of pollution. Thus, like their rural cousins, people mired in urban poverty live close to the line in terms of their ability to adequately provision themselves. Because competition for access to natural capital and economic opportunity is so intense, violence is closer to the surface in peri-areas than in the enclaves, where provisioning processes are taken more or less for granted.

To illustrate the potential for conflict inherent in competition over provisioning in the conditions of ecological scarcity that now afflict the global community, it is helpful to revisit the ambitions of Ahmed, the travel guide we talked about in Part 1. He and his family are captives of the limited provisioning mechanisms of the urban poor. He is not alone. The 3 billion people who earn less than $2 per day and who each consume less than one-twentieth the natural capital of individuals in advanced economies share his aspirations for a better life. Ecological scarcity overhangs their existence. At any moment, it can tip them from deprivation into the cauldrons of despair. They, like Ahmed, are industrious people. But the only way they can escape their inadequate and precarious provisioning processes is to build themselves in to at least the edges of the provisioning networks of the global economy. And they can't do that without increasing their consumption of natural capital. Ahmed's ambitions, and those of billions of his fellow impoverished, are predicated on being able to access vastly more abundant sources of ecological goods and services.

It is easy to see how the scale of their collective aspirations can lead to violent competition over scarce local resources. But the threat to social stability is not limited to 'old style,' localized wars. If ecological decline continues, if solutions to the equitable provisioning of the world's peoples are not found, competition for scarce natural capital could quickly escalate into a global confrontation between the rich and the poor – between those fully participating in Round Five and the excluded.

Differences in how technologies and forms of organization are used in order to meet provisioning needs are at the root of many of the world's cultural confrontations. As the patterns of technology use, social organization, and economic growth that are the hallmarks of Round Five are spread around the world, they become conduits for cultural change and eventual conformity.

This does not mean that all societies must be or ever will be identical. The past is part of current culture. History, traditions, language, and other attributes of national heritage are perpetuated through the actions of governments and cultural and religious institutions. Nevertheless, to the extent that societies employ common technologies, there will be similarities in their forms of social organization and thus common patterns of social behaviour and attitudes. These cultural similarities are most noticeable in the relatively well-off urban enclaves of Third World countries where cross-border similarities in provisioning processes are most pronounced. The cultural gaps between the formal and informal economies within cities appear to be growing at the same time that differences between enclave cultures around the globe are shrinking.

Indeed, if the cultural gaps between the enclaves and peri-areas widen, nations may soon find that those living in the relatively affluent consumer-oriented and outward-looking enclaves have more in common with other enclaves and with the cultures of advanced economies than with the cultures of their informal sectors. Those in the enclaves may find people from other 'cultures' who share their technologies, behaviour, and forms of social organization easier to deal with and understand than people living just a short distance away in the confines of the peri-areas of their own city and rural communities.

In the end, the adoption of common approaches to provisioning and the resulting reorganization of societies around new technologies may be a stronger builder of common interest than tribal, cultural, or national factors. The world seems to be tracking not so much toward clashes between civilizations as it is toward bipolar cities in bipolar nations in a bipolar world. If civilizational conflicts are really on the horizon, it is more likely that they will be between the wealthy participants in the provisioning processes of Round Five and the rest.

The Road Ahead

The Fifth Round in the evolution of provisioning – the global economy – is beset with a huge, complex intermingling of sources of tension and conflict. Changes to the economic and power relationships between nations have uncertain implications. Everywhere the gaps between the well-off and the poor are growing. The world seems to be fragmenting along tribal, cultural, and religious fault lines. The integration capacities and social cohesion of cities, the bonds of nationhood, and systems of governance are all being tested.

When ecological scarcity is added to the already volatile mix of cultural, religious, political, and historical differences and the challenges of poverty, the potential for conflict is significantly enhanced. People tend to strengthen their ethnic, racial, religious, and cultural bonds – and perhaps their civilizational links – in order to enhance their greater power to compete for access to sources of natural capital. And overarching all of these sources of tension is the prospect that the world is coalescing into two broadly competing camps: participants in the provisioning processes of Round Five, and those still locked into the provisioning mechanisms of earlier rounds.

What makes the current situation so fraught with danger is that the pivotal role of ecological scarcity in precipitating social conflict is often hard to identify. Diverse sources of human activity around the world are having pernicious yet virtually unseen effects on both natural systems and human societies. Ecological scarcity is showering all of these interlocking sources of social tension with the sparks of perceived grievance that could easily ignite human passions.

Everything is now connected. Ecological decline is no longer mainly a local or regional issue; we must deal with the erosion of ecosystems on a global basis. Everyone is now competing for the same diminishing sources of ecological goods and services. Like the spread of economic collapse or a monetary crisis, the effects of ecological pressures are now rippling around the world. They are eventually felt everywhere, but their effects are rarely identified, priced, or taken into account in decision making.

Ecological scarcity is the ultimate catalyst of human disaster. If the world continues on its present track, the great train of economic growth, on whose rails ride the only hope for a better human future, will be derailed on the downslope of social dislocation caused by competition between and within societies for access to increasingly scarce sources of natural capital. To avoid this, the world must once again reorganize its basic provisioning processes to meet the demands of growth and equity.

PART IV

The War to Provision the World

The battle plan for waging a global war to provision societies by mobilizing national and international efforts on the six battlefields of technological innovation.

Chapter 12

Our Common Enemy

The world community must declare war on ecological decline and mobilize global resources to fight this war.

This war must be fought to stabilize the human prospect on earth. The survival of natural systems is the reason for fighting the war, but nature is not the enemy and the war is not being fought to further bend natural systems to meet human needs. Rather, it is a war to bring about dramatic changes in the ways human societies provision themselves in conditions of global ecological scarcity. This will not be a conventional war fought with weapons of mass destruction. It will be a war against our own actions and a war that can only be fought with the weapons of technological advance and related social adaptation.

All societies, consciously or not, have always organized around the technologies available to them to secure access to necessary inbound flows of natural capital and to the ecological services required to decompose and absorb outbound flows of pollution.

The relationship between technology, population growth, and provisioning arrangements has followed a consistent pattern. To the extent that societies succeeded in augmenting flows of natural capital, populations grew until new shortages arose, thus forcing outreach to new sources. This tendency to exhaust or despoil the local environment and then reach out to the more distant has been at the heart of most migrations and conflicts throughout human history.

Four earlier rounds and some three hundred years of experimentation and technological innovation led to the private-sector networks and economic integration of the Fifth Round. The evolution in thinking about how to promote economic and social development through the application of neoclassical economic principles is a triumph of human ingenuity, and the global community has been the beneficiary of the most powerful and broadly dispersed growth dynamic in human history. The technologies and business networks of Round Five have enabled leading societies to access the global sources of natural capital on which economic advance depends and are extending this capability and its corresponding benefits around the world. Earlier periods of rapid wealth creation and generalized improvements in human well-being touched the lives of only thousands or hundreds of thousands of people – millions during the Industrial Revolution – and these gains were local or regional. In contrast, billions of people from all corners of the world are enjoying the gains brought about by the provisioning mechanisms of the Fifth Round, and the prospect of full participation in the global economy has become a beacon of hope for the remaining legions of the impoverished.

At the same time, the gains conferred by growth and the enormous potential to enhance human well-being through participation in the global economy are being compromised. The world has now reached a new and unprecedented impasse between continued economic growth and ecological decline. There are no more distant sources of natural capital to which humanity can reach out. Humans are tapping the outer edges of, and in many instances exceeding, the world's ecological capacity, and as a result, all societies now find themselves locked together in the common challenge of meeting their provisioning requirements from the same stressed ecological envelopes. The consequences of ecological scarcity are closing in on all of us.

Those living close to the margins, especially hunter-gatherer societies and the rural and urban poor, tend to depend almost exclusively on local resources and are affected immediately by shortfalls. For this reason, they are more prone to violent reaction than those in leading economies and wealthy urban enclaves, who have diversified and flexible means of accessing ecological goods and services as well as the wealth, political power, and military strength to protect their supply lines. However, because ecological scarcity is now a global phenomenon, the effects of pollution and excessive pressure on ecological systems in one region are being diffused through other ecosystems and societies around the world.

From this inequitable, ecologically diminished, and socially precarious base, the world must somehow respond to a rapid bunching of natural capital provisioning requirements that will add enormously to the present, already unsustainable levels of demand for ecological goods and services. By 2025 the world is going to be challenged to provision a global economy that could be two or three times as large as it is now and to secure additional natural capital to meet the needs of another two billion people. The latter task will be compounded by the fact that urban growth is accelerating faster than that of the overall world economy. Another 3 billion people could be added to the ranks of urban dwellers, and their requirements for ecological goods and services are going to be significantly greater on a per capita basis than those of rural dwellers. Moreover, if efforts to reduce global poverty are to succeed, we must first confront a further, enormous expansion in per capita provisioning requirements. Given that most of the world's ecological systems are already in some stage of human-induced decline, the cumulative increases in demand for ecological goods and services, if met through existing provisioning mechanisms, could require access to the ecological resources of three or four worlds by 2025.

Within this time frame, the full impact of these incremental sources of ecological stress will have run their course:

- The consequences of limits to water availability, the depletion of major aquifers, and declines in water quality as a result of widespread pollution will have come to a head, with all that this entails for agricultural output, industrial production, the social well-being of rural and urban residents, and relations between nations that share common water resources.
- Human-induced loss of biological diversity will have reached its zenith. There may be little viable forest, coral reef, and other protective habitat left. Aquaculture will have peaked because our ability to provide fish meal from the wild and to access more land and water resources to support the growth of the industry will have been exceeded. Thousands of other less dramatic limits on ecological supply capability will have been reached, or losses will have occurred.
- Accelerated global warming – the result of another doubling of greenhouse gases (GHGs) from human activity – will have significantly altered weather patterns, with serious implications for global food production and social stability.

The global economy is immersed in self-limiting patterns of ecological exploitation. Thus, well before 2025 we will know whether humanity's provisioning needs have precipitated catastrophic, growth-ending ecological and social flips that are causing the competition between and within nations for natural capital to spin wildly out of control.

If human pressures on ecosystems are not alleviated, ecological scarcity will spark intense social and cultural strife. Conflicts that now arise mainly within nations will spread across borders. As competition for access to scarce natural capital mounts, and as ecosystems begin to collapse, economic growth will stop and the world will be plunged into chaos and despair.

The common enemy of all the world's peoples is ecological decline. The scale of the threat it presents for all societies and the time available for restructuring provisioning processes are such that the global community must mobilize as if for war in order to fight this decline. The nations of the world must collectively declare and wage this war with an unbending commitment to victory. The alternative is to watch the rich and the poor of the world compete and eventually fight for access to increasingly scarce natural capital.

The Battlefields of Technological Innovation

The choices available to societies for dealing with provisioning shortfalls are few, and the consequences of the different options are stark. The means of outreach are limited to four: migration; trade; the use of force (i.e., war, colonial occupation, and other forms of political and economic coercion); and technological advance.

Unlike earlier societies, we cannot look to untapped sources of natural capital to bail us out. Nor can people migrate to unoccupied lands, although millions of economic migrants are already attempting to move to regions more favoured than theirs. On a local basis, some groups can take natural capital from their neighbours, perhaps using the appalling techniques of ethnic cleansing practised in the Balkans and Rwanda. The better off can take such capital in more peaceful ways through the application of economic power backed by superior technology and, if necessary, military strength. But neither trade nor war can increase the global availability of natural capital or the absorptive capacity of ecological systems. Thus, these avenues are only available if the peoples using them are prepared to show moral indifference to the suffering of vast numbers of deprived people. Moreover, those relying on trade, economic power, and war to satisfy their provisioning needs cannot evade the fact that provisioning options are steadily being foreclosed.

This leaves only one viable course of action. As in all five previous rounds of human provisioning, societies must once again reorganize around new, leading-edge technologies and practices that enable them to significantly augment useable flows of natural capital. Technological innovation is the glue that must eventually bind the sustainable development puzzle together, and it is on the battlefields of technological innovation and related social reorganization that ecological decline will have to be fought. In this respect, the war will be decided on six battlefields of technological advance:

- Better management of the world's natural resource base through the development of technologies and practices leading to the integrated management of bio-regions, and the conversion of political mandates to facilitate this transition.
- The development of new agricultural technologies and practices that will integrate productivity gains with reductions in agriculture's contributions to climate change, water depletion, and pollution.
- The development of the diverse technologies and management practices of industrial ecology. This will enable all industry sectors to move toward systems of closed-loop production and life-cycle materials management.
- The development of the technologies and practices of eco-urban management. This will transform cities, like industries, into closed-loop processors of natural capital. At the same time, it will allow new approaches to providing infrastructure services designed to create wealth and mass employment for the urban poor.
- The development of 'green' energy technologies that will wean global energy infrastructures from dependence on carbon-based forms of energy (as is now occurring in response to the FCCC).
- The development of regional and global monitoring and forecasting technologies to track signs of regional ecological stress or collapse and systemic changes in global ecological systems. Societies will then be better able to respond – again, through improved technologies.

It is essential to recognize that these are all highly specific battle-grounds: advances on other technology fronts will not slow ecological decline. In this respect, New Economy innovation that is now driving the global economy has been largely a result of a narrow focus on immediate market needs and opportunities in specific industrial sectors as well as the idiosyncratic pursuit of scientific inquiry. As a result, patterns of technological advance lack direction and social coherence. The narrow pursuit of economic growth and the random patterns of New Economy innovation are unlikely to produce solutions to the challenge of equitably provisioning human societies from rapidly deteriorating ecosystems.

From Skirmishes to All-Out War

A severe imbalance exists between the opportunistic directions of New Economy innovation and the specific technological requirements of waging the war for ecological sustainability (see Table 1).

Progress in closing this innovation gap will not come easily. New Economy innovation efforts have generated great momentum based on more than fifty years of cumulative development of relevant science and technology (S&T) and market infrastructures. These advances have been driven by increasingly clear visions of technology's future (e.g., the 'wired world,' the 'human genome') and by the perception – shared by most governments – that leading-edge communications and information technologies and New Economy science, technology, and education infrastructures constitute the essential base of national competitiveness.

These powerful market pressures and opportunities are now driving New Economy innovation and enabling it to command most private-sector investment. Leadership is being provided by large, established companies with global market linkages. The innovation thrust is supported by a sophisticated, well-entrenched S&T support infrastructure. Education and human resource training facilities are in place. Sophisticated venture capital firms, merchant banks, and other investment and market development mechanisms have been created over the years to channel resources into New Economy technologies and companies.

In contrast, the innovation required to provision societies is constrained by a serious lack of strong market drivers. Outside of the energy field, where innovation is being driven by the FCCC, there is

TABLE 1

The Innovation Divide

New Economy Innovation Trends *	Innovation for Ecological Sustainability**
1. Increased computer speed and capacity	1. Integrated bio-region management
2. Communications and Internet functionality	2. Comprehensive agricultural management
3. Software, artificial intelligence, smart machines	3. Eco-urban management
4. Medical technologies	4. Industrial ecology
5. Chemicals, aerospace, new materials, engineering	5. 'Green' energy and transportation technologies
6. Basic science	6. Preparedness re CC and ecological 'surprises'
	7. Application/use of CITs***

* Source: from chapter 8
** Derived from earlier discussion
*** These are not watertight compartments. The overlap is especially noteworthy in the areas of computer and communications technologies, agro-biotechnology, engineering, and basic science.

little pure market demand for investment in ecological sustainability. Venture capital firms and equity markets show minimal interest. Structural impediments exist in the relevant portions of industry: leadership by large MNEs depends on continued energy-efficiency and other cost savings. Most technology suppliers are small firms, and there is little innovative R&D. Serious institutional constraints also exist: the investment criteria for urban environmental infrastructure are risk-averse; ecodesign capacity is limited; incentives are minimal; and national subsidies to industry are overwhelmingly biased toward resource and carbon-intensive energy use.[1] There are also huge knowledge gaps that will need to be addressed if ecological sustainability is to be realized. These gaps are most pronounced in relation to our knowledge of how natural systems operate and how those systems must be managed.[2] As a result of these knowledge gaps, there aren't enough people capable of doing the relevant innovation work.

Present market forces and government policies are not pushing global innovation and technological advance toward the needs of ecological sustainability. And as the WBCSD put it, 'if basic framework conditions push us in the wrong directions, then that is the way society will go.'[3] Thus, if a better balance between New Economy needs and the technological imperatives of provisioning societies is to be achieved, national governments and the international community will have to make a serious commitment to make this happen.

The world cannot rely on market forces to bring about necessary change. The operation of free markets is necessary to promote and to meet inbound provisioning needs. However, as the discussion in Part III illustrated, market prices respond too slowly to the effects of ecological stress, and only *after* the fact to outright flips. We cannot rely on market mechanisms alone to slow the rate of ecological decline unless these mechanisms are specifically geared to doing this. Governments must create conditions that will stimulate the necessary levels of innovation in support of ecological sustainability; they must also foster the changes in social organization that will be required to embrace new provisioning arrangements. Redressing the innovation divide in this manner does not mean that New Economy innovation must be constrained: the demand for existing innovation efforts will continue to exert a strong market pull. Rather, it means that additional, massive, innovative effort in support of ecological sustainability must be created.

The task facing the global community goes far beyond markets and the performance of private-sector actors. Changing the ways that business networks access, process, and consume ecological goods and services will be necessary for ecological sustainability, but insufficient in itself. Societies themselves must also reorganize, especially when it comes to their approaches to managing bio-regions and urban areas. The world can no longer tolerate political and institutional arrangements that hamper efficient provisioning processes. To overcome the tyranny of policies, mindsets, and institutions that were entrenched in a different era to address different issues, the world must come to see and accept that fighting ecological decline through a balanced and heavily strengthened approach to innovation will lead to more growth, greater social equity, and a more peaceful future.

In a conventional war, the weapons and tactics differ between the battles fought on land, on sea, and in the air, but each of these theatres must be co-ordinated within the overall strategy for the conduct of the war. In a similar manner, the tactics used in the war against ecological decline must be tailored to the unique conditions that prevail on each of the six battlefields of technological advance, and these battle plans must be organized within the framework of national strategies and specific war objectives. As well, because in all dimensions this is truly a *global* war, the ways that national actions are supplemented by co-ordinated international effort will have a defining influence on its outcome.

Chapter 13

Mobilizing Nations for War

As nation-states place themselves on a war footing, they will need to mobilize to fight on each of the six battlefields of innovation. They will need to encapsulate the vision of innovation for ecological sustainability in specific national war objectives and program thrusts and these will have to be supported by policy tools and tactics that are appropriate to each of these battlefields.

In the energy field, most nations already have the semblance of a battle plan. The drivers here include long-standing market forces – including the health and environmental side effects of fossil fuel production and use – and the FCCC, which is generating a powerful demand for cleaner energy forms, including renewables. For this reason, the following discussion will pay only limited attention to this key battlefield. Similarly, the discussions of agricultural innovation and monitoring and preparedness will also be limited as these war plans are best drafted in the context of bio-region management strategies. In sum, the discussion of national mobilization will be limited mainly to three battlefields: industrial ecology, integrated bio-region management, and eco-urban management.

The Battle for Industrial Ecology

The war on the battlefield of innovation in industrial ecology must be fought by using market incentives. To mobilize investment in industrial ecology, we will have to change the investment climate in ways that create specific private-sector opportunities. Investment in industrial ecology must be made more attractive.

Most governments in advanced economies are already experimenting with a broad range of policy tools and programs designed to induce greater corporate investment in industrial ecology. These options vary from traditional command-and-control approaches to voluntary programs. As we have seen, companies are already beginning to respond. Leading companies are testing new patterns of innovation, new industrial processes, and new management regimes with the potential to produce gains in the efficiency of resource use. They are also moving toward zero-emission production processes and utilizing ecodesign and life-cycle management approaches that involve the full recycling of products and their constituent materials. These efforts are being supported by the development of environmental management standards, notably the International Standards Organization's ISO 14000 series and new corporate accounting and reporting procedures such as the Global Reporting Initiative (the GRI).[1]

The most important market drivers for speeding up innovation in industrial ecology include the following:

- Relevant portions of national S&T infrastructure, including education and training facilities, research and product development support programs, and venture capital and other funding mechanisms, which are required to commercialize and market new technologies.
- Voluntary measures and codes of conduct that induce corporations to adopt triple bottom-line management practices, including reporting systems such as GRI and compliance with relevant standards and certification procedures.
- Fiscal measures, including carbon and other 'green' taxation initiatives, tax shifting, and subsidies (e.g., shifting incentives and subsidies from resource extraction to environmental protection).
- Innovations in equity and financial markets such as ethical investment funds, as well as government rules and regulations that set minimum investment targets.
- Tradable permits to create market demand for the collection and sale of toxic and environmentally harmful materials (e.g., the use of tradable permits in the United States to help address the acid rain problem, the beginnings of a carbon-trading regime, and California's use of tradable permits to allocate scarce water resources between competing uses).

- Corporate and government 'green procurement' policies based on qualifying products through certification, ecolabelling, and life-cycle cost estimating.
- Trade policy and border measures, including consumer boycotts of offending goods.
- Health regulations.
- Municipal regulations and standards regarding the management and disposal of pollutants.
- The direct creation of market demand through incentive programs to encourage municipalities to experiment with innovative infrastructure technologies.
- Actions to incorporate environmental costs into the price of consumables.
- The further development and use of use of sustainable development systems of national accounting and other forms of indicators to publicize and manage progress toward sustainability.

In the absence of a clear, forward-looking vision and strong market signals, most of these measures are contentious, and it is difficult to make a compelling case for them using established market-evaluation criteria. To illustrate the problem, carbon taxes – provided they are part of a tax-shifting mechanism as opposed to an add-on to existing tax structures – can truly make a difference quickly. If all other taxes used by governments to raise equivalent revenues were replaced by a tax on carbon consumption, the world would move rapidly from its heavy reliance on carbon-based fuels. That is the upside, but there are plenty of strong political constraints to such drastic action. At a minimum, some industrial sectors would be severely harmed. Furthermore, what would happen to government revenues when societies moved to less carbon-intensive energy forms?

Given the variety of industry needs (including the unique requirements of smaller firms), and given the scale of innovation effort required (aside from tax levers), few of the measures listed above are powerful enough to generate strong market pull on their own. On the other hand, the sheer range of possible market levers for encouraging greater investment in industrial ecology bodes well for their successful use if they are applied in combination. For example, the appeal of voluntary industry measures can be greatly enhanced by the complementary introduction of sustainable-development accounting practices, green procurement policies, and technology demonstration programs. Regardless, a full basket of national measures is going to be required.

To create the clear vision and market momentum in which a basket of these measures can begin to take root and drive corporate behaviour, governments must be explicit about why they are introducing these new market levers, and what expectations and targets they have set for their use, and they must express a commitment to sustained change. To translate all of this into a coherent battle plan, governments must present their objectives, expectations, and tools as a unified, national industrial-ecology program. These national battle plans will likely produce more effective and technologically more creative solutions if they allow private enterprise the flexibility to develop specific technologies. Governments, however, must drive the process by creating sufficient market pressures and opportunities to bring about change.

The introduction of coherent national battle plans for bio-region and eco-urban management will also create powerful incentives for investment in industrial ecology. These plans will help shape new market opportunities and establish directions for long-term social and technological advance. However, the framework for fighting the battles for industrial ecology will be of little help in waging war on the bioregional, agricultural, and eco-urban management fronts. These may prove to be more difficult challenges, as they will require the adoption of new management regimes as well as social and political reorganization.

The Battles for Integrated Bio-Region and Eco-Urban Management

Any vision of how nation-states might reorganize political mandates to equitably provision societies will have to take into account the relationship between rural and urban areas in provisioning processes and in the processes of employment and wealth creation.

Urban societies rely on the productivity of rural areas. Cities are the great concentrators of natural capital consumption and depend totally on inbound flows, largely from rural areas. Profligate and growing urban demand for continuous flows of natural capital long ago consigned rural areas to the role of provisioning urban areas. Since the founding of the first cities, the production of natural capital surpluses for urban consumption has been the key driver of rural development and the basis for the accumulation of rural wealth. This is, perhaps, most evident in the agricultural sector, but it applies equally to all primary industries, including forestry, mining, fishing, energy, power generation, and the provision of water.

As the urban age unfolds and global interdependence tightens, the task of provisioning urban areas will continue to dominate rural development and shape its direction. The role of rural areas can no longer be limited to provisioning only local or national populations. Increasingly, rural areas must be managed by nation-states in ways that maximize the efficiency of global provisioning processes.

The flip side of urban reliance on rural productivity is that urban demand for flows of natural capital is responsible for most forms of rural ecological stress. Roughly 80 per cent of economic growth is urban-based, and this percentage will increase as the percentage of the global population living in cities increases. It is the provisioning of this concentrated urban economic activity that is spreading ecological stress into the outer reaches of the biosphere.

Advanced economies source natural capital from every corner of the world in order to provision their cities. They import food, raw materials, and semiprocessed and finished goods, and they rely on global ecosystems to absorb their wastes. What is true for them is no less a reality for most developing countries, whose urban populations are rapidly expanding, whose food and other natural capital needs are increasingly being met through international exchange, and whose industries and urban areas are now competing with advanced economies on a global scale for access to scarce ecological absorptive capacity. The larger cities become, and the wealthier, the greater their outreach to more distant sources of natural capital. At the global level, *all* forms of ecological disruption are caused by the provisioning of urban populations.

In less than twenty-five years, as many as four worlds could be required to meet the global demand for natural capital, so it is clearly an inadequate response simply to maximize the efficiency of provisioning efforts from rural areas. Cities must dramatically reduce the pressures that their demands for natural capital are placing on global ecosystems.

The only way they can do this and still meet the provisioning needs of growth and poverty reduction is to reduce their citizens' demands on ecosystems through technologies and forms of social organization that will allow them to continuously recycle flows of natural capital derived from primary sources, until the need for absorptive services is driven down to almost zero.

Rural and urban areas are also bound tightly together by employment chains and by the vastly greater capacity of cities to generate wealth and jobs. It would be a cruel hoax to encourage false optimism regarding the potential of rural areas to meet the employment needs of the population surges expected by 2025. Regardless of the potential for small-scale farmers to increase output, sooner or later necessary productivity gains and the imperatives of organizing to channel food and produce to urban consumers will reduce the number of people that given parcels of land will be able to employ directly. Surplus rural populations will have to migrate to other sources of opportunity. To the extent that these opportunities exist, they will be in urban locations.

The creation of mass employment opportunity is an urban phenomenon. Cities, if properly organized, can be powerful engines of wealth and employment generation. Only in cities can technology and infrastructure services create the need for specialized skills and job functions that diversify employment opportunity. Rural poverty cannot be addressed in any other way than through the creation of urban jobs. Thus, rural development strategies must be linked to urban employment strategies if progress is to be made. This is the *quid pro quo* for accepting urban provisioning as the ultimate driver of rural production processes.

Thus, both rural and urban areas have vital, interconnected roles to play in enhancing the overall efficiency of provisioning processes and in dramatically increasing the availability of usable flows of natural capital. Equity issues must also be resolved by accelerating the transition from rural to urban employment and the re-engineering of urban infrastructure to create wealth and employment diversification. These binding linkages define the nature of the battle plans that must be developed if rural and urban areas are to contribute their maximum to the war effort.

Bio-Region Management

Few regions of countries are now managed on a bio-region basis; even so, the pressures to move to this form of management are pervasive. They result from the growing recognition that holistic approaches must be taken to sector-specific management decisions and from the fact that actions taken in one sector cannot but affect actions taken in others.

In the case of water management, the problem can be illustrated by the slow death of Lake Chapala in Mexico's parched west-central highlands. One of the country's most important sources of water, this lake is drying up rapidly as a result of uncontrolled water draws. Agricultural demands drained 30 per cent of the lake in the early 1900s, and since then the amount of farmland in the region under irrigation has expanded from around 161,000 acres to well over 2 million. At the same time, urban demand – mainly from Guadalajara, more recently from Mexico City, and continuously from other surrounding municipalities – has exploded. The result is that the lake now contains less than 20 per cent of the water it held at its peak, fish stocks have plummeted, tourist revenues are declining, and agricultural production and urban development are being threatened in several nearby states. The management challenges facing Mexico's Lake Chapala region are being replicated in a discouraging number of regions around the world. And the challenges of managing water resources are hardly confined to developing and mid-level economies. The United States is also tumbling toward a water crisis, according to 'America's Most Endangered Rivers of 2003,' a report prepared by the conservation group American Rivers.

These challenges are not new, and although policy solutions have been framed, they have rarely if ever been implemented. The conclusions arising from years of international deliberations can be summarized as follows: Access to clean water and sanitation at an affordable price is a basic human right. 'The future of many millions of people demands immediate and effective action' based on holistic approaches to managing land and water across 'the whole of a catchment area or ground water aquifer.' These approaches must involve 'users, planners and policy makers at all levels' engaging in thorough public consultations and collaborative decision making. It must be recognized that 'water has an economic value in all its competing uses' and needs to be managed as an 'economic good' in order to achieve efficient and equitable use' and to encourage 'conservation and protection of water resources.'[2]

Obviously, water quantity and water quality are both affected by industrial and urban growth, by agricultural technologies, by forest management practices, and by human actions that affect climate change and weather variability. Thus, it is not possible to manage water resources without managing everything else, including forestry, agriculture, and the technologies that underpin urban and industrial growth.[3] The failure to mediate carefully among these competing demands leads to land-use patterns that are unsustainable and to the irreversible degradation of water resources. In effective management practices are already placing major agricultural areas at risk and are leading to intense competition for access to water between cities and rural areas. Concerns over water access are also intruding on relations between countries that share catchment areas.

A similar situation prevails with respect to forestry management: decisions cannot be made solely on the basis of forest interests. Short-term gains from forest exploitation must be balanced against the functioning of ecosystems. Management decisions have implications for biodiversity, for water conservation, and for the contribution of forests as CO_2 sinks and the reduction of pressures on climate change. The FAO's report 'State of the World's Forests 2003' puts all of this into perspective by pointing out that the loss of forest cover and the conversion of forested land to other uses is degrading supplies of fresh water, damaging the environment, and threatening the survival of millions of people. The report's demanding conclusion reads, in part, that 'solutions have to be sought to change human values, social relations and activities' and will require 'deep policy and institutional reforms' at 'sub-national, national and international levels.'[4]

When phrased as a sector-specific requirement, sustainable forest management is perhaps unattainable since this ambition places forestry issues and other sector demands in competition with one another for political and public attention. A better approach is to see forestry issues for what they really are: part of a broader challenge of integrated bio-region management. Once we sharpen our focus from tens or hundreds of discrete, competing management challenges to one political imperative, perhaps forestry issues will finally get the attention they merit.

All of these considerations come to a head in decisions regarding agriculture's contribution to national economic and social welfare. The main agricultural challenge facing the world over the next twenty-five years is to devise strategies for producing the surpluses required to meet the growing needs of urban dwellers in ways that are far more ecologically benign than current practices. As noted earlier, this must be achieved in the context of competing demands for land and water resources from a multitude of users. The needs of cities must be factored in, but so must the needs of forests and of biodiversity. And so must the effects of agriculture on climate change, and on international relations in situations where agricultural lands are part of river basins or other ecosystems that span national borders. For example, balancing the water demands of even two sectors – agriculture and forestry – has to involve the complicated harmonization of social and economic demands. In the tropics, for example, agricultural expansion has accounted for some 60 per cent of rapid deforestation.[5] This clear-cutting by impoverished farmers migrating into forest zones is contributing to reductions in the effectiveness of water catchment areas, to soil erosion and siltation and to downstream flooding. The same effects result from poorly controlled logging practices.

The choice of agricultural technologies is of paramount importance, because technological advance shapes patterns of job creation, strongly influences population movements, affects distributional equity, drives cultural change, and adds to or ameliorates ecological stress. Technology choices must be made in the context of intense pressures for agriculture to contribute to equity and employment goals, related infrastructure investment requirements, and the market implications of different approaches. Furthermore, they must be made in full awareness of the employment opportunities generated by urban growth.

Finally, urban areas must be included in the structures established to manage bio-regions. The relinking of rural and urban societies in the common management of provisioning processes is critical, and so is the need to introduce an integrated approach to job creation that spans the rural/urban employment continuum. This may tend to vest more urban power over rural affairs than many would think warranted, but the reality is that far more people will soon be living in cities than in rural areas. As well, deliberately making urban management part of ecosystem management and linking rural aspirations to urban employment opportunities should more than compensate for any downsides.

Given how much technological and social change must occur if ecological and equity issues are to be effectively addressed, piecemeal, fragmented, sectoral approaches to decision making seem doomed to failure. Everything is connected, and decision-making and management systems can reflect this fact *only* if a 'whole area' view is taken. The resolution of these conflicting pressures needs to be managed though political processes that balance competing demands in the overall framework of bio-region capacity.

Organizational constraints to bio-region management. The challenge of managing ecosystems to maximize natural capital flows cannot be met in conditions of competing mandates and great organizational and jurisdictional complexity. Yet these are the conditions in which most nations in the world now approach the task of natural capital management. Responsibility tends to be spread among sectoral ministries and disparate political jurisdictions. Separate departments are charged with agricultural development, management of the forestry and fishing industries, mineral extraction and processing, and energy. Subunits within all of these deal with specialized crops, specific minerals, and specific habitats and species. Rural and urban interests are separated into distinct administrative units, and responsibility is further divided among national, state or provincial, and local administrations. On a regional basis, administration is fractured between town councils and so on.

All of these disparate entities tend to operate within their own narrowly defined mandates and areas of responsibility without consideration for the interests of other sectors and jurisdictions. Management has become the domain of segregated sector specialists. This has led to a confusing mix of conflicting policy and program initiatives, serious delays in necessary decision making when issues fall between jurisdictions, and frequent failures to take any action whatever. The minutiae of sector issues are dissected and debated at great length, while interactions among sectors and with overall management considerations are largely ignored.

This situation leads to contradictory government policies. It also diverts attention from the looming threat of global ecological scarcity and from the social chaos that competition for scarce natural capital holds in store. It condemns the world to continue on its self-destructive path. It makes it easier for decisions regarding natural capital flows to be influenced by immediate economic opportunity and local or national political considerations. Sustainable farming systems can easily be undermined by landlords and short-term profit seekers, as well as by urban demand. Political insiders become client groups for competing government departments that ought to be making joint decisions on resource allocations.[6] Jurisdictional barriers and the absence of organizational coherence and mission also seriously constrain the capacity to generate political awareness of global and local ecological and provisioning challenges.[7]

Creating political accountability for bio-region management. In most nation-states, the present profusion of overlapping administrative responsibilities and political jurisdictions almost precludes the rational management of the natural resource base. This organizational complexity and the confusion surrounding decision-making processes are largely hangovers from earlier times, when limited communication and transportation links forced greater self-reliance on local communities and when narrow sector interests could be accommodated by abundant land areas and still forgiving ecosystems.

We must free ourselves from the constraints of these outdated organizational modes and mindsets and learn to manage the human draw on the ecological resources of specific bio-regions in ways that maintain essential ecosystem functionality in the face of the cumulative pressures of human demands, whatever their source. We have to break out of our sectoral and discipline boxes and manage bio-regions on a holistic basis. The expert knowledge of sectoral specialists is still needed, but it must be applied in a cross-disciplinary management framework.

The overarching requirement for effective ecological resource management must drive the next iterations of political organization. If the integrated management of land, water, and other environmental resources is to develop, specific political accountability for making this transition must be created. New political mandates are needed that clearly allocate responsibility for bio-region management, and this commitment must be backed by funding and by decision-making authority.

Individual nation-states will need to determine the bio-regions around which this restructuring can take place. Appropriate choices will often involve cross-border collaboration. As most people live on or near water systems (more than one-third of the world's people live within 100 kilometres of a seacoast, and more than 40 per cent are squeezed into river basins that cross national boundaries so)[8], freshwater drainage areas, water basins, and coastal zones are likely to predominate.

New management systems cannot be imposed without taking into account the social realities of the people affected, so national governments will have to exercise leadership.[9] Democratic decision-making may make it difficult to push from the centre; even so, it is only national governments that can drive these processes of change and fully mobilize diverse civil-society organizations around new political agendas. Local management and political control is ultimately the goal, but this can become an obstacle to progress if people lose sight of the reasons for the reorganization. Thus, the transition must at first be directed by national governments, which must clearly articulate the goal, which is to manage bio-regions as if they are part of the global heritage. The first step is to generate a commitment to the big objectives. Local circumstances and concerns can then be accommodated while the changes are being implemented.

Bio-region management systems will create a powerful requirement for detailed knowledge of how ecosystems actually work. They will also create a need for enhanced ecosystem monitoring mechanisms and technologies and for better analytical and decision-support tools. National actions to develop and use this capability will thus become important elements in the process of assembling the information required to assess how national actions are contributing to the success of the global war effort.

Eco-Urban Management

Cities are places of human accomplishment and cultural complexity in a way that rural areas are not. Cities are also where the fate of humanity will be decided. They are the crucible of hope for a better future, yet they are also the source of most of the major ecological and equity issues that are now threatening growth and social stability. There can be no sustained progress toward a more secure and prosperous human future if the ecological impacts of urban provisioning are not dramatically softened.

So it is one of the great paradoxes of our era, and one of its great problems, that even though the world's most pressing environmental and social challenges are encountered in cities or generated by them, the power to develop and implement solutions is entrenched elsewhere. Cities were long ago subsumed under the authority of national or regional governments. Their present circumscribed roles and responsibilities were defined in relation to the conditions that existed toward the end of the Middle Ages and have not followed step with the ensuing centuries of social evolution. Thus, cities are ill equipped to cope with the mounting challenges they presently face.

Differential access to provisioning processes underpins all forms of economic disparity. Raising several billion urban dwellers out of the poverty pit, and preventing several billion more from falling into it in the next twenty-five years, will require significant increases in access to sources of natural capital. The first critical transition point for increased demand occurs when people migrate from rural to urban areas.

Demand then increases exponentially as people escape the restraints of informal-sector activity by finding employment in the formal economy. Clearly, then, there is a binding relationship between social equity and the ways that urban societies are organized to meet their provisioning needs. Neither global inequities nor ecological decline will be alleviated until cities are empowered with clearly defined political mandates to alter the ways they access and use natural capital and dispose of waste products. Urban provisioning processes must be designed specifically to accelerate the ability of the impoverished to access natural capital. Only then will they be able to create wealth and benefit from the technology-related processes of employment diversification. For these reasons, a new urban agenda is needed to shape new roles for cities in the provisioning of societies.

Mining urban natural capital. The necessary starting point for shaping the urban battle plan is to present cities with the same challenge as was presented to industry: cities must find ways to decouple their growth from ever-increasing demands for natural capital.

As a first step, urban areas must be included in bio-region management arrangements. By reorganizing political authority so that ecozones have a central place in citizen consciousness, we will help reintegrate rural with urban planning. We will also help control the negative impacts of urban provisioning on local environments.

However, because urban provisioning is global in scale, we must also find ways to dramatically reduce the demands made by urban provisioning on ecological systems around the world. This will require radical reductions in the urban draw on ecological goods and services. Cities, like private companies, must become closed-loop machines for processing natural capital. The concepts and principles of industrial ecology must be applied to the management of entire urban areas.

These concepts are now being applied in a handful of city initiatives to establish 'eco-industrial parks.'[10] These operate like any industrial park, but with the important difference that efforts are made to attract industries so that the waste products of one are essential material inputs for others. Ramping this concept up to become the basis for a new form of 'eco-urban management' would involve designing and organizing urban waste flows on a citywide basis by taking all final industrial and municipal wastes and channelling them as inputs to other local or more distant production processes.

This has important implications for how technologies are chosen and how urban infrastructures are organized to deliver essential water, energy, power, transportation, and other hard services to urban consumers. All must be designed for endless recycling and for the minimization of all forms of waste. The goal must be nothing less than 'mining' urban sources of natural capital through the use of technologies and management practices that enable circular systems of use and reuse until nothing is left of the original flow that can be reused or that will harm the environment if discarded.

Obviously, cities will have to work closely with local industries in order to bring this about. They will have to play a vigorous role in shaping a new urban infrastructure of natural capital recycling; this will have to include developing new waste-capture technologies, collection and processing facilities, and market-arbitration mechanisms. The latter will be needed to help local companies find markets for their 'captured waste' products. If local markets cannot be found or created for local waste, regional or broader intercity markets will have to be sought. Failing this, the use of noxious substances will have to be banned from municipal areas.

Jobs and wealth creation. Cities, especially in the Third World will also have to create massive new employment opportunities for their citizens. Thus, the technologies for eco-urban management will have to be developed in concert with employment strategies. This will require the building of infrastructure tailored to the needs of the poor and the creation of asset wealth for those aspiring to escape the informal sector.

Equity, ecology, and job creation all intersect around the technologies that drive urban infrastructure and the tailoring of infrastructure services to people's needs. Hard infrastructure (e.g., water and sanitation delivery, waste removal, energy and transportation systems, pollution control technologies) creates access to enhanced flows of natural capital by extending the reach of urban residents to more distant and higher-quality sources or by enabling greater use of existing sources (e.g., cleaner air). Soft infrastructure (e.g., education and legal and financial services) provides access to knowledge and value-added personal or business services. There is considerable potential to introduce new forms of highly decentralized urban infrastructure that simultaneously address ecological concerns and the employment and wealth-creation needs of the urban poor.[11]

Of particular note, many decentralized water, waste-management, and energy technologies now exist that cannot be fully utilized within the framework of centralized water and waste-treatment facilities on which the concept of 'trickledownism' is based. For example, it is possible to pipe dirty water into an urban slum area, clean it on site for drinking purposes and all first-level household needs, and recirculate semicleaned water for secondary use while recovering and composting all of the organic pollutants for sale as fertilizer; in fact, this process can be continued endlessly until the only water effluent released is evaporation. Similar technological capability exists to recirculate industrial wastewater on site while separating organic and toxic waste streams for on-site processing and reuse or easier collection and removal. These new, decentralized infrastructure technologies have particular relevance for Third World cities, where the uncontrolled growth of urban slums makes it difficult to plan and pay for the extension of large infrastructure corridors and where the immediate requirement for basic infrastructure services is pressing.[12] As these decentralized technologies come into play, they will provide a natural base for expanding the soft infrastructure services that are essential to channelling additional technologies and that create the conditions for diversifying employment opportunity.

Constraints to Eco-urban Management

The promise of eco-urban management is a long way from being fulfilled. There are few signs anywhere that provisioning is playing any role in the organization of urban areas. Nor is there widespread recognition of the key role played by tailored infrastructure services in creating wealth and diversifying employment. Urban investment priorities are skewed to the needs of advanced enclaves and international market linkages. There is a major disconnect in thinking about the role, design, and choice of infrastructure technologies and services and the integrated promotion of equity and ecological preservation. Progress toward eco-urban management systems is constrained by the tyranny of the installed base of technology and related mindsets, the narrow pursuit of New Economy economic opportunities, and the preservation of outdated political mandates and organizational structures.

The most visible evidence of the constraints imposed by existing technologies is the fact that the car still rules urban design. The unrestrained growth of suburban areas makes expanded road networks and reliance on cars a necessity. Expressways are being built into city centres with a corresponding fouling of the air; meanwhile, workers and their families are trading off the lower costs of suburban living against the tedium of commuting.

The consequences of this type of urban expansion for global provisioning are profound. To give just two examples, low-density housing is 'about 2.5 times more materials intensive per inhabitant than high density development,'[13] and suburbs as presently designed seldom create the population densities required to support mass-transit systems.[14] These two factors alone dramatically increase provisioning requirements while locking in patterns of automobile use and condemning civic administrations to endlessly subsidizing public transportation.

Yet the octopus-like growth of cities into surrounding regions continues everywhere. In all parts of the world, urban tentacles are spreading out in all directions, a result of human addiction to the automobile. The entire Atlantic seaboard of the United States from Maine to Florida is slowly evolving into a formless urban blob where the private automobile is a necessity.[15] A similar infill has been developing for years between Rotterdam and Amsterdam and is being replicated across Europe. In Asia, a 1500 kilometre urban belt extending from Beijing to Tokyo by way of Pyongang and Seoul now 'connects 77 cities of over 200,000 inhabitants each. More than 97 million residents live in this urban corridor, which, in fact, links four separate megalopolises in four countries in one.'[16]

But railing against the car is unlikely to lead to reduced dependence on it, at least not quickly. Powerful new motive technologies are waiting in the wings that may reduce dependence on the internal-combustion engine, but it may be years before they actually step onto the stage. Even then, precious few alternatives exist to seriously reduce global reliance on the private automobile. The car is here to stay, and planning decisions will have to continue to work within this basic reality.

A more fruitful approach is to try to deal with the mindset that now drives the centralized provision of urban infrastructure. This fixation began over 2,500 years ago, when the ancient Romans first began building water systems, only now it revolves around the car. The full range of hard infrastructure services – water and sanitation, power lines, natural gas connections, communication cables, and the like –

are generally delivered as a package along with the extension and upgrading of road networks.

The focus of urban planners on the extension of centralized urban infrastructure is strengthened by the growing competition between cities for investment and by the need to build services and linkages that tie cities into international markets. These new forms of competition are setting urban investment priorities. The global business networks of the New Economy have largely bypassed national governments by directly linking enclaves in cities around the world. As macro-economic and trade policies at the national level are gradually harmo-nized, the competition for investment, corporate presence, and mobile people is increasingly influenced by city-specific considerations.

The result is that the extension of advanced urban enclaves is the key to the commercial success of cities. The requirements of the en-claves and international business connections provide the focus for the extension and upgrading of urban infrastructure, and almost by default, 'trickledownism' becomes the means for addressing urban poverty. All of this constrains experimentation with new infrastruc-ture technologies, besides leading to risk-averse city administrations that refuse to consider alternative approaches. New Economy infra-structure commandeers the money, but it fails to move urban manage-ment toward the next levels of ecologically appropriate, decentralized infrastructure, and it fails to reach the poor. This dominant pattern of investment must change if progress toward eco-urban management is to be made.

New patterns of investment in eco-urban infrastructure are unlikely to emerge until strong political mandates are created for implement-ing a clear vision of how cities must be reorganized. This vision pres-ently does not exist, and the potential for creating it has been compro-mised by the centuries-long, random, largely unplanned transfers of political authority from municipalities to other levels of government.

The old monopolies that cities once enjoyed and the political control that went with those monopolies have been erased: power is now located elsewhere, and local investment decisions are regulated largely by the state. There are few exceptions around the world. Some of the consequences are listed below:

• The management of the interactions between cities and surround-ing bio-regions is not clearly lodged. The divisions are enforced by diverse bureaucratic mandates that separate the management and mindset of civic administrations and urban residents from those of rural interests.

- There is no power base for the urban environment: primary mandates for environmental protection are located at the national or provincial/state level. Concern for global ecological management is divorced from the purview of cities. There is little pressure on cities to reduce their global ecological footprints.
- Responsibility for equity and employment generation is located elsewhere. The role of cities in employment generation has been reduced to implementing social assistance programs that are largely designed and funded by other levels of government.
- Municipalities must work with industry, which takes root in the fabric of urban societies, yet responsibility for industrial regulation is largely outside of municipal control.
- Technological innovation takes place within institutions and businesses located in cities, yet policy responsibility and investment priorities are largely shaped by macro-economic and tax policies at the national and provincial/state levels.
- The great majority of infrastructure investment takes place in cities, yet a high proportion of infrastructure funding comes from other sources and is subject to the dictates of funding agencies. Underfunded cities lack political power and must stand in line, hat in hand, in order to attract infrastructure investment.
- The often chaotic and fragmented mishmash of political jurisdictions within cities limits the capacity to bring a 'whole city' perspective to bear on urban management and undermines the capacity to shape a vision around the notion of eco-urban management. This problem is especially acute in the Third World, where the boundaries of cities are often drawn in ways that exclude large portions of the peri-areas, which house informal-sector economic activity.[17]

Creating political accountability for eco-urban management. It is difficult to conceive how urban challenges of the magnitude expected in the next several decades can be addressed without a substantial realignment of political authority.

In terms of the constitutional division of powers, the requirements of eco-urban management imply a need to expand existing city mandates in the areas of ecology, employment, industrial regulation, market development, technological innovation, and the design of hard and soft infrastructure. Cities also need to be given the authority and taxation powers to raise requisite financing.

Wars, of course, are fought not just to alter the division of political authority but to achieve specific social objectives. So it is essential that the transfer of political power to cities take place within the framework of carefully defined responsibilities. The change of political mandates needs to be driven by the task of provisioning societies in conditions of global ecological decline. This has to be clearly spelled out if political accountability is to be meaningful. More specifically, urban politicians must be given responsibility for controlling the natural capital draws of their cities and local industry and for transforming urban areas into giant employment-creating and materials-recycling machines. To accomplish this, city administrations must quickly be made politically accountable for the following:

- Dramatically reducing the urban throughput of natural capital from primary sources through the development of a new urban infrastructure of recycling – one that includes both the technologies of secondary recovery and local, regional, and broader market mechanisms for facilitating the reuse of recovered natural capital.
- Fully integrating municipal activities related to provisioning and waste flows in the context of broader political mandates for bioregion management. This includes establishing clear targets for managing urban industrial pollution in the framework of local ecological carrying capacities and for controlling the impacts of city-provisioning processes on global ecosystems. Cities must control production and natural-capital reprocessing technologies; they must also be responsible for related spatial planning and zoning decisions.
- Designing infrastructure technologies and services in ways that maximize wealth creation and employment. In particular, this includes the design of hard and soft infrastructure services that meet the needs of people living in the informal economies of the peri-areas of Third World cities.

Obviously, profound differences exist between cities. They begin the processes of transformation from different starting points, their growth prospects differ, and the scale of local environmental and equity challenges varies widely. No 'one size fits all' prescriptions are possible. Nevertheless, all cities are in competition for the same global sources of limited natural capital and all must reorganize their affairs if the provisioning of global growth and poverty reduction are to happen. The adoption of eco-urban management practices is the only way cities can contribute to meeting these objectives.

This type of management approach must eventually be replicated around the world. When this occurs, and especially when the bioregion management and industrial ecology components are added, the global community will have an enormously strong capability for provisioning all societies while stabilizing human intervention in the operation of regional and global ecosystems.

Chapter 14

Mobilizing the International Community

Regardless of the desire of nation-states to mobilize for the war on ecological decline, the scope and effectiveness of their efforts will be limited in the absence of international co-ordination. Ecological decline must be fought on a global basis.

This is more than just a matter of generating the national political will to wage war. It is a reflection of the fact that we live in a world in which the ecological and economic links between nations are increasingly strong. This reality constrains the scope for independent national action. It creates a 'not me first' syndrome that can only be overcome if most nations act in unison.

The dilemma facing national politicians in moving the sustainable development agenda forward was captured with elegant clarity in a comment by one of the participants at a meeting of OECD environment ministers. After noting his government's commitment to the principle of sustainable development, he went on to say that 'whenever he tries to promote the behavioural and technological changes necessary to move in that direction, i.e., when he attempts to internalize the costs of environmental pollution and resource degradation, he is branded a "green protectionist" outside his country, and a destroyer of national competitiveness at home.'[1]

This schizophrenic reaction accurately reflects the divided mindset that most countries and international companies reveal when questions of national competitiveness and market access arise in the context of calls for more stringent environmental protection measures. Industry may *drive* growth, but it is markets that set the directions for investment. Thus, voluntary actions by industry can only be effective within the parameters set by market conditions and opportunities.

Companies can only operate within the limits of profitability: they cannot get too far out of step with their competitors. In turn, governments have a limited ability to act independently without hurting their industries.

This 'not me first' syndrome permeates both corporate and national thinking about environmental protection. Without strong, co-ordinated international action to enhance the market pull of ecological sustainability, most industries and most governments will resist all-out commitment to the war effort. As a result, national action will be most effective if it is co-ordinated within the framework of a unified, global plan for the conduct of the war.

The Framework Convention on Provisioning (the FEP)

It is in the international arena that the war against ecological decline must ultimately be declared. The challenges and consequences of ecological decline can only be fully comprehended in global terms, and it is only in this context that specific national responsibilities for the conduct of the war can be allocated.

As in the case of national actions, a lack of clarity, focus, and vision constrains international action to address the pressures leading to ecological decline. What now motivates international effort is the elusive concept of sustainable development, but the specific enemy that the world must mobilize to fight has not been explicitly defined. The international sustainable-development agenda is becoming more complex and has failed to differentiate between causes and effects. Furthermore, it identifies ecological decline as only one of many social and economic challenges to be overcome. It fails to recognize that all issues are not equal and that continued economic growth, poverty reduction, human rights, and social peace all depend on the ability to continue provisioning societies with essential ecological goods and services. Not surprisingly, international mobilization around the objective of halting ecological decline has been half-hearted. Thus, the war is being lost without having really been declared. To turn this situation around, international programs and funding must be redirected to the support of national plans for fighting ecological decline on each of the six battlefields of technological advance.

In Round Five, responsibility for managing ever more complicated provisioning functions was turned over to private enterprise, and nation-states lost their capacity to control the cumulative impact of provisioning activities on global ecosystems. National regulations and changes in resource management practices can limit the impacts of specific pollutants or weaknesses in resource management. However, no mechanisms other than the negotiation of multilateral environmental agreements (MEAs) have yet been developed to control the cumulative effects of residual demands on global ecosystems that result from the hundreds of thousands of individual investment decisions being taken every day in all corners of the world.

Thus, to co-ordinate and launch the war, a new multilateral agreement, the Framework Convention on Provisioning (FCP), must be negotiated. The preamble to the FCP would amount to a declaration of war by the international community on ecological decline. The programs, policies, co-ordination mechanisms, and enforcement arrangements encapsulated in the FCP would constitute the global plan for waging the war.

Below, I outline the organization of the proposed FCP:

The International Declaration of War

As befits a Declaration of War, the preamble to the FCP should break the mould of typical UN and other international communiqués by being written as a simple expression of the global resolve of national leaders, along the following lines:

> We, on behalf of the world's peoples, and in recognition of the fact that the loss of ecosystem viability now and forever threatens the ability to provision the world community in conditions of peace and broad social equity, do hereby commit our nations to co-operate in waging unrelenting war against ecological decline.
>
> To this end, we have entered into formal agreement to wage this war through national actions aimed at developing and utilizing the weapons of technological advance and related changes in the manner in which corporations and public authorities manage their interface with natural systems. It is only through directed technological advance that the global community can provision the ongoing requirements of growth and poverty reduction while avoiding the suffering and conflict that will accompany the continued, human-induced erosion of global ecosystems.
>
> These national efforts will be co-ordinated on an international basis through the implementation of this Framework Convention on Provi-

sioning, the purpose of which is to control, prevent, and reverse all aspects of global ecological decline.

The Global Battle Plan

The program framework of the FCP must also be kept simple and focus on the essential tasks of waging the war. In this respect, the battle plan of the FCP should be organized around four components:

- A program for the international control and maintenance of ecosystem viability, built around the establishment of specific national performance targets for controlling pollutants.
- An enhanced global ecological monitoring and crisis response capability, built around the development of requisite monitoring and forecasting technologies.
- Specific technology development and management programs to support national actions, to develop and apply ecologically sustainable technologies and to implement bio-region and eco-urban management systems.
- These activities should be backed by an ecological dispute resolution mechanism (EDRM) to mediate and enforce agreed solutions to ecological management disputes or conflicts that arise between societies competing to provision themselves from the same sources of natural capital.

A central objective of the FCP is to provide an umbrella for rationalizing and consolidating most existing sustainable development programs and agreements. The FCP would transform the present scattered, unfocused, and confusing mélange of international sustainable development efforts into a highly targeted, clearly defined international war effort. In this respect, almost all of the more than 350 existing international cross-border or common-pool environmental agreements would fit easily within the program framework proposed for the FCP.[2]

The International Maintenance of Ecosystem Viability

The first component of the FCP battle plan would involve the mobilization of international effort to manage and reduce levels of human-induced stress on ecological systems.

This would be achieved by setting global targets for pollution reduction, for eliminating the use of toxic materials, for raising the percentage of waste products to be recycled, and so on, and the translation of these into specific national targets with time frames for their achievement.

The organization of this component would be similar to that of the MEAs developed over the years to control pollutants on an international basis. Existing programs such as the Montreal Protocol would be brought under the umbrella of the FCP, and new programs would be added as additional pollutants are targeted.

Ecosystem Monitoring and Preparedness

The process of setting global and national targets and monitoring the progress of the war would be supported by monitoring and preparedness arrangements. These would enable nation-states to track progress, as well as to react to signs of growing ecological stress and possible flips.

'Preparedness' is mainly a national responsibility, yet there is much the international community can do to help societies forced to cope with ecological instability. The world has developed a strong capability to co-ordinate the flow of relief and assistance to peoples of the world affected by natural disasters or displaced by war. However, the same world has yet to develop a strong capacity to monitor, forecast, and assist with adjustments to longer-term, systemic, ecological change.[3]

All societies must become more vigilant in tracking and evaluating changes in ecosystems. More refined indicators of change need to be developed in order to anticipate both short-term fluctuations in natural systems and more fundamental, longer-term changes. The resources available to national environmental-monitoring activities must be augmented. International collaboration based on the integration of existing monitoring and modelling programs could lead to the development of an enhanced early warning system to alert countries of impending crises. As in the case of other MEAs, and in particular the FCCC, the monitoring arrangements would be backed by the mobilization of relevant scientific capability and the development of related modelling and forecasting technologies. This component of the FCP could build on existing efforts to create an international pollution register that would require participating countries to collect and publish information on the quantities of pollutants released from certain industrial sources. A step in this direction is being developed by a working group within the UN Economic Commission for Europe (UNECE), under the Aarhus Convention.

Besides tracking specific pollutants, the monitoring infrastructure would operate in close collaboration with the implementation of the technology and management elements of the FCP described below – in particular, with the innovation thrusts aimed at bio-region and eco-urban management. Data developed within the framework of these national technology and management programs would flow into the global monitoring system and be used to help evaluate the conduct of the war on each battlefield as well as the overall war effort.

Programs to Develop Sustainable Technologies and Management Systems

The objective of mobilizing at the national level to fight the war on the six battlefields of technological innovation for ecological sustainability provides the basis for structuring the third component of the FCP battle plan. This would focus on the development and application of technologies and management systems in each of these areas of innovation; also, it would be designed to support the efforts of national governments to fight their own innovation battles.

Significant new layers of innovation effort will be required in order to produce the kinds of transformations in industry processes and social infrastructure that will give natural capital many consumption lives. Broad social and political change is also anticipated as societies and organizations adopt the management systems required to apply the new technologies effectively. For these reasons, all of the FCP's technology innovation program areas should contain capacity-building components that will assist countries in their efforts to overcome roadblocks to effective national mobilization.

A brief outline of the key programs for supporting innovation for ecological sustainability follows:

Energy and the FCCC. The battle to transform global energy infrastructure has already been joined under the FCCC and related national efforts. There are valid arguments for leaving this innovation thrust out of the ambit of the FCP, but there are stronger ones for including it; in particular, bringing the entire FCCC under the FCP umbrella as a distinct program unit would add to the credibility of the global Declaration of War and help clarify its intent. In the course of doing this, the disparate approaches to controlling the release of greenhouse gases (GHGs) that exist between the United States and signatories to the Kyoto Protocol could be integrated into a coherent, collective approach that includes specific commitments by Third World nations to full and urgent participation.

A global bio-region management program. This program would focus the nations of the world on moving toward the integrated management of the world's ecological resources. It would support the reconfiguration of subnational political jurisdictions into bio-region management units, and it would help build corresponding government mandates and capacity to augment flows of natural capital from primary sources in ecologically responsible ways. The emphasis would be on the integrated management of land, water, and air corridors and all ecosystem biota, as well as on social and economic interactions within specific bio-regions. Goals would include building stronger rural/urban links and simplifying relevant administrative and political management structures.

The new agriculture. This program would help bring about the next generation of agricultural technologies and assist in their global application. Only through international co-operation will global agriculture be able to make the productivity gains required to feed the world's growing population. It is only through international cooperation that agriculture can be converted from being 25 per cent of the climate change problem, 70 per cent of the global water problem, and a major source of pollution to a significant part of the solution to climate change, the source of huge volumes of water that can be made available for other uses and an environmentally benign industry.

Industrial ecology. Innovation on an international scale is going to be required to develop viable industrial ecology technologies. The use of these technologies will then have to be co-ordinated within and across industrial sectors (e.g., in forestry, mining, manufacturing, and services). Corporate incentives to invest in relevant technologies and business practices must be enhanced by changing the pull of market forces, and governments will have to work hard to encourage this. A practical, international industrial-ecology program could provide the conditions under which the world's nations might develop and adopt a uniform basket of market drivers, thus providing powerful market incentives for relevant investment.

A global eco-urban management program. A global, multifaceted management and technology development program would support the creation of new political mandates and build the management and technological capacity required to reduce the urban throughput of natural capital. It would help transform cities into closed-loop consumers and reprocessors of natural capital by reconfiguring urban infrastructures and by creating markets for reprocessed materials. It would co-ordinate the development and diffusion of the tailored hard- and soft-infrastructure services required to meet the employment and wealth creation needs of the urban poor.

Managing Conflicts over Natural Capital: EDRM

The world is faced with global ecological scarcity and the challenge of equitably meeting the provisioning needs of all societies. To make matters worse, many ecological problems are cross-border in nature. For these reasons, in the next twenty-five years the world can expect a dramatic increase in conflicts over access to natural capital and in disputes over differences of view regarding the merit of environmental management practices. A strong, international ecosystem dispute resolution mechanism (EDRM) to address and help reduce these bilateral and international tensions will be an essential part of the global war against ecological decline and a necessary component of the FCP.

At present, there are no generally accepted mechanisms for mediating international disputes over the management of environmental resources – none that have the power to enforce consensus-based solutions.[4] There has been considerable discussion of this issue in recent years, most of it focused in a rather unproductive manner on the WTO's role as arbitrator of trade policy and environmental protection measures. At present, environmentalists are furious that WTO decisions seem to be limiting the ability of nation-states to impose import restrictions on goods and products that do not accord with national environmental standards during production or harvesting.[5] They are stymied, because trade sanctions are the preferred option for enforcing MEAs when negotiations between contesting parties break down, and the WTO is the only international mechanism for enforcing such sanctions.

The WTO may have a role to play in refereeing disputes between trade and the environment, but it cannot and should not be the only player involved in making and enforcing international environmental-protection decisions. To look to the WTO for this purpose would be to distort the true nature of environmental issues. At the same time, in the absence of recourse to the power of the WTO enforcement mechanism or a viable alternative, the weak – and even many of the not so weak – have little leverage for changing the behaviour of offending countries. As well, the 'not me first' syndrome is aggravated by the threat that trade action could be taken against national environmental management initiatives that are regarded as trade limiting. As a result, many cross-border environmental issues are simply not dealt with, and otherwise unacceptable environmental management practices are allowed to continue.

An EDRM that is an integral part of the FCP will go far in breaking through these limitations and lead to effective arbitration mechanisms. This is because in signing the FCP Declaration of War on ecological decline, nation-states will be committing themselves to implement the provisions of the FCP battle plan. They will be committing themselves to managing national bio-regions in ways that maximize their contributions to global provisioning requirements and to participating in the development and application of solutions in the six key areas of technological and management innovation required to move toward ecological sustainability. Furthermore, they will be committing themselves to abide by the decisions of the EDRM.

Regarding how the EDRM would operate, it is important to recognize that environmental management issues are just that. They are not trade or legal issues. They are issues that must ultimately be resolved by reference to the principles of sound ecological management. As such, the key requirement for their resolution must involve bringing expert knowledge to bear.

In this respect, a growing body of international experience suggests that most environmental disputes – not all, but most – can be resolved through negotiation and by developing a common understanding of management issues based on scientific knowledge and evidence.[6] The best solutions can often be reached by arriving at a common understanding of the problem with the help of objective third-party experts. This suggests that the EDRM should be organized on the assumption that most cross-border environmental management disputes are ame-nable to resolution through negotiation.

Yet expert knowledge will not resolve enforcement issues if nations fail to support the war effort, fall short in meeting their obligations and commitments under the FCP, or refuse to implement EDRM rec-ommendations. If this new war were like old-style wars, the enforce-ment mechanisms and punishments inflicted on those nations which failed to engage the enemy would be severe – death by firing squad for dereliction of duty springs to mind. However, outside of military intervention – which we are trying to avoid – there is really no power-ful penalty that can be imposed other than trade sanctions, and their use is governed by the WTO.

To get around this impasse, we will need to separate EDRM deci-sions regarding ecological management, and specifically regarding com-pliance, from the WTO's enforcement mechanisms.

Thus, the EDRM would function mainly as a mediation service for countries involved in disputes with their neighbours relating to dam-aging environmental practices. The EDRM could also assist nation-states in subnational conflicts over access to natural capital. For ex-ample, it could offer its ecosystem knowledge during the mediation process.

The mediation service would be designed to bring the parties to the negotiating table. It would operate, like the WTO, through indepen-dent panels of experts charged with assembling the information re-quired to reach a common understanding of the problem, its severity and effects, the options for resolution, and the obligations of the par-ties to implement remediation measures. The EDRM would then pro-vide the services of an arbitrator to facilitate negotiations leading to desirable actions. The EDRM would also have the capacity to monitor the implementation of its recommendations.

Mediation would need to proceed in a timely fashion to avoid de-lays in curbing inappropriate environmental practices and to prevent countries from using mediation as a delaying tactic. Thus, the entire process should take no more than a year from the time the dispute is first lodged to the time implementation begins.[7]

If the moral or peer-group pressure that results from public disclo-sure of the panel's conclusions does not precipitate remedial action, the EDRM would then quantify the scale of punitive damages to be imposed on the offending country and authorize the aggrieved party to approach the WTO to set and impose appropriate trade sanctions that reflect the scale and consequences of the ecological mismanage-ment. As all nations are now either directly or indirectly affected by ecological mismanagement, the trade sanctions should be applied on an international basis when the damaged party lacks the economic weight to make the sanctions meaningful.

Chapter 15

Round Six: The Age of Global Provisioning

The fundamental challenge now facing the global community is to find the means to provision societies in conditions of global ecological scarcity. The world must quickly make the transition to new technologies and new patterns of social organization if it is to succeed in securing access to the ecological goods and services on which growth, poverty reduction, and social peace all depend.

The world has evolved through five rounds in provisioning arrangements. These have culminated in the Fifth Round, our present global economy, which relies disproportionately on the organizational strength of international business networks and New Economy technologies to access almost all sources of natural capital in the biosphere. The economic integration mechanisms of Round Five have demonstrated their power to spread the benefits of growth around the world, but they do not provide the organizational or technological capability to adequately provision the more than 6 billion people now living and the 8 billion who will be inhabiting the planet in less than twenty-five years. The technologies underpinning present provisioning arrangements are grinding down the world's ecological systems and placing at risk continued growth and efforts to reduce global poverty. A continuation of opportunistic approaches to technological advance will not produce solutions to the specific challenge of finding new ways to equitably provision human societies from depleted global ecosystems.

In earlier chapters I summarized the evidence that has been assembled by the international scientific community regarding the pervasive erosion of ecosystem viability already wrought by human provisioning efforts, and I tried to quantify the incremental demand for natural capital that will accumulate by 2025. If forecasts of population, economic, and urban growth prove accurate, and if the goal of reducing global poverty is to be met, the demands of human societies for increased flows of natural capital – including the services required to dispose of human wastes – could require the ecological resources of three or four worlds; by 2050, the requirement could increase to ten worlds.

There is little in this assessment that is new. All of the compelling evidence of ecological decline has failed to stop the world's nations from pursuing growth at the expense of the environment. The international agenda remains dangerously unbalanced. Almost all countries are now actively seeking fuller engagement in the global economy in order to derive the benefits of more diversified and prolific provisioning mechanisms. The lure and requirements of participation in the global economy have commandeered most efforts at innovation as well as most of the attention of politicians. As a result, the world is trapped in a downward spiral toward ecological Armageddon. The solution to hunger is rightly seen as more food; the solution to poverty is rightly seen as more growth; the solution to global inequity is rightly seen as greater participation in the global economy. But all of these solutions require increased consumption of natural capital, which now has to be drawn from sources already severely eroded by the relentless pressure of human demand.

Seeing the Enemy

If existing knowledge of the extent of ecological decline has not been enough to cause the global community to take decisive action, there is little hope that continued dialogue around sustainable development issues will result in adequate responses to the challenge of provisioning the world in time frames that matter. It is as if decision makers are waiting for some catastrophic event to remove all lingering doubt regarding the scale and immediacy of the threat presented by ecological decline. As in the prelude to most wars, we are waiting for the enemy to clearly define itself through an action that turns the tide of opinion in favour of full mobilization.

This situation bears an eerie resemblance to events leading to the final dénouement of the appeasement movement. On 1 September 1939, Germany invaded Poland. The British had a mutual defence pact with the Poles and so were already technically at war with Germany. The following day, Neville Chamberlain, the British prime minister, rose to address the joint Houses of Parliament. As he began to repeat the arguments for appeasement that had led to past accommodations with Germany, he was stopped cold by a backbench MP named Greenwood, who angrily shouted, 'Speak for England, Neville!' Forced to change tack, Chamberlain acknowledged his country's obligations, and the following day, Britain formally declared war.

Appeasement had a bad name that day, not because its objectives were wrong but because its practitioners vastly underestimated the implacable evil facing the world. Chamberlain and his fellow appeasers were attempting to negotiate solutions to what they saw as the great issues that could potentially drag Europe into another all-out war: the question of reparations, the remilitarization of Germany, the right to occupy the Rhineland and the Sudetenland, and Germany's long-standing demand for the return of the Danzig corridor. In pursuing a peaceful resolution of these issues, they lost sight of the true character and ambitions of Nazi Germany. Because of this, it took a succession of events, culminating in the invasion of Poland, to force Chamberlain to commit the British people to war.

More recently, the world failed to respond to the growing signs of a rise of global terrorism because of ambiguities surrounding the strength and intent of different groups. For years, terrorists had been honing their skills, building organizational strength, probing the edges of the security apparatus of Western nations, and identifying loopholes. They had detonated bombs, killed hundreds of people, and seen how the United States – perhaps held back by the more timorous among its NATO allies – lacked the resolve to respond with powerful force. Terrorism was emboldened. Western democracies had failed to come to grips with the true nature of the enemy. The reality of terrorism had not permeated the public consciousness, nor had it received the focused attention of politicians, before the attacks on the World Trade Center and the Pentagon on 11 September.

The political leaders of the 1920s and 1930s failed to look objectively and realistically at the challenges to peace, and seventy years later another generation of political leaders failed to see the extent of the threat of terrorism. In the same way, today's politicians seem to be almost wilfully ignoring or underestimating the coherence and implacable consequences of ecological decline for humankind.

Ecological decline is not like other enemies, and the war against it is not going to erupt or be fought like other wars. There are no historical precedents for the challenge now facing the global community. The threat is not at all comparable to an enemy eyeing someone's oil fields or agricultural lands or to a clash of ideologies or civilizations. Nor can the world expect or wait for a defining event to tip the balance of opinion in favour of war. The full effects of the enemy's power are not going to appear over a weekend. There is not going to be an ecological equivalent to the invasion of Poland or the destruction of the World Trade Center towers that will force the world onto a war footing. All there will be is a slow accretion of ecological loss.

The evidence of ecological decline abounds, but its effects are diffused around the world. Societies are not all affected in the same manner. Changes in ecosystems take place slowly. The small increments of destruction are often difficult to quantify, and the interconnections between events often escape detection. The sudden flips that occur as a species dies off or an ecosystem drops to a lower level of productivity are still regarded as isolated events or as local or regional issues. Yet in conditions of global ecological scarcity, everything is connected. If a local ecosystem fails, and if local provisioning capability is impaired, the human challenge is no longer limited to suffering the decline in provisioning capacity through the decades required to reverse the loss. The challenge is complicated by the fact that the loss, even if temporary, will immediately lead to increased pressure on other ecological systems as humans shift the focus of their provisioning efforts. Moreover, once environmental change begins it can take decades for catastrophic changes in global ecosystems to unfold. And once that has begun, there is often nothing that humans can do except adjust to conditions of reduced or altered ecological productivity.

Global ecological decline is much like the old practice of inflicting death through a thousand cuts. Depending on how long the executioner is prepared to wait for the victim to die, the defining slice could be any one of the thousand, yet the result is the same. Human provisioning efforts are slicing into natural systems, and the world cannot expect and dare not wait for a defining ecological slice to precipitate the decision to wage war.

If the world's political leaders are not yet prepared to heed the formidable evidence, and if we cannot count on a cataclysmic event to tilt opinion toward waging war, then we need a new way of talking about ecological decline that makes the threat urgent and sufficiently compelling to cause serious mobilization. Looking at the world from the perspective of provisioning does this. It forces us to see more clearly the scale and consequences of ecological decline for human societies, and it provides insights into how to fight ecological decline in ways that will help provision humanity's future.

Provisioning human societies is the great imperative of our times. We have reached the point in the long struggle to provision human societies where all of the world's peoples are now competing for the same sources of global as opposed to local or regional ecological goods and services. Everything is now connected: the consequences of inequitable provisioning arrangements and ecological decline are diffused through the entire global community. The world's ecosystems are already in disrepair, and incremental demands will soon cause irreversible collapse. In these circumstances, when environmental disruption strikes hard at one corner of the world, all of us share in the consequences, for the capacity to provision everyone has been diminished. Ecological scarcity is now the single greatest constraint to continued growth, to our ability to reduce global poverty, and to world peace. It is now the common enemy of all peoples because these ambitions and all other dimensions of continued human progress must be provisioned. The entire global population must now declare and wage war against ecological decline.

Choosing Our Wars

Focusing on the challenge of provisioning the rapid expansion of present societies also provides a clear indication of the actions required to fight ecological decline. If provisioning is the need, if there are no significant untapped sources of natural capital remaining, and if existing sources are already stretched beyond sustainable limits, then there is only one way to fight the war. It must be fought through directed technological change and related management practices that have the power to augment useable flows of natural capital. The war must be waged on the battlefields of technological innovation. Only on those battlefields will the big, replicable solutions to the challenge of provisioning societies be secured.

This has profound implications for the choices societies make regarding how they organize themselves. All societies must engage themselves in these battles and implement the new provisioning arrangements. The world must move away from past methods of portioning out responses.[1] Third World nations cannot argue that the advanced economies are responsible because of their disproportionate consumption of natural capital and then, in the next breath, disregard the implications of their burgeoning populations for the coming challenges. In an interlocking world where everything connects, *all* nations are affected by ecological scarcity, and *all* must participate in the search for solutions. Fragmented international efforts will not be enough to win the war.

Finally, placing the task of provisioning human societies at the centre of political decision making will help clarify the consequences of a failure to halt ecological decline.

We know from the earlier rounds of provisioning how dangerous ecological scarcity can be to the established social order. Eras of increased competition for access to essential natural capital have tended to be eras of human conflict. Ecological scarcity has often led to war; sometimes it has been the sole cause, and other times it has contributed to the coalescing of peoples along ethnic, national, cultural or religious lines. The consequences of competition for access to natural capital have been especially devastating during transitions between rounds: one group gains economic advantage or military power that enables it to meet its provisioning requirements at the expense of other groups that are still locked into the provisioning arrangements of earlier rounds.

So far, the trade-based provisioning arrangements of Round Five have been quite benign compared to the strife that accompanied the transitions between earlier rounds. In large measure this is because war is now proving to be a less effective means of provisioning societies than trade and economic integration. However, the tensions inherent in Round Five have yet to fully play out, and earlier provisioning arrangements – 'hangovers' from previous rounds – are creating a potentially volatile situation. These differences in provisioning arrangements are what is now determining the place of tribes, cities, and nation-states within the global community; they underlie the hierarchies of wealth and power which presently exist around the world. These differences are also preparing the ground for the 'old style' conflicts that could erupt if the world's peoples are forced to compete for the same declining global sources of natural capital.

Those societies within the global community whose provisioning arrangements still reflect earlier rounds are less well off than those fully participating in Round Five. The poorest among them are more likely to resort to violence when faced with ecological decline. People living in poverty tend to rely disproportionately on local sources of natural capital, and they are immediately susceptible to shortfalls caused by environmental disruption or by the actions of their neighbours. When this happens, ecological scarcity or constrained access to natural capital can trigger wars between peoples who have organized to provision themselves from the same local sources of natural capital. These old-style wars tend to be fought within tight geographical boundaries, usually at the subnational level, and they are fought with deadly intent.

In contrast, those participating in the advanced provisioning mechanisms of Round Five, the global economy, enjoy a diversity of provisioning mechanisms that insulate them from local ecological disruption. If they cannot access a particular source for an essential commodity, they can find it elsewhere. But they are not off the hook. Local wars can spill across international borders, and the rich and powerful participants in Round Five are not immune from the effects of global ecological disruption or from the growing competition for access to increasingly scarce natural capital. In this respect, if history is any guide, the coalescing of warring parties over access to scarce global resources is likely to pit those fully engaged in the provisioning processes of Round Five against those organized in less advantageous ways to meet their provisioning requirements. This may seem like a total mismatch, but unlike the transitions between earlier rounds, there are significant constraints on the ability of the leading economies to wield their economic and military power. Global interdependence makes the economic performance of leading economies increasingly sensitive to their trade and investment ties with Third World nations. These market realities temper the independent exercise of economic or military power. Furthermore, the poor have new weapons at their disposal, as the terrorist threat now illustrates. Thus, the prospect of Round Five deteriorating into a series of violent, tribal-like confrontations will grow if ecological decline continues to constrain global provisioning capacity. But these old-style wars cannot provide solutions to the challenge of provisioning the world's people from declining sources of natural capital. Nor can the economic and military power of leading economies and of the advanced enclaves in poorer nations protect the wealthy in conditions of continued ecological decline. For neither trade nor war can increase the availability of global sources of natural capital.

For these reasons, the peoples of the world can either fight one another for privileged access to ecological goods and services, or they can collectively declare war on global ecological decline. This choice could not be more stark. In old-style wars of competition for natural capital, victory can be achieved only by continuing the slaughter until populations have been reduced to levels that can be provisioned using existing technologies and mechanisms. In contrast, the war to provision the world will not be fought with swords, bombs, or propaganda. It will be fought through co-ordinated technological innovation that creates enormously powerful mechanisms for rationalizing human interactions with the natural environment and for securing the ongoing flows of natural capital required to meet social and economic objectives. It will not be a war of human carnage but rather a war for human survival in which we are all on the same side. And it will be a war the world's peoples must mobilize to fight with desperate urgency, for it must be won within several decades.

To bring about the scale of change required in provisioning processes in time frames that matter, the global community must fight on each of the six battlefields of technological innovation. Only in this way can ecological decline be halted. I propose that the war effort be co-ordinated through a global battle plan under a new Framework Convention on Provisioning (FCP). This convention will clearly mark ecological decline as the enemy. It will make it possible for the world to mobilize effectively at both the national and international levels. It will give the world the power to unlock the puzzle of promoting sustained growth, and it will advance the cause of international equity in conditions of global ecological scarcity. It will give the world a road map for achieving a sustainable future.

The World Summit on Global Provisioning

To move this new, highly focused agenda forward, I propose that the next world summit be called to declare and launch the global war against ecological decline. This World Summit on Global Provisioning (the WSGP) should be organized around the specific actions the world must take to meet the growing provisioning needs of societies in conditions of accelerating ecological scarcity and uncertainty, and on nothing else! The intervening years should be used to prepare for the summit and to lay the groundwork for the ensuing war.

This means that the arguments I have made in this book must be put to the test. It is obviously beyond the realm to think that a few pages will be able to alter prevailing political opinion when forty years of intense international dialogue around the same themes have failed to place the provisioning of societies at the heart of political decision making. Nor can a couple of chapters do justice to the topics of ecological decline, social equity, and human conflict. On the other hand, all it takes to break out of the present stasis that bedevils the global dialogue on sustainable development is a small shift in the angle of vision that will force us to think more directly about the provisioning challenges that face us all. So, I propose the following actions for moving the dialogue on provisioning forward and for laying the groundwork for the WSGP.

Document the scale of provision requirements by 2025. The starting point is to fully assess the growth of the global provisioning requirements that will arise in less than twenty-five years and to verify the implications of these requirements for global ecological decline. This is essential in order to unambiguously establish the scale and nature of the enemy and the short time available for taking definitive action. It is vital for coherent decision making that world leaders know whether the scale of global provisioning effort will, in fact, require the ecological resources of three or four worlds within this short time frame. Alternatively, if only two or perhaps five worlds are required, they need to know whether the basic argument for urgent action advanced in this book still pertains.

Accelerate investment in innovation for ecological sustainability. A critical requirement in the lead-up to the summit is to begin to rebalance the international agenda so that innovation for ecological sustainability is given weight at least equal to that of present dominant patterns of technological advance. Existing technologies are now shaping provisioning processes and setting the directions of growth, and this must change.

The six battlefields of innovation on which the war must be fought are not new. Especially in the field of alternative (i.e., non-carbon) energy, substantial research has already been done. However, placing all of these innovation requirements in the framework of the challenge of provisioning our societies will add considerable impetus to these efforts. The immediate need is to flesh out the specific technological requirements of provisioning and to dramatically accelerate investment in these areas of innovation. To this end, nation-states must change the balance of innovation incentives to enhance the appeal of innovation for ecological sustainability, and they must establish the international policy-co-ordination mechanisms, programs, and incentives required to overcome the 'not me first' syndrome that now constrains international innovation efforts. These actions will build momentum for change in the lead-up to the WSGP. They are not aimed at diverting investment from existing, market-driven innovation efforts: these already benefit from well-developed investment support infrastructure and from market demand that will continue. Rather, the objective is to create comparable or greater investment incentives for essential technology developments related to ecological sustainability. The goal is to find ways to fully release the power of human ingenuity so that it can focus on the specific innovation requirements for provisioning the human community.

Assess the effects of innovation for ecological sustainability on employment, wealth creation, and the reduction of poverty. Objections are likely to be raised to the suggestion that innovation effort must be directed to purposes not immediately driven by market demand. It will be pointed out that this will impede growth and cause economic and employment loss. These assumptions need to be questioned, and the case for investing in innovation for ecological sustainability needs to be defended.

In this respect, it is important to emphasize that the intent in all this is not to stop growth but rather to make it possible. Growth must be provisioned if it is to continue and if the world is to derive the benefits that only growth can confer. Obviously, finding technologies that will enable growth is not going to mean less growth. If the war against ecological decline is successful, it will mean more growth but of a qualitatively different and environmentally benign kind.

In particular, we need to review the arguments about the roles that provisioning infrastructure and innovation for ecological sustainability play in generating wealth and creating jobs. Technological innovation creates jobs because it leads to greater specialization and more differentiated employment opportunities. This helps explain the beneficial effects of existing and expected New Economy innovation. Well, if it works for New Economy technologies, it should work in exactly the same way with innovation for ecological sustainability. Indeed, there are grounds for believing that these innovation efforts may lead to even greater employment gains.

Times of significant change in technological and social infrastructure have historically been times when employment opportunities have vastly expanded. This occurred with advances in maritime technologies in the ancient world, with the invention of the steam engine and the railways, with the electrification of nation-states, with the introduction of the telegraph and telephone, with the invention of the internal combustion engine, and with the huge transportation and energy infrastructure transformations that followed. It occurred with jet planes, which shrank the world. It is happening now as new communication and information technologies combine through the Internet to drive whole new patterns of social, economic, and cultural integration and employment opportunity. And it should happen again with innovation for ecological sustainability, since this will have an enormous impact on the nature, design, and organization of infrastructure technologies and services in every country in the world.

The employment gains associated with the dramatic overhaul of social infrastructure will occur through the retooling of national and municipal energy and transportation infrastructure and through the combined effects of industrial and urban efforts to create secondary markets for reprocessed natural capital. The effects will be especially evident in cities, where the technologies, practices, and market systems of eco-urban management will basically overhaul the core infrastructure of all municipalities. Further employment gains and wealth generation will accompany the development of infrastructure technologies and services to meet the specific needs of people engaged in informal-sector activities, including the design of highly decentralized urban water and waste management systems and the range of soft infrastructure services required to build asset wealth and to help people move up the ladders of technological and employment sophistication. In the process, the poor will be integrated into the broader, more diversified provisioning arrangements that enable these progressions.

The economic benefits derived from this more balanced base of innovation activity may also be augmented by the potential synergy between technological advance leading to ecological sustainability and the drivers of New Economy investment. Global business investment is hampered by social instability, urban crime, and pollution. Thus, growth requires the right infrastructure but also requires that ecological and equity issues be addressed. The war to provision the world could produce a vital symbiosis with New Economy investment by providing the antidote to the ecological and equity derailers of continued growth.

As well, once the new directions of technological advance have been set, it is reasonable to assume, based on past experience, that a rapid multiplication of new directions in human invention around the world will spin out beneficial surprises and that societies will adapt in productive ways that we cannot yet foresee.

Clearly define rural and urban roles in regard to provisioning and wealth and job creation. In the lead-up to the WSGP, the implications of global ecological scarcity for the roles of rural and urban areas in provisioning societies and in creating employment need to be thought through, and appropriate policy options for building on these roles need to be assessed. The Urban Age is arriving in conditions of global ecological scarcity and intense pressure on rural provisioning capacity. Rural areas must find ways to manage their resources so as to meet the world's rapidly growing urban requirements. The *quid pro quo* of this is for urban areas to become generators of mass employment. As well, urban areas are the main source of demand for natural capital, so they also have an enormous role to play in augmenting usable flows of natural capital and reducing the demands being made on the waste disposal services of ecological systems.

For these ideas to be put into practice, rural areas must be reorganized on the basis of integrated bio-region management, and cities must be reorganized around the concept of eco-urban management. The challenge in the lead-up to the WSGP is to begin to think through how these dominant priorities for each area can be integrated into national thought processes and planning.

Build the case for bio-region management. Nation-states must begin to define the appropriate geographical units on which the transition to integrated bio-region management can be based. Part of this challenge will involve developing the administrative and decision-making mechanisms required to foster holistic interactions between industry sectors and the ecology of bio-regions. Also, political accountability for managing bio-regions must be portioned out in the context of the global requirement to produce surplus flows of natural capital to meet urban provisioning needs.

On an international basis, steps must be taken to define cross-border bio-regions. For these, co-ordinated action will be essential to effective management. In bio-regions, ineffective management can lead to conflict both within and among nations. Ways must be found and implemented to assist nation-states in adopting bio-region management practices.

Build the case for eco-urban management. There are four main actions that cities and nation-states around the world must take in order to begin the transition to eco-urban management systems:

- To document the initial potential for managing urban flows of natural capital on a closed-loop basis, cities around the world must undertake studies to determine the broad patterns of inbound streams of natural capital going into production and consumption processes as well as of outbound waste streams. This citywide materials flow analysis will provide the starting point for evaluating options for matching waste streams to inbound needs and also for evaluating the technology and market challenges that need to be overcome if the negative environmental impacts of these and other wastes are to be neutralized.
- To address the pressing need to find alternatives to the slow, expensive spread of centralized infrastructure, the technological and economic feasibility and the employment and wealth-generating impacts of decentralized, urban infrastructure technologies and approaches need to be assessed. Pilot projects must be mounted.
- Greater experimentation is required relating to the provision of social-service infrastructure specifically geared to the employment and wealth creation needs of the urban poor.
- Efforts presently being made to augment the political and financial authority of local governments must be accelerated, with the goal of having them assume responsibility for making the transition to eco-urban management. Specific financial and political accountability for meeting this management challenge must be created.

Place social issues in the context of provisioning. It is unrealistic to think that we can ignore or wish away other legitimate issues that currently clutter the international agenda. It may be possible, however, to build on some of these concerns and give them greater practical focus by integrating them with the new discussion framework which centres on provisioning processes. Those now active in a wide array of social causes (e.g., gender equity, citizen engagement, and, above all, poverty reduction and employment) should be challenged to redefine those causes in the context of provisioning as the catalyst for social and economic change.

Address the need to control population growth. In past transitions between rounds, the greater abundance of natural capital made available by more productive forms of social provisioning led to significant expansions of human populations. The three-hundred-year transition to Round Five resulted in by far the most dramatic explosion of human populations. Recent evidence suggests that the full inclusion of more people in the economic benefits of global provisioning will temper continued expansion; even so, the huge numbers of people still excluded will continue to force the pace of population growth for another thirty to fifty years. Given the scale of projected provisioning needs, the world must control population growth or risk losing the war on ecological decline. In preparation for the WSGP, the UN should try again to develop a global action plan to hold the line on population growth. This time, however, the task should be placed in the context of equitably provisioning growth and reducing poverty. A specific target of halting population growth at 8 billion within twenty-five years should be the basis on which the plan is prepared. Those who on ethical, moral, practical, or religious grounds are opposed to population-control measures should be invited to provide input to the summit in the form of proposed solutions to the challenge of provisioning the world's people.

Accelerate efforts to document global pollution levels. Though it is politically dicey, because it involves allocating responsibility, efforts to set up a global pollution register under the Aarhus Convention should be accelerated so that this composite picture will be available before the World Summit.

Begin rationalizing international institutional structures. In anticipation of the eventual coming into force of the FCP, the UN should do the following:

• Define the types of program initiatives that can be usefully introduced to help develop appropriate technologies and practices and to assist nation-states in making the political and social transition to bio-region and eco-urban management systems.

- Develop the concepts and steps required to fold existing sustainable development programs, other MEAs, and institutional arrangements into a consolidated framework for waging global war on ecological decline, under the umbrella of the proposed framework convention.
- Build on existing arrangements for ecological monitoring. Ecological uncertainty is at present a virtual certainty, so the world must improve its ability to anticipate, prevent, and respond as necessary to environmental change.
- Begin designing an effective ecological dispute resolution mechanism (EDRM) to address (or help avoid) conflicts arising within and among nation-states over provisioning needs and the management of bio-region resources. Part of this work must involve establishing inducements for complying with EDRM decisions, as well as penalties for not doing so. It is especially important that the EDRM include procedures for intervening to pre-empt old-style wars. These vicious forms of human conflict – even when small and localized – are diversionary, in that they distort priorities and reduce the world's capacity to wage the greater war on ecological decline.

If all of these actions are well organized and pursued with diligence in the lead-up to the WSGP, it will then be possible to integrate the results into a comprehensive proposal for the FCP and the Declaration of War, which would become the basis for negotiations at the summit. These actions would launch the beginning of the global effort to make the transition to the Sixth Round, the Age of Global Provisioning.

The defining characteristics of this new age will emerge when the physical infrastructure of human societies is reorganized around new technologies and political mandates. It will be an age during which humans dramatically change the way they think about the world and their place in it. It may also be the age when economic growth finally unleashes the full potential of the world's peoples, including the billions who might otherwise live in poverty.

For all its benefits, the transition to Round Six promises to be difficult. If past transitions are any guide, strong resistance to new technologies and new forms of social organization can be expected from entrenched cultural beliefs and social values. The need for rapid change in order to dramatically increase provisioning capacity will stiffen resistance still more. As well, all of the world's nations will have to participate. Thus, the war effort will involve collaboration between partners, who will be approaching the effort from radically different starting points and levels of technological competence. Not all countries and peoples will be affected equally: some are likely to benefit disproportionately from the war effort; others could be left far behind, at least temporarily. The risk that the rich will dominate will be ever present; the poor, the disadvantaged, and the technologically deprived will be especially vulnerable.

Even though the war is essential in order to make the provisioning of the poorest countries possible, and even though these countries have the most to gain in the long term, they may have precious little appetite for the war. It is precisely in these countries that the challenges of cultural and social adaptation to common provisioning practices will be greatest. It is here where the commitment to change can lose out to the immediate preoccupations of people living on the cusp of despair. Involvement in technological innovation and adaptation tends to make leading economies more open to social change. It is in the technologically deficient countries that resistance to the war effort will be most stubborn. Ultimately, however, change is the price that the world and its people will have to pay if we are to adequately, with a semblance of equity, and in relatively peaceful conditions, provision the 8 billion people who will inhabit this planet by 2025.

The success of the war effort will be hard to measure. The effects of human assaults on natural systems and of the attempted remedies may be slow to appear. The war effort may be diverted by sudden ecological flips and by social upheaval. The world, while the war continues, will be an unpredictable place and made all the more so by the approach of ecological limits that could make 'preparedness' a vivid and compelling necessity. The war will not be over until the global community has reorganized its diverse societies around the use of technologies and management practices that allow them to peacefully meet the provisioning requirements of growth and poverty reduction.

The scale of the challenge of moving the world into Round Six is unprecedented, and time is ridiculously short. Yet powerful momentum can be generated through just a small shift in perspective and by developing a consensus around social and technological objectives. The truly remarkable accomplishments of the past three centuries of economic development and social evolution – especially the accelerating pace of technologically induced change in the past 150 years and the immense technological innovations of the past several decades – suggest what human ingenuity can do when properly organized.

The world has come to a fork in the road, and both alternatives take us toward war. Yet the two choices have entirely different consequences for human societies. One leads to an unpredictable series of old-style conflicts precipitated by competition for access to increasingly scarce sources of natural capital, and to human suffering associated with ecological flips and constrained growth. The other leads to a declaration of war on ecological decline and the eventual transition to the Age of Global Provisioning, and it can be taken with optimism and great hope. If nations can mobilize over the course of a weekend to fight military wars aimed at slaughtering their neighbours, the world should be able to mobilize over the next twenty-five years to wage a technological war on ecological decline. This latter road offers the only option for securing long-term human survival, prosperity, and social peace.

Notes

Preface

1 The WEHAB papers can be found at www.johansburgsummit.org (under UN documents/WSSD documents).
2 See, for example, Hawken (1997).
3 See, for example, Daniel Deudny in Deudny and Mathew (1999) and Hastings (2000). The latter argues for active non-violence as a way of overcoming environmental degradation.

1. A Shift in the Angle of Vision

1 This is the medium variant in the forecast of population growth made in the United Nations (2000) report.
2 The Factor Ten Institute defines this challenge this way: as it would take a two-fold reduction in materials consumption to stop the present degradation of the biosphere, and as meeting Third World materials needs implies a five-fold increase, the net result is that the industrialized world needs to achieve at least a ten-fold reduction in materials consumption. Thus, the Factor Ten target for the 'dematerialization' of societies; see Schmidt Bleek (1998). The World Wildlife Federation estimates that the ecological footprint of the world's peoples now exceeds the regenerative capacity of the Earth by about 20 per cent and that, at the current rate of consumption – that is, just continuing to do what we are now doing – 'the Ecological Footprint of all humankind will reach twice the regenerative capacity of the Earth by 2050' (WWF, 2002). The case made in this book says the same thing but turns the challenge around and puts a specific time frame on the need for action: if the challenge of equitable growth is to be met, the global community must find ways to meet provisioning requirements that, using

present technologies and forms of social organization, will require the ecological resources of three or four worlds by 2025.

3 The World Commission on Environment and Development (1987) (*Our Common Future*, popularly referred to as the Brundtland Report). An excellent source of information on sustainable development is the website for the International Institute for Sustainable Development (www.iisd.org).

4 Final text of agreements negotiated by governments at the United Nations Conference on Environment and Development, 3–14 June 1992, Rio de Janeiro, Brazil.

5 The list of initiatives and organizations is long. The following is meant to be indicative and is limited to organizations not specifically identified elsewhere in this book. National governments are experimenting with green taxation and tax shifting; taking tentative steps toward market-determined pricing mechanisms for environmental services, especially water; exploring a range of initiatives for decoupling growth from natural capital consumption; experimenting with ecodevelopment parks; and supporting modest R&D initiatives, most of which are related to alternative energy options. Leadership is also being provided by a number of private-sector organizations and by civil-society groups such as The Natural Step (TNS), based in Sweden. BP was the first major oil company (and is still almost the only one) to embrace renewable energy options. The World Business Council on Sustainable Development emphasizes decoupling growth from rising energy consumption. Also providing leadership are the Worldwatch Institute, the Earth Council, the World Wildlife Federation, and the World Resources Institute.

6 The problem of growth outstripping gains in environmental protection measures is clearly identified in OECD (2001: 10), where it is noted that total OECD energy use is expected to increase by over 35 per cent by 2020 despite the concerted efforts being made to improve energy efficiency.

7 The Washington Consensus is discussed in chapter 6. The decisions of G8 ministerial meetings can be found at www.g8.gc.ca. The agenda and record of decisions of the WSSD can be found at www.UN.org (conferences and events).

8 In terms of the relationship between growth and the environment, Bailey (1997: 171) argues that 'anything that retards economic growth also retards ultimate environmental cleanup' and suggests there are per capita income thresholds that must be achieved before countries will begin to invest seriously in environmental protection. *The Economist* ('Economic Man, Cleaner Planet,' 29 September 2001) makes a similar argument.

9 See Rees (1992, 2001) and Wackernagel and Rees (1995). For further applications of the concept, see 'The Footprint of Nations Study' at www.rprogress.org.

10 The websites for The Natural Step are organized on a national basis (see, for example, the Canadian site at www.naturalstep.ca, and especially the paper 'Strategic Sustainable Development: Selection, Design and Synergies of Applied Tools.' See also Nattrass and Altomare (1999). For natural capitalism, see Hawken (1997) and Hawken, Lovins, and Hunter Lovins 1999. The Zero Emissions Research Institute is a good source of information on zero emission technologies: see www.ZERI.org.

2. Provisioning Societies

1 Korten (1995: 152–3).
2 De Soto (2000: 35).
3 UNHCS (1986).

3. Round One: The Spread of Hunter-Gatherer Societies

1 Wilson (1992: 183–6).
2 Ibid.: 24.
3 Ibid.: 133.
4 Ibid.: 131–62.
5 Ibid.: 95.
6 Bronowski (1973: ch. 1).
7 Wilson (1992: 5–6).
8 Bronowski (1973); Barber (1999: 183–4).
9 *The Economist* (1 July 2000: 11).
10 Suzuki (1999).
11 Hartmann (1998: 1).
12 Debeir et al. (1991). This book provides insights into the relationship between social organization and sources and patterns of energy use from earliest times to the present day.
13 Diamond (1999: ch. 1); Barber (1999: ch. 3).
14 Ibid.: ch. 1.
15 The uncertainty surrounding the origins is documented in Pringle (2001) and Dewar (2001).
16 Diamond (1999: 27).
17 *The Economist* (1 July 2000: 11).
18 Ibid.: 12–13.
19 Obviously it is not possible to verify this. However, behavioural traits of a number of remaining hunter-gatherer societies suggest this is the case. See, for example, Diamond (1999: chs. 2, 14).
20 Sahlins (1972).

21 Diamond (1999: 45) suggests the maximum population of hunter-gatherers in the Americas would have been 10 million. Bronowski (1973) suggests a figure of 20 million for the world (ch. 1). These estimates were never fulfilled, of course, as the rise of agricultural and other pastoral societies overlapped with the late years of the spread of hunter-gatherer societies.
22 Godwin (2001).
23 Brody (2000: 312).
24 Toynbee (1972: 132–5).
25 Huntington (1997).

4. Round Two: The Rise and Spread of Agricultural Societies

1 Diamond (1999: chs. 8, 9).
2 Ibid.
3 Ibid.: 98.
4 Ibid.: ch. 14.
5 Barber (1999: 26).
6 Ibid.: 27, Diamond (1999: 97–8).
7 Barber (1999: 158).
8 Bronowski (1973: 48).
9 Ibid.: 79–89; Barber (1999: 159).
10 Barber (ibid.); Langer (1962: 121, 136, 143–5, 158, 174, 211).
11 White (1962: 65).
12 Russel (1986: 67).
13 Ibid.: 61; Claster (1982); Gies (1990).
14 Diamond (1999: ch. 17); Brody (2000: 156).
15 Diamond (1999: 388).
16 Ibid.: 400.
17 Gordon (1981); Davidson (1959); Hull (1976).
18 Diamond (1999: 375).
19 Langdon (1999: 26).
20 Ibid.: 26–35.

5. Round Three: Urbanization

1 Bronowski (1973: 64–73).
2 National Geographic Society (1979).
3 Edwards (2000).
4 Mumford (1961: 33).
5 Hall (1998: 44).

6 Mumford (1961: 104).
7 Langer (1952: 27).
8 Grove (1997: 28–35).
9 Hall (1998: 51).
10 Ibid.
11 See Mumford (1961: 46–54); Diamond (1999). Chapter 14 of this book discusses why large societies must replace band mentalities and organization.
12 Mumford (1961: 35–9).
13 Follain (2001).
14 Debeir et al. (1991: 23).
15 Barocas (1972: 9–12).
16 Grove (1997: 34).
17 Hall (1998: 35–7).
18 Mumford (1961: 186).
19 Ibid.: 52–4.
20 Ibid.: 124, 131.
21 Grove (1997: 70–3).
22 Hall (1998: 49).
23 Debeir et al. (1991: 29).
24 Mumford (1961: 153).
25 Hall (1998: 39, 45, 47).
26 Ibid.: 49.
27 Ibid.: 65.
28 Mumford (1961: 153).
29 Debeir et al. (1991: 34).
30 Mumford (1961: 205–10).
31 Ibid.
32 Fernand Braudel, *Civilization and Capitalism*, quoted in Russel (1986: 67). See also Claster (1982: ch. 5) and Gies (1990).
33 Claster (1982: 237).
34 Russel (1986: 66–77).
35 Ibid.: 68; Claster (1982: 228–36).
36 Russel (1986: 70).
37 Debeir et al. (1991: 34).
38 Russel (1986: 75).
39 Ibid.: 76–7.
40 Ibid: 78.
41 Hibbert, *The Rise and Fall of the House of Medici*, quoted in Russel (1986: 83).

42 Hall (1998: 81–4).
43 Ibid.: ch. 3; Claster (1982: 228–36).
44 Grove (1997: 194).
45 Debeir et al. (1991: 92).
46 Hall (1998: 119).
47 Reich (1983: 24).
48 Debeir et al. (1991: 98).
49 Mumford (1961: 528).
50 Ibid.: 529.
51 Reich (1983: 30).
52 Ibid.
53 Hall (1998: chs. 10, 11, 13).
54 Ibid.: ch. 12; Thurlow (1999: 18–20).
55 Rogers and Gumuchdjian (1997: 27).
56 Hall (1998: 746–7).
57 Rogers and Gumuchdjian (1997: 41).
58 Ibid.: 28.

6. Round Four: From City-States to Nations

1 Smith (1991).
2 Toynbee (1967: 15).
3 Mumford (1961: 143).
4 Diamond (1999: 266).
5 Langer (1962: 244–6).
6 Rich (1977: 82).
7 Theories abound as to why. Diamond (1999) points to the necessary administrative and cultural changes that must accompany population growth. Others, such as Kellas (1998) and Gellner (1983), see nations and nationalism resulting from modernization and industrial growth as these require particular forms of organization, technologies, and cultures. Gellner in particular rejects the role of nationalistic philosophy, arguing instead that nations and nationalism simply emerged in concert with the times.
8 Hirst and Thompson (1999: 19).
9 Toynbee (1967: 25).
10 Rich (1977: 77).
11 Grove (1997: 194).
12 Hirst and Thompson (1999: 20).
13 See, for example, Rich (1977: 103–7); Schafer (1955); Gellner (1983); Kellas (1998); and Smith (1991).

14 See Anderson (1991).

15 See Kedourie (1960).

16 Thurow (1999: 35).

17 Harris (1987; esp. ch. 4); Reich (1983: 121–7).

18 Kennedy (1987: 413–46). The formation of international joint ventures and strategic partnerships continued throughout the 1980s and 1990s.

19 Concerns over jobless growth throughout this and other periods are well documented in Rifkin (1996).

20 Thurow (1999: 53).

21 Russel (1986: 125).

22 Ibid.

23 The arrival of the Information Age in the United States was heralded by the statistical analysis of national accounts undertaken by Mark Uri Porat in 1975 when he wrote: 'We are now in an information economy ... Over half our wages and nearly half our GNP originate with the production, processing, and distribution of information goods and services. Over half of all labor income is now earned by workers whose tasks are primarily informational' (quoted in Russel [1986: 146]). Daniel Bell's 1973 *The Coming of Post–Industrial Society* covered some of the same ground, and Yoneji Masuda's 1983 *The Information Society* added international breadth and legitimacy to the concept.

24 Russel (1986: 126).

25 Williamson (1993).

26 See, for example, Carson (1962), Hardin (1968), Ehrlich (1970), Schumacher (1976), and Meadows et al. (1972).

27 For a critique of the precautionary principle, see Shaw (2001).

7. Round Five: Reliance on Global Business Networks

1 Russel (1986: 93).

2 Reich (1983: 26).

3 Ibid.: 27.

4 Thurow (1999: 19).

5 Ibid.: 19–22; Reich (1983: 22–44).

6 Hertner and Jones, eds. (1998: chs. 1, 2); also Teichova et al. (1986).

7 Teichova et al. (1986: 362–73).

8 Streeten (1998: 20). The figures are taken from a UNRISD study released in 1995. Presumably the numbers will have grown in the interval.

9 Rich (1977: 169).

10 A very strong presentation of this confluence is made by Marber (1998).

11 WTO, 'Seattle Press Pack, Facts and Figures.' (1999)

12 Thurow (1999: 23).

13 Moore et al. (1998).

14 Chernow (1998).

15 One of the strongest critics of the dominant role of MNEs was Jean-Jacques Servan-Schreiber; see his *The American Challenge* (1967). Also see Hertner and Jones, eds. (1998) and Dunning (1988). For a dissenting view, see Doremus et al. (1998).

16 The UN economic development agencies were a hotbed of these sentiments throughout the 1960s and 1970s. The views of Raul Prebisch, head of the Economic Commission for Latin America, were typical. He argued that 'the natural operation of the market works against developing countries because of a long-term decline in developing countries' terms of trade and because of Northern protectionism. What is needed is a redistribution of world resources to help the South: restructuring of trade, control of multinational corporations and greater aid flow' (in Marber [1998: 49]).

17 For a discussion of the NIEO see Teichova et al. (1986).

18 See Rosencrance (1999).

19 Based on personal involvement of OECD discussion of the issue in the late 1970s.

20 The impracticality of the Tobin Tax idea is discussed in Eichengreen (1999: 88–90).

8. The Organization and Potential of Round Five

1 Data tabled at APEC meeting, Beijing, 1985.

2 These requirements are discussed in World Bank, *Private Sector Development in Low-Income Countries* (1995: chs. 2, 3, and 4).

3 Moran (1999).

4 This was one of the main conclusions reached after a year-long consultative process managed by the author involving ten major cities across Canada on 'Gearing Up the Technology Engine at the Community Level.'

5 Detailed information on the organization and operation of the IMF can be found at www.IMF.org.

6 See www.WTO.org.

7 See www.wb.org and links to the Asian, African, and Latin American Development Banks.

8 Streeten (1998: 16).

9 Bhalla (1998: 2).

10 Ibid.

11 Ibid.
12 Marber (1998: 30–7).
13 Ibid.: 37.
14 World Bank, *World Development Report (2000/2001): Attacking Poverty* (2001: 154).
15 Thurow (1989: 51).
16 This is not meant to imply that the system cannot be improved. In this respect, there is considerable international discussion. See, for example, Noland et al. (1998); Eichengreen (1999); and Rodrik (1997).
17 OECD, *Science, Technology and Industry Scoreboard 1999* (1999: 3). See also Schwartz, Leyden, and Hyatt (1999).
18 Marber (1998: 13).
19 Ibid.: 15.
20 Marber (1999: 34–6).
21 Ibid.: 193.
22 OECD, *Science, Technology and Industry Scoreboard 1999* (1999: 7).
23 This summary is drawn from the following sources: McDonough and Braungart (1998); Frosch (1995); *The Economist* (24 June, 5 August, and 9 September 2000); Government of Canada background papers on 'Energy Technology Futures' (available through www.strategis.gc.ca under 'climate change'); Levy (1999); Drucker (1999); a Special Report in *Scientific American* (September 1995); *The Economist* (1 July 2000); the Center for Energy and Climate Solutions (2000); Cetron and Davies (2001); Maddox (1999); Patterson (1995); Pearson (2000); and the OECD (1998).
24 See www.africaone.com.
25 International Institute for Management Development (1995).
26 International Development Research and Policy Task Force (1996). See also Kennedy (1987: ch. 8).

9. From Egalitarian Tribes to Global Inequity

1 See, for example, Kay et al. (1999).
2 See Kay and Regier (1998).
3 Rees, William (1999).
4 Thurow (1999: 49).
5 See Mumford (1961: 130) and Hall (1998: 40–2).
6 Ibid.: 220.
7 Mumford (1961: 215).
8 Ibid.: 217.
9 Ibid.: 218–19.

10 Morris (1998).
11 *The Economist* (28 September 1996: 7).
12 *Vancouver Sun* (27 March 2000).
13 Hall (1998: 85).
14 Mumford (1961: 322).
15 Ibid.: 290.
16 Ibid.: 291.
17 Ibid.: 528.
18 Hall (1998: 675).
19 Ibid.: 695.
20 Ibid.: 706–11.
21 Ibid.: 5.
22 Ibid.: 746–68.
23 Thurow (1999: 13).
24 Parkes (2000).
25 World Bank (2000: 45).
26 Langdon (1999: 25–35).
27 World Bank (2000: 51).
28 UNDP (1999: 2–3).
29 Bhalla (1998: chs. 2, 3).
30 Bernstein, J., et al. (2000).
31 Anderson, John (2001).
32 Bhalla (1998: 8).
33 The high-income countries and their Gini index are as follows: Norway
    25, Denmark 23, Germany 23, U.S.A. 40, Belgium 25, France 33, the
    Netherlands 32, Sweden 25, Finland 26, Austria 34, Italy 31, the U.K. 33,
    Canada 32, Ireland 36, Spain 33. The Asian countries selected were Nepal
    36.7, Vietnam 35.7, India 29.7, Pakistan 31.2, China 41.5, the Philippines
    42.9, Thailand, 46.2, Malaysia 48.4. The countries included from LAC were
    Bolivia 42, Guatemala 59, Ecuador 46, Jamaica 41.1, El Salvador 49.9,
    Colombia 57.2, Peru 44.9, Costa Rica 47, Venezuela 46.8, Mexico 50.3,
    Brazil 60.1, Chile 56.5. Source: World Bank (1998: 68–71).
34 Discussion with Romanian pensioner and workers.
35 Discussion with Indian software workers in New Delhi (1997).
36 Dollar and Kray (2000).
37 WTO (2000) (www.wto.org – see Trade and Development/Research and
    Analysis).
38 U.S. Congressional Budget Office (1999). Summary in *National Post*
    (2 October: E1).
39 Maxwell (2002).

40 World Bank (2000: ch. 1).

41 Ibid.: 17.

42 United Nations (2002).

43 Ibid.: 4.

44 United Nations Conference on Human Settlements (1986: 58).

45 A stark description of this segregation of the wealthy in armed urban enclaves is found in Langewiesche (1999).

46 Other analysts have reached similar conclusions based on economic divisions that are occurring in a globalizing world. For example, Jorge Castañeda notes the split in Mexican society between those 'plugged into the US economy' and those that are not. This, he argues, separates Mexicans into those 'who remain on the margins of global flows of capital, goods and services ... and those who are being steadily integrated into these flows' (quoted in Rodrik [1997: 71]).

10. Ecological Roadblocks to Growth and Poverty Reduction

1 World Resources Institute (*People and Ecosystems*) (2000).

2 Easterbrook (1995: 14).

3 UNDP 2000 (forests).

4 See Wilson (1992: 280, 346).

5 UNDP (1999: GEO Report).

6 Munro (2001).

7 Wilkening and Barrie (2000).

8 Intergovernmental Panel on Climate Change (1990, 1995, 2001).

9 Trenberth (1997); Pawlowicz (1999); Lemonick (2001); Krajick (2001).

10 Intergovernmental Panel on Climate Change (1990).

11 Trenberth (1997).

12 See Federation of Red Cross and Red Crescent Societies (1999) and Abramovitz (2001).

13 These reports can be accessed through www.ipcc.ch.

14 Hawken et al. (1999: 243–4).

15 Karl and Trenberth (1999: 101).

16 Shaviv and Veizer (2003).

17 See Parry and Carter (1998: 13–16), and Trenberth (1997: 201).

18 See Charlson et al. (2001).

19 The role of phytoplankton is described in Falkowski (2002).

20 Suess et al. (1999).

21 Kerr, *Warnings Unpleasant Surprise* (1998).

22 Suess et al. (1999).

23 Hawken et al. (1999: 240).
24 Karl and Trenberth (1999: 100).
25 For details on the Kyoto Protocol, see www.UNFCCC.org.
26 Kerr (2002) reviews the U.S. government's plan. The critique noted in the text is found in Mintzer et al. (2003).
27 Hertsgard (1997: 114).
28 Debeir et al. (1991: 50).
29 Ibid.: 232.
30 Drennen and Erickson (1998).
31 Debeir et al. (1991: 232).
32 Flavin and Dunn (1999: 27).
33 Ibid.: 23.
34 Ibid.: 24.
35 Editorial, *National Post*, 31 March 2001, A15.
36 Michael MacCracken, Director of the National Assessment Office of the U.S. Global Change Research Program; quoted in Borenstein (2000). See also Bolin (1998).
37 The discussion of water issues in Turkey is based on an assessment of water management markets undertaken by the author in 1997.
38 Leslie (2000: 38).
39 Sampat (2000).
40 World Commission for Water (2000: 13).
41 Postel (1999); Brown and Halweil (1998).
42 Sampat (2000, 2001).
43 World Resources Institute (2000), 'Freshwater Systems in Peril.'
44 McGinn (1999: 85–6); Moffat 1998. See also Baron (2000) for a discussion of toxic algae blooms.
45 Lindgren (2000).
46 Starnes (2001).
47 Postel (2000: 23–4). Also see the first Report of the World Commission for Water.
48 Brown (1999).
49 Food and Agricultural Organization (1995). Referenced in Barraclough and Ghimire (2000: 18). This marked a radical departure from the past in terms of per capita agricultural land. Between 1700 and 1980, cropland increased from about 2 per cent of the Earth's land area to over 11 per cent, or roughly proportional to the rate of population increase. Per capita agricultural land is now in steep decline. See also the Wildlife Conservation Society website: www.wcs.org/humanfootprint.
50 Myers (1996: 74).

51 Langdon (1999: 90).
52 Brown (1999).
53 Manning (2000). The figures come from the Consultative Group on International Agricultural Research.
54 McKibben (1998: 60).
55 Brown (1999: 123–5).
56 Hawken et al. (1999: 204).
57 Ibid.: 205.
58 Parry and Carter (1998: 118–20). For a more recent and more pessimistic analysis, see the World Wildlife Fund examination of the regional impacts of global warming at http:/wwf.org (newsroom, 10/19/99).
59 National Assessment Team (2000), 'Climate Change Impacts on the United States.' U.S. Global Change Research Program, Office of Science and Technology Policy, Washington, D.C. (www.us-gcrp.gov). The WWF modelling exercise (see note 57) provides a harsher view.
60 Hawken et al. (1999: 208–12).
61 Ibid.: 196.
62 The Gallon Environment Letter, 2000: Special Report on Concerns over Feedlots. Canadian Institute for Business and the Environment, 16 October 2000. See www.gallon.elogik.com.
63 See especially the 2003 study by the Hubbard Brook Research Foundation, *Nitrogen Pollution in the Northeastern United States: Sources, Effects and Management Options.* Also Moffat (1998); Bright (1999).
64 Brown and Halweil (1998); Hawken et al. (1999: 190–212); *The Economist* (25 March 2000); Schillhorn van Veen et al. (1996); Srivastava et al. (1996); and Brown (2002).
65 Hawken et al. (1999: 205).
66 An agri-pulp project of note is one run by a small Vancouver company, Arbokem, which converts agricultural fibre from Saskatchewan farms into paper and biofuels. The project networks a great diversity of organizations in an exemplary manner (www.agripulp.com).
67 Hawken et al. (1999: 2002).
68 Mann (1999).
69 Goodstein (1999) debunks the myth that environmental regulations lead to high costs and the loss of jobs.
70 McGinn (1999: 83).
71 Food and Agriculture Organization (2002).
72 Ibid.
73 Spears (2000).
74 McGinn (1998).

75 World Resources Institute (www.wri.org/trends/fishfarm.html).
76 Ibid.
77 Brown (2001: 56).
78 Ibid.
79 Alroy (2001).
80 Ecological economics has sprung from the writings of a great many analysts, foremost among them being Herman Daly. A leading proponent is Robert Costanza, Director of the University of Maryland Institute for Ecological Economics (www.cbl.umces.edu) and a founder of the International Society for Ecological Economics (www.ISEE.org). Information on the American GPI initiative can be found at www.redefiningprogress.org.

11. The Catalysts of Calamity

1 See, for example, Rosecrance (1999).
2 Fukuyama (1992).
3 Mander and Goldsmith (1996); quoted in Marber (1998: 3).
4 These writers include Connor Cruise O'Brien, Daniel P. Moynihan, Mark Juergens-Meyer, William Pfaff, Robert Kaplan, and Benjamin Barber. Sadowski (1998: ch. 2) summarizes the views of the 'chaos' theorists.
5 Martin Van Crevald quoted in Kaplan (1994: 73).
6 This conclusion is supported by both Sadowski (1998) and Homer-Dixon (1999).
7 Homer-Dixon (1999: 155–68).
8 See, for example, Obudhu (1997: 314).
9 See Kaplan (1994). As the poor evolve their own unique cultures of impoverishment, of the misplaced, the hopeless, the uneducated, and the rootless, they separate themselves from the cultures of those living in technologically advanced and economically advantaged enclaves. As slum areas come to harbour resentment and anger, as the values and standards of the people and groups they contain diverge from the attitudes and civility of wealthy enclaves, as criminal elements flourish, social harmony within the ranks of the poor also breaks down. Old grievances re-emerge; cultural and religious divides are exacerbated as separate groups – tribes if you like – coalesce in the struggle to gain economic and political advantage.
10 See Kurth (1994) and Moynihan (1993).
11 Kaplan (1994: 26).
12 Huntington (1997).

13 Ibid.: 321.
14 Homer-Dixon (1999: 179).
15 Sadowski (1998: 5).
16 Homer-Dixon (1999: 166).
17 Ibid.: 179.
18 Debeir et al. (1991: 232).

12. Our Common Enemy

1 In the energy field, for example, subsidies amount to between $70 and $80 billion per year in Western countries. These go mainly to support the market position of coal, oil, nuclear power, and natural gas. Energy subsidies in Third World countries are even more significant, with one 1991 estimate placing them in the range of $270 to $330 billion, although these may have been reduced by as much as $100 billion by reforms in Russia and China. See de Moor and Calamai (1997: 29–34).
2 Benyus (1998).
3 Stigson (2001). Stigson is president of the World Business Council for Sustainable Development.

13. Mobilizing Nations for War

1 Examples of private-sector investment in industrial ecology can be found in Hawken et al. (2001: ch. 1). Information on ISO 14000 can be found at www.iso.org, on the Global Reporting Initiative at www.globalreporting.org.
2 Calder (1999: 51–80); World Commission for Water (2000: 5–11).
3 Ibid.: 8.
4 Barraclough and Ghimire (2000: 2).
5 World Bank (1992).
6 This has happened, for example, in government policies that have accentuated deforestation and the pursuit of short-term commercial profit by vested interests or favoured groups and accompanying graft as an alternative to more progressive land reform. It occurs when good crop-land is lost to urbanization, thus forcing the upgrading or opening of marginal lands to meet agricultural needs. It contributes to uncontrolled logging and unstructured demands on rural lands. It helps perpetuate unresolved land tenure arrangements that lead to the disenfranchisement of the rural poor and competition among small landholders for access to land, water, and agricultural inputs.

7 It is not at all surprising to find, for example, that in the Philippines, local populations, local officials, and politicians have little or no knowledge of water resource problems or strategies, and little or no access to relevant information, and do not take a holistic approach to decision making; see Calder (1999: 141) Or that in China, many local people do not see themselves being disadvantaged by deforestation as they benefit from tree plantations. Thus, they see the protection and regeneration of the natural forest as the responsibility of the state; see Barraclough and Ghimire (2000: 80).

8 Biswas (1996: 7).

9 Progress will be influenced by the extent of public awareness of the need for change. The same is true at the implementation stage. In this respect it is especially important that the rural poor be engaged. It is not possible to deal in an arbitrary manner with people and expect their support for new land use rules: progress on all fronts will be limited if land access is precarious, if titles are unclear, or if there is simply insufficient incentive to cause people to link their self-interest with the processes of change. However, this does not negate the need for strong central direction and the creation of binding frameworks for organizing social engagement.

10 An excellent source of information on efforts to set up and operate eco-industrial parks can be found in the website for the Cornell University Center for the Environment (cfe.cornell.edu/wei/EIDP/design.html). The September 1998 edition of the *Journal of Cleaner Production* is also devoted to the subject.

11 This immediately raises the spectre of having one type of infrastructure for the rich and another – perhaps seen as less worthy – for the poor. In the short run this may be the case. Decentralized technologies may be the only way to quickly extend essential infrastructure services into urban slum areas, and these must be different types of extensions from the core services or completely separate from them. However, if the challenge is seen as the creation of appropriate infrastructure, and a longer-term view is taken, this becomes a non-issue. The poor also need lower-cost access to things such as potable water and cleaner air, which improve health and are essential to the creation of wealth based on property; however, they have little capacity to pay for them. Nevertheless, the pressures on water supplies in all countries will eventually lead to the same types of technological solutions, and the decentralized infrastructure technologies of poverty reduction will eventually become the technologies of eco-urban management.

12 A report prepared by the giant water management company Lyonnaise Des Eaux summarized the situation: 'A decade ago it would have been

unthinkable to offer anything other than the western model for drinking water and sanitation. It is now unthinkable to offer only this model to mega-cities in developing countries'; see Lyonnaise Des Eaux (1998: 7).

13 Gardner and Payal (1999: 58).
14 Roseland (1992).
15 Mumford (1961: 541).
16 Yeung and Lo (1996: 41).
17 For example, the city of Buenos Aires has the status of a province, but its borders have been drawn to exclude twenty surrounding municipalities, most of which are poor.

14. Mobilizing the International Community

1 Nördstrom and Vaughan (1999).
2 Well over 350 and perhaps as many as 500 CPR and cross-border environmental agreements have been signed to date. These range from the broad statements of intent found in big MEAs such as the Montreal Protocol, the Climate Change and Biodiversity Conventions, and the Law of the Sea, to a host of bilateral and multistate commitments to address cross-border pollution and the sharing of natural capital. The latter include statements of high purpose such as the principle of good neighborliness enshrined in Article 21 of the Stockholm Declaration (nations should avoid actions that cause damage to the environment of other states); more structured arrangements such as the Canada/U.S. agreement on management of the Great Lakes; and a variety of other agreements covering issues such as coastal zone management, water sharing or river and airshed management, and biodiversity and wildlife corridor agreements. Others are also pending (e.g., a global forest protocol) or anticipated (e.g., few of the two hundred major river basins in the world are now covered by co-operative institutional arrangements for their management. The World Water Forum has recommended an ecosystem approach to water management, which implies a need for additional multistate agreements.)
3 There is at present no internationally designated authority with the mandate or resources to monitor global ecological stress. Even in the field of climate change, data are compiled from networks of satellites, sensors, and other forms of equipment that are being operated for other purposes such as short-term weather forecasting or space research (Karl and Trenberth, 1999). The difficulty faced by UNEP in pulling together the GEO 2000 Report, and the limitations of that report, attest to the need for an enhanced capacity to comprehensively monitor and evaluate human impacts on the natural world.

4 The International Court of Justice in the Hague recently set up a facility to deal with environmental cases, most of which are likely to deal only with liability issues. In contrast, the issues in most cross-border environmental disputes involve questions of management, not of law.

5 The strengths and weaknesses of the WTO as an arbiter of cross-border environmental disputes are discussed in French (1999). A summary of specific decisions made by the WTO can be found at www.WTO.org.

6 The consensus for action to control acid rain reached in both Europe and North America certainly indicates that knowledge can be a great motivator for finding common ground and proposing solutions. The Convention on the Conservation of Antarctic Marine Living Resources (CCAMLR) moved to better enforcement based on improved scientific understanding and the ability to demonstrate to fishing nations the unsustainability of their practices. Most bilateral environmental agreements such as the highly successful Canada–U.S. Great Lakes agreement base dispute resolution on some form of negotiation. Public disclosure of shortfalls in national action has also proven to be an effective tool for pressuring signatory states to comply with their commitments under the Montreal Protocol. See Litfin (1998: 1–27) and Ward (1998).

7 By way of comparison, the WTO dispute resolution process takes, at most, one year to complete; a further three months is allowed for appeals.

15. Round Six: The Age of Global Provisioning

1 Almost all UN resolutions on issues related to environmental protection or sustainable development lead off with lengthy preambles that include reference to Principle 7 of the Rio Declaration on Environment and Development. In a very ambiguous way that essentially lets Third World nations off the hook for doing anything they don't wish to do. This principle undermines the brave words related to commitments by referring to 'common but differentiated responsibilities' for cause and implementation.

Bibliography

Abramovitz, Janet N. 2001. 'Averting Natural Disasters.' *State of the World 2001*. New York: W.W. Norton.

Abu-Laban, Baha, ed. 1989. *University Research and the Future of Canada.* Ottawa: University of Ottawa Press.

Alger, Chadwick F., ed. 1998. *The Future of the United Nations System: Potential for the Twenty-First Century.* New York: United Nations University Press.

Allahar, Anton L., and James E. Cote. 1998. *Richer and Poorer: The Structure of Inequality In Canada.* Toronto: Lorimer.

Alroy, John. 2001. 'A Multispecies Overkill Simulation of the End-Pleistocene Megafaunal Mass Extinction.' *Science* (8 June): 1893–6.

Anderson, Arthur. 2000. 'Best Cities Survey: Fortune's Best Cities: 1999.' *Fortune.*

Anderson, Benedict. 1991. *Imagined Communities: Reflections on the Origin and Spread of Nationalism.* London/New York: Verso.

Anderson, John. 2001. 'Beyond the Wealth Divide.' Toronto: Centre for Social Justice.

Annan, Kofi A. 2000. *We the Peoples. The Role of the United Nations in the 21st Century.* New York: UN Department of Public Information.

Atehity, Kenneth S., ed. 1996. *Renaissance Reader.* New York: Harper Perennial.

Austin, Duncan. 1997. *Climate Protection Policies: Can We Afford to Delay?* Washington, D.C.: World Resources Institute.

Bailey, Ronald. 1997. 'A Clean and Comfortable Planet without Global Regulations.' *Delusions of Grandeur: UN and Global Intervention.* Washington, D.C.: CATO Institute.

Bailey, Ronald, ed. 1995. *The True State of the Planet.* New York: Free Press.

Baker, Dean, Gerald Epstein, and Robert Pollin, eds. 1998. *Globalization and Progressive Economic Policy*. Cambridge, U.K.: Cambridge University Press.

Barber, Elizabeth Wayland. 1999. *The Mummies of Urumchi*. New York and London: W.W. Norton.

Barkin, Samuel, and George E. Shambaugh, eds. 1999. *Anarchy and the Environment: The International Relations of Common Pool Resources*. Albany: State University of New York Press.

Barocas, Claudio. 1972. *Egypt*. New York: Grosset & Dunlap.

Baron, Nancy. 2000. 'The Cells from Hell.' *Saturday Night* (3 June): 30–6.

Barraclough, Solon L., and Ghimire Krishna. 2000. *Agricultural Expansion and Tropical Deforestation*. London: Earthscan Publications.

Bartone, Carl, et al. 1994. *Toward Environmental Strategies for Cities: Strategic Options for Managing the Urban Environment*. Washington, D.C.: The World Bank.

Beck, Nuala. 1995. *Excelerate: Growing in the New Economy*. Toronto: HarperCollins.

Bell, Daniel. 1973. *The Coming of Post Industrial Society*. New York: Basic Books.

Benyus, Janine M. 1998. *Biomimicry: Innovation Inspired by Nature*. New York: HarperCollins.

Bernard, Ted, and Jora Young. 1997. *The Ecology of Hope*. Gabriola Island, B.C.: New Society Publishers.

Bernstein, Jared, Lawrence Mishel, and Chauna Brecht. 2000. *Any Way You Cut It*. Washington: Economic Policy Institute.

Bernstein, Paul M., W. David Montgomery, and Thomas F. Rutherford. 1996. *The International Impact Assessment Model*. Washington, D.C.: Charles River Associates.

Bhalla, A.S., ed. 1998. *Globalization, Growth and Marginalization*. Ottawa: International Development Research Centre.

Birchard, Bill. 1999. 'Finance: A Pragmatic Activist.' *Tomorrow* (July–August): 28.

Biswas, Asit K., ed. 1996. *Management and Development of Major Rivers*. Madras: Oxview Press.

Blinder, Alan S. 2000. 'Eight Steps to a New Financial Order.' *Foreign Affairs* 78(5): 50–63.

Bolin, Bert. 1998. 'The Kyoto Negotiations on Climate Change: A Science Perspective.' *Science* 279 (16 January): 330–1.

Bongaarts, John. 1998. 'Demographic Consequences of Declining Fertility.' *Science* 278 (16 October): 419–20.

Borenstein, Seth. 2000. 'You Can't Stop Global Warming.' Washington, D.C.: Knight Ridder Newspapers (reported in the *Ottawa Citizen*, 21 February: C15).

Boyer, Gabriela. 1999. 'Riches in Rags.' *Urban Age* (Spring): 10.

Boyle, David. 1999. 'Finance: Flexible Ethics.' *Tomorrow* (July–August): 16–17.

Boyle, Robin, et al. 1999. 'The Devastation of Cities.' *Urban Age* (Spring): 12–13.

Boyle, Timothy J.B., and Boonchoob Boontawee, eds. 1995. *Measuring and Monitoring Biodiversity in Tropical and Temperate Forests*. Bangor, Indonesia: Centre for International Forestry Research.

Bradford, GiGi, Michael Gary, and Glenn Wallach, eds. 1999. *The Politics of Culture*. New York: The New Press.

Brandel, Fernand. 1992. *Civilization and Capitalism*. Berkeley: University of California Press.

Breslin, Patrick. 2000. 'From Mud to Markets.' *Urban Age* (Spring): 4–22.

Bright, Chris. 1999. 'The Nemesis Effect.' *World Watch* (May–June): 12–23.

Brody, Hugh. 2000. *The Other Side of Eden*. Vancouver and Toronto: Douglas & McIntyre.

Bronowski, J. 1973. *The Ascent of Man*. Boston and Toronto: Little, Brown.

Brown, Dennis, ed. 1998. *The Culture/Trade Quandary. Canada's Policy Options*. Ottawa: Centre for Trade Policy and Law.

Brown, Kathryn. 2000. 'The Human Genome Business Today.' *Scientific American* (July): 50–5.

Brown, Katrina, et al. 1993. *Economics and the Conservation of Global Biological Diversity*. Working Paper No. 2. Washington, D.C.: The Global Environment Facility.

Brown, Lester R. 1999. 'Feeding Nine Billion.' *State of the World 1999*. New York and London: W.W. Norton.

– 2001. 'Eradicating Hunger: A Growing Challenge.' *State of The World 2001*. New York and London: W.W. Norton.

Brown, Lester R., and Brian Halweil. 1998. 'China's Water Shortage Could Shake World Food Security.' *World Watch*. July/Aug:10–21.

Brown, Lester R., Michael Renner, and Brian Halweil. 1999. *Vital Signs 1999: The Environmental Trends That Are Shaping Our Future*. New York: W.W. Norton.

Brown, Lester R., et al. 1999. *State of the World 1999*. New York: W.W. Norton.

– 2000. *State of the World 2000*. New York: W.W. Norton.

Brown, Paige, ed. 2002. *Sustainable Agriculture and Common Assets: Stewardship Success Stories*. Redefining Progress (www.redfiningprogress.org).

Brown-Humes, Christopher. 1999. 'Finance: From Niche to Mainstream.' *Tomorrow* (July–August: 20).

Buckles, Daniel, ed. 1999. *Cultivating Peace: Conflict and Collaboration in Natural Resource Management.* Ottawa: International Development Research Centre.

Business Council for Sustainable Development. 1992. *BCSD: Report on Technology Cooperation.* Geneva: Business Council For Sustainable Development.

Calder, Ian R. 1999. *The Blue Revolution; Land Use and Integrated Water Resources Management.* London: Earthscan Publications.

Canadian Environmental Assessment Agency. 2000. 'The Canadian Environmental Assessment Act: Cumulative Effects Assessment.' http://www.ceaa.gc.ca/publications_e/cumul/training.

Canadian Museum of Nature. 1998. 'Global Biodiversity: An International Forum on the Variety of Life on Earth: Research, Conservation and Wise Use' 7(4). Ottawa.

Carpenter, Ted. *The UN and Global Intervention.* Washington, D.C.: Cato Institute.

Carpenter, Ted, ed. 1997. *Delusions of Grandeur: The UN and Global Intervention.* Washington, D.C.: CATO Institute.

Carson, Rachel. 1962. *Silent Spring.* New York: Alfred A. Knopf.

Castilleja, Guillermo, Peter J. Poole, and Charles C. Geisler. 1993. *The Social Challenge of Biodiversity Conservation.* Working Paper No. 1. Washington, D.C.: The Global Environment Facility.

Center for Energy and Climate Solutions. 2000. 'The New Energy Economy.' www.cool-companies.org.

Cervero, Robert. 1995. 'Why Go Anywhere?' *Scientific American* (September): 118–19.

Cetron, Marvin J., and Davies, Owen. 2001. 'Trends Now Changing the World: Technology,' *Futurist* (March–April): 27–42.

Chan, Vincent W.S. 1995. 'All-Optical Networks.' *Scientific American* (September): 72.

Charlson, Robert J., et al. 2001. 'Reshaping the Theory of Cloud Formation.' *Science* 292 (15 June): 2025–6.

Chatterjee, Patralekha. 1999. 'Portrait of a City: Hyderabad, India.' *Urban Age* 6(4): 23–5.

Chayes, Abraham, and Antonia Handler Chayes. 1995. *The New Sovereignty: Compliance with International Regulatory Agreements.* Cambridge, MA: Harvard University Press.

Chernow, Ron. 1998. *Titan: The Life of John D. Rockefeller, Sr.* New York: Random House.

Chi, Yingying. 2000. 'China's Rural Challenge. Prospects for the Spread of Village Democracy.' *Harvard International Review* 22(2) (Summer): 34–7.

Chossudovsky, Michel. 1998. *The Globalization of Poverty*. New York: Zed Books.

Claster, Jill N. 1982. *The Medieval Experience: 300–1400*. New York: New York University Press.

Cleveland, Harlan, Hazel Henderson, and Inge Kaul, eds. 1995. *The United Nations: Policy and Financing Alternatives. Innovative Proposals by Visionary Leaders*. New York: Apex Press.

Cline, William R. *Trade and Income Distribution*. 1997. Washington, D.C.: Institute for International Economics.

Cobb, Clifford, Gary Sue Goodman, and Mathis Wackernagel. 1999. *Why Bigger Isn't Better: The Genuine Progress Indicator – 1999 Update*. San Francisco: Redefining Progress.

Conger, Lucy. 1999. 'Entitled to Prosperity.' *Urban Age* (Autumn): 7–11.

Cote, Raymond P., and E. Cohen-Rosenthal. 1998. 'Designing Eco-Industrial Parks: A Synthesis of Some Experiences.' *Journal of Cleaner Production* (September): 181–8.

Daggart, Douglas. 1995. 'Satellites for a Developing World.' *Scientific American* (September): 94.

Davidson, Basil. 1972. *The Lost Cities of Africa*. Rev. ed. Boston: Little, Brown.

David Suzuki Foundation. 2000. *Power Shift: Cool Solutions to Global Warning*. Vancouver: David Suzuki Foundation.

Day, Rob, and Matt Arnold. 1999. 'The Business Case for Sustainable Development.' *Sustainable Business.com*. June. www.sustainablebusiness.com.

Debeir, Jean-Claude, Jean-Paul Deléage, and Daniel Hémery. 1991. *In the Servitude of Power: Energy and Civilization through the Ages*. London: Zed Books.

Decanio, Stephen J. 1997. *The Economics of Climate Change*. San Francisco: Redefining Progress.

De Moor, Andre, and Peter Calamai. 1997. *Subsidizing Unsustainable Development. Undermining the Earth with Public Funds*. Toronto: Earth Council.

De Soto, Hernando. 2000. *The Mystery of Capital*. New York: Basic Books.

Deudny, Daniel H., and Mathew, Richard A. 1999. *Contested Grounds*. New York: State University of New York Press.

De Villiers, Marq. 1999. *Water*. Toronto: Stoddart.

Dewar, Pringle. 2001. *Bones: Discovering the First Americans*. Toronto: Random House.

Diamond, Jared. 1999. *Guns, Germs, and Steel: The Fates of Human Societies*. New York: W.W. Norton.

Dollar, David, and Kray, Art. 2000. 'Growth Is Good for the Poor.' Washington D.C.: The World Bank, March 2000.

Doremus, Paul N., et al. 1998. *The Myth of the Global Corporation*. Princeton: Princeton University Press.

Douthwaite, Richard. 1999. *The Growth Illusion*. Gabriola Island, B.C.: New Society Publishers.

Drabrowski, Andrea, et al. 1999. 'A City of Traders.' *Urban Age* (Spring): 18–19.

Drennen, Thomas E., and Jon D. Erickson. 1998. 'Who Will Fuel China?' *Science* (6 March): 1483.

Drucker, Peter F. 1999. 'Beyond the Information Revolution.' *The Atlantic Monthly* (October): 47–57.

Dunning, John H. 1988. *Multinationals, Technology and Competitiveness*. London: Unwin Hyman.

Easterbrook, Gregg. 1995. *A Moment on the Earth: The Coming Age of Environmental Optimism*. New York: Penguin Books.

Edwards, Mike. 2000. 'Indus Civilization.' *National Geographic* (June): 108–30.

Ehrlich, P.R. 1969. *The Population Time Bomb*. New York: Ballantine.

Ehrlich, Paul R., et al. 1997. 'No Middle Way on the Environment.' *The Atlantic Monthly* (December): 98–104.

Eichengreen, Barry. 1999. *Toward a New International Financial Architecture: A Practical Post-Asia Agenda*. Washington, D.C: Institute for International Economics.

Evans, Kyla. 1999. 'Latest State-of-the-Art Climate Scenarios Show Futures to Avoid.' *WWF Global Network: Press Release*. 19 October. www.panda.org.

Ezzell, Carol. 2000. 'Beyond the Human Genome.' *Scientific American* (July): 64–9.

Economist, The. 1996 (28 September). 'Making Waves': 7–8.

– 2000 (25 March). 'A Survey of Agriculture and Technology': 1–16.

– 27 May. 'Business: The Wiring of India': 63–6.

– 27 May. 'Finance and Economics: Growth Is Good': 82.

– 27 May. 'Finance and Economics: Only Connect': 75–6.

– 27 May. 'Poverty in America: Out of Sight, Out of Mind': 27–30.

– 3 June. 'Argentina: No Fund of Love for the IMF': 39.

– 24 June. 'The Next Revolution: A Survey of Government and the Internet': 3–34.

– 1 July. 'A Survey of the Human Genome': 1–16.

– 5 August. 'The Electric Revolution': 19–20.

– 19 August. 'The Caucasus: Where Worlds Collide': 17–19.

– 19 August. 'The Failure of New Media': 53–4.

- 2 September. 'Asia. The State That Would Reform India': 38–9.
- 9 September. 'Biometrics: The measure of Man.'
- 2001 (26 February). 'E-Commerce: Shopping around the Web': 5–50.
- 29 September. 'Economic Man, Cleaner Planet': 73–5.

Falkowski, Paul. 2002. 'The Oceans Invisible Forest.' *Scientific American* (August): 54–61.

Federation of Red Cross and Red Crescent Societies. 1999. *World Disasters Report: 1999*. Geneva: Continental Printing.

Fisher, Anne. 1999. 'Best Cities for Business: What's So Great about Dallas?' *Fortune* (29 December).

Fisheries and Oceans Canada. 1994. *Aquaculture*. Canada: Fisheries and Oceans.

Flavin, Christopher, and Seth Dunn. 1999. 'Reinventing the Energy System.' *State of the World 1999*. New York and London: W.W. Norton.

Follain, John. 2001. 'China to Build 300-Storey Vertical City.' *Ottawa Citizen* (25 February): A1.

Food and Agriculture Organization. 1995. 'State of Food and Agriculture 1995' Rome: FAO.

- 2002. '*Projection of World Fishery Production in 2010*' and '*Trends in Global Aquaculture Production: 1984–1996.*' *www.FAO.org*.

French, Hillary. 1999. 'Challenging the WTO.' *World Watch* (November–December): 22–7.

Friedman, Thomas L. 1999. *The Lexus and the Olive Tree*. New York: Farrar Straus Giroux.

Frosch, Robert A. 1995. 'The Industrial Ecology of the 21st Century.' *Scientific American* (September): 178–82.

Fukuyama, Francis. 1992. *The End of History and the Last Man*. New York: Free Press.

Gardner, Gary, and Sampat Payal. 1999. 'Forging a Sustainable Materials Economy.' *State of the World 1999*. New York and London: W.W. Norton.

Garfield, Donald. 2000. 'Cultural Capital: Is There an Economic Value to Culture?' *Urban Age* (Winter): 7–9.

Garman, Julie. 1999. 'Finance: How They Measure Up.' *Tomorrow* (July–August): 27.

Gellner, Ernest. 1983. *Nations and Nationalism*. Ithaca, NY: Cornell University Press.

Gies, Francis, and Gies, Joseph. 1990. *Life in a Medieval Village*. New York: Harper and Row.

Gilbert, Richard, et al. 1996. *Making Cities Work: The Role of Local Authorities in the Urban Environment*. London: Earthscan Publications.

Glenn, Edward P., J. Jed Brown, and James W. O'Leary. 1999. 'Irrigating Crops with Seawater.' *Scientific American* (August): 41–50.

Godwin, Peter. 2001. 'Bushmen.' *National Geographic* (February): 90–117.

Goodman, Ann, and Peter Knight. 1999. 'Finance: Lobbying the Lenders.' *Tomorrow* (July–August): 15.

Goodstein, Eban. 1999. *The Trade-Off Myth: Fact and Fiction about Jobs and the Environment.* Washington, D.C.: Island Press.

Gordon, René. 1981. *Africa: A Continent Revealed.* New York: St Martin's Press.

Government of Canada. 1996. *Science and Technology for the New Century: A Federal Strategy.* Ottawa: Industry Canada.

– 1998. *Sustainable Strategies for Oceans: A Co-Management Guide.* Ottawa: Renouf Publishing.

– 1999. *Retrospective Analysis of the 1994 Canadian Environmental Review.* Ottawa: Department of Foreign Affairs and International Trade.

Grove, Noel. 1997. *National Geographic Atlas of World History.* Washington, D.C.: National Geographic Society.

Guratz, Jaurequin Bereriartu. 1994. *Decline of the Nation State.* Sigh. XM de Espana, eds. Reno: University of Nevada Press.

Guruswamy, Lakshman D., and Brent R. Hendricks. 1997. *International Environmental Law in a Nut Shell.* St Paul, MN: West Publishing.

Hall, Edward T. 1981. *Beyond Culture.* New York: Anchor Books.

Hall, Peter. 1998. *Cities in Civilization.* London: Weidenfeld & Nicolson.

– 1999. 'Cycles of Creativity.' *Urban Age* (Fall): 13–15.

Hansen, James E., et al. 1998. 'Global Climate Data and Models: A Reconciliation.' *Science* 281: (14 August): 930–2.

Hardin, Garret. 1968. 'The Tragedy of the Commons.' *Science* (December): 1243–8.

Harris, Nigel. 1987. *The End of the Third World: Newly Industrializing Countries and the Decline of an Ideology.* London: Penguin.

Harrison, Nick. 2000. 'Linking Africa's Farms and Cities.' *Urban Age* (Winter): 4–6.

Hartmann, Thom. 1998. *The Last Hours of Ancient Sunlight.* Northfield, VT: Mythical Books.

Hastings, Tom. 2000. *The Ecology of Peace and War.* Boston: University Press of America.

Hawken, Paul. 1994. *The Ecology of Commerce.* New York: HarperCollins.

– 1997. 'Natural Capitalism.' *Mother Jones* (March-April): 40–53.

Hawken, Paul, Amory Lovins, and L. Hunter Lovins. 1999. *Natural Capitalism.* New York: Little Brown.

Henderson, Hazel. 1996. *Creating Alternative Futures: The End of Economics.* West Hartford, CT: Kumarian Press.

– 1999. *Beyond Globalization: Shaping a Sustainable Global Economy.* West Hartford, CT: Kumarian Press.

Hertner, Peter, and Geoffrey Jones, eds. 1998. *Multinationals.* New York: Gorver.

Hertsgaard, Mark. 1997. 'Our Real China Problem.' *The Atlantic Monthly.* (November): 97–114.

Hibbert, Christopher. 1979. *The Rise and Fall of the House of Medici.* New York: Penguin.

Hillner, Jennifer. 2000. 'Venture Capitals.' *Wired* (July): 258–69.

Hirst, Paul, and Grahame Thompson. 1999. *Globalization in Question.* Malden, MA: Policy Press.

Hollantiai, Vladimir, et al. 1999. 'China, Africa, Russia, India – One of the Planet's Foremost Think-Tanks Considers Global Scenarios.' *Whole Earth* (Spring): 96–100.

Holmberg, John. 1998. 'Backcasting: A Natural Step in Operationalising Sustainable Development.' *Greener Management International* 23 (Fall): 30–51.

Homer-Dixon, Thomas F. 1999. *Environment, Scarcity, and Violence.* Princeton: Princeton University Press.

Houghton, J.T., B.A. Callander, and S.K. Varney, eds. 1992. *Climate Change 1992: The Supplementary Report to the IPCC Scientific Assessment.* Cambridge, UK: Cambridge University Press.

Houghton, J.T., G.J. Jenkins, and J.J. Ephraums, eds. 1993. *Climate Change: The IPCC Scientific Assessment.* Cambridge, UK: Cambridge University Press.

House, Richard. 1999. 'Finance: Battle of the Benchmarks.' *Tomorrow* (July–August): 12–13.

Howard, Ken. 2000. 'The Bioinformatics Gold Rush.' *Scientific American* (July-August): 58–63.

Hubbard Brook Research Foundation. 2003. *Nitrogen Pollution: From the Sources to the Sea.* Hanover, N.H.: Hubbard Brook Research Foundation.

Hull, Richard W. 1976. *African Cities and Towns before the European Conquest.* New York: W.W. Norton.

Hulme, Mike, and Nicola Sheard. 1999. *Global Climate Change Scenarios.* Norwich, U.K.: Climate Research Unit. http:www.cru.uea.ac.uk/~mikeh/research/wwfscenerios.html.

Huntington, Samuel P. 1997. *The Clash of Civilizations and the Remaking of World Order.* New York: Simon & Schuster.

Ignatieff, Michael. 1993. *Blood and Belonging: Journeys into the New Nationalism.* Toronto: Penguin.

Industry Canada. 1998. *Winning in Global Infrastructure Markets: Solutions through Partnership.* Ottawa: Service Industries and Capital Projects Branch.

Inoguchi, Takashi, Edward Newman, and Glen Paoletto, eds. 1999. *Cities and the Environment: New Approaches for Eco-Societies.* New York: United Nations University Press.

Institute for Latin American Integration.1994. *The Latin American and Caribbean Integration Process in 1992/1993.* Publication No. 425. Buenos Aires, Argentina: Inter-American Development Bank Institute for Latin American Integration.

Intergovernmental Panel on Climate Change. 1990. *Climate Change: The IPCC Scientific Assessment.* Cambridge and New York: Cambridge University Press.

International Development Research and Policy Task Force. 1996. *Connecting with the World: Priorities for Canadian Internationalism in the 21st Century.* Ottawa: Canadian International Development Agency.

International Environment Technology Centre. 1996. *Environmental Risk Assessment for Sustainable Cities.* IETC Technical Publication Series, Issue 3. Osaka/Shiga: UNEP International Environment Technology Centre.

International Institute for Management Development. 1995. *The IMD World Competitiveness Yearbook 1995.* Geneva: IMD.

International Institute for Sustainable Development. 1996. *The World Trade Organization and Sustainable Development: An Independent Assessment.* Winnipeg: International Institute for Sustainable Development.

Jacobs, Michael. 1993. *The Green Economy: Environment, Sustainable Development and the Politics of the Future.* Vancouver: UBC Press.

Kahn, Jeremy. 2000. 'Best Cities for Business: The Global Greats.' *Fortune* (20 December).

Kaiser, Jocelyn. 1998. 'Climate Change: Possible Vast Greenhouse Gas Sponge Ignites Controversy.' *Science* 282 (16 October): 37–8.

Kaplan, Robert D. 1994. 'The Coming Anarchy.' *The Atlantic Monthly* (February): 46–76.

Karl, Thomas R., and Kevin E. Trenberth. 1999. 'The Human Impact on Climate.' *Scientific American* (December): 100–5.

Kay, James J., and Henry A. Regier. 1998. 'An Ecosystemic Two-Phase Attractor Approach to Lake Erie's Ecology.' *The State of Lake Erie (SOLE) – Past, Present and Future.* Netherlands: Backhuys Academic Publishers.

Kay, James J., et al. 1999. 'An Ecosystem Approach for Sustainability: Addressing the Challenge of Complexity.' *Futures* (Fall): 2–25.

Kedourie, Elie. 1960. *Nationalism*. New York: Hutchison.

Kellas, J.G. 1998. *The Politics of Nationalism and Ethnicity*. 2nd ed. New York: St Martin's Press.

Kendall, Henry W., et al. 1995. *Meeting the Challenges of Population, Environment, and Resources: The Costs of Inaction*. Environmentally Sustainable Development Proceedings, Series No. 14. Washington, D.C.: The World Bank (4 and 9 October).

Kennedy, Paul. 1987. *The Rise and Fall of the Great Powers*. New York: Random House.

– 1994. *Preparing for the Twenty-First Century*. New York: Vintage Books.

Kepel, Gilles. 2000. 'Islamism Reconsidered: A Running Dialogue with Modernity.' *Harvard International Review* 22(2) (Summer): 22–7.

Kerr, Richard A. 1998. 'Warming's Unpleasant Surprise: Shivering in the Greenhouse.' *Science* (10 July): 156–7.

– 1998. 'West Antarctica's Weak Underbelly Giving Way?' *Science* 281 (24 July): 199–500.

– 2000. 'The Hottest Year, by a Hair.' *Science* 279 (16 January): 315–16.

– 2001. 'It's Official: Humans Are Behind Most Global Warming.' *Science* 291 (26 January): 566.

– 2001. 'Rising Global Temperature, Rising Uncertainty.' *Science* 292 (13 April): 192–4.

– 2002. 'More Science and Carrot, Not a Stick.' *Science* 295 (18 February): 1439.

Khalilzad, Zalmay, and Ian O. Lesser, eds. 1998. *Sources of Conflict in the 21st Century: Regional Futures and U.S. Strategy*. Washington, D.C.: RAND.

Kiernan, V.G. 1998. *Colonial Empires and Armies: 1815–1960*. Montreal: McGill-Queen's University Press.

Komisar, Randy, and Kent Lineback. 2000. *The Monk and the Riddle*. Boston, MA: Harvard Business School Press.

Korten, David C. 1995. *When Corporations Rule the World*. West Hartford, CT: Kumarian Press.

Kottelat, Maurice, and Tony Whitten. 1996. *Freshwater Biodiversity in Asia with Special Reference to Fish*. World Bank Technical Paper No. 343. Washington, D.C.: The World Bank.

Krajick, Kevin. 2001. 'Arctic Life, on thin Ice.' *Science* 291 (29 January): 424–5.

Krugman, Paul. 2000. *The Return of Depression Economics*. New York: W.W. Norton.

Kumar, Anjali, et al. 1997. World Bank Discussion Paper No. 377. *Mobilizing Domestic Capital Markets for Infrastructure Financing: International Experience and Lessons for China*. Washington, D.C.: The World Bank.

Kuperman, Alan J. 2000. 'Rwanda in Retrospect.' *Foreign Affairs* (January–February): 94–118.

Kurth, James. 1994. 'The Real Clash.' *National Interest* (Fall).

Landes, David S. 1999. *The Wealth and Poverty of Nations.* New York: W.W. Norton.

Langdon, Steve. 1999. *Global Poverty, Democracy and North-South Change.* Toronto: Garamond Press.

Langer, William L., ed. 1962. *An Encyclopedia of World History.* Boston: Houghton Mifflin.

Langewiesche, William. 1999. 'Eden: A Gated Community.' *The Atlantic Monthly* (June): 84–5.

Laxer, James. 1999. *The Undeclared War: Class Conflict in the Age of Cyber Capitalism.* Toronto: Penguin Books.

Lemonick, Michael D. 2001. 'Life in the Greenhouse.' *Time* (9 April): 18–23.

Lenat, Douglas B. 1995. 'Artificial Intelligence.' *Scientific American* (September): 80.

Leslie, Jacques. 2000. 'Running Dry. What Happens When the World No Longer Has Enough Freshwater?' *Harpers* (July): 37–52.

Levy, Steven. 1999. 'The New Digital Galaxy.' *Newsweek* (31 May): 37–55.

Lindgren, April. 2000. 'Environmental Disasters in Waiting.' *Ottawa Citizen* (12 June): A4.

Litfin, Karen T., ed. 1998. *The Greening of Sovereignty in World Politics.* Cambridge, MA: MIT Press.

Lo, Fu-chen, and Yue-man Yeung, eds. 1996. *Emerging World Cities in Pacific Asia.* Tokyo, New York, and Paris: United Nations Press.

Lovins, Amory B., L. Hunter Lovins, and Paul Hawken. 1999. 'A Road Map for Natural Capitalism.' *Harvard Business Review* (May–June): 146–58.

Lyonnaise Des Eaux. 1998. *Alternative Solutions to Water and Sanitation in Areas with Limited Financial Resources.* Nanterre: Lyonaise Des Eaux.

MacNeill, Jim, Pieter Winsemius, and Taizo Yakushiji. 1991. *Beyond Interdependence. The Meshing of the World's Economy and the Earth's Ecology.* New York: Oxford University Press.

Maddox, John Sir. 1999. 'The Unexpected Science to Come.' *Scientific American* (December).

Maes, Patti. 1995. 'Intelligent Software.' *Scientific American* (September): 84.

Mann, Charles C. 1999. 'Crop Scientists Seek a New Revolution.' *Science* 283 (15 January): 310–14.

Manning, Anita. 2000. 'Report Finds Much of the World's Soil Is Seriously Degraded.' *USA Today* (22 May): 5A.

Marber, Peter. 1998. *From Third World To World Class: The Future of Emerging Markets in the Global Economy.* Reading, MA: Perseus Books.

Markham, Adam. 1999. 'Global Warming and Atlantic Hurricanes.' World
Wildlife Fund Background Paper, September, 1999. http:/wwf.org/news/
attachments/floyback.cfm.

Martin, Hans-Peter, and Harald Schumann. 1997. *The Global Trap. Globalization and the Assault on Democracy and Prosperity*. Montreal: Black Rose
Books.

Masuda, Yoneji. 1981. *The Information Society*. Washington, D.C.: World
Future Society.

Maudes, Jerry, and Edward Goldsmith, eds. 1996. *The Case against the Global
Economy*. Washington: Sierra Club Books.

Maxwell, Judith. 2002. *Smart Social Policy – Making Work Pay*. Ottawa:
Canadian Policy Research Network. www.cprn.org.

Mazur, Jay. 2000. 'Labor's New Internationalism.' *Foreign Affairs* (January-
February): 79–93.

McCready, Ken, David O'Brien, and Arthur Sawchuk. 1994. *Climate Change: A
Strategy for Voluntary Business Action*. Ottawa: Business Council on National
Issues.

McDonough, William, and Michael Braungart. 1998. 'The Next Industrial
Revolution.' *The Atlantic Monthly* (October): 82–92.

McGinn, Anne Platt. 1998. 'Blue Revolution: The Promises and Pitfalls of Fish
Farming.' *World Watch* (March–April): 10–19.

– 1999. 'Charting a New Course for Oceans.' *State of the World 1999*. New
York and London: W.W. Norton.

McKibben, Bill. 1998. 'A Special Moment in History.' *The Atlantic Monthly*
(May): 55–78.

Meadows, D.H., et. al. 1972. *The Limits to Growth*. New York: Universe Books.

Mesarovic, Mihajlo, and Eduard Pestel. 1974. *Mankind at the Turning Point:
The Second Report to the Club of Rome*. New York: E.P. Dutton.

Miller, Kenton R. 1996. *Balancing the Scales: Guidelines for Increasing
Biodiversity's Chances through Bioregional Management*. Washington, D.C.:
World Resources Institute.

Minoque, K.R. 1967. *Nationalism*. London: B.T. Batsford.

Mintzer, Irving, ed. 1992. *Confronting Climate Change: Risks, Implications and
Responses*. Cambridge, U.K.: Cambridge University Press.

Mintzer, Irving, Amber J. Leonard, and Peter Schwartz. 2003. *U.S. Energy
Scenarios for the 21st Century*. Washington, D.C.: Pew Center on Global
Climate Change.

Mitchell, Jennifer D. 1998. 'Before the Next Doubling.' *World Watch* (January–
February): 21–7.

Moffat, Anne Simon. 1998. 'Global Nitrogen Overload Problem Grows
Critical.' *Science* 279 (13 February): 988–9.

Moore, Geoffrey, Tom Kippola, and Paul Johnson. 1998. *The Gorilla Game: An Investor's Guide to Picking Winners in High Technology*. New York: Harper Business.

Moran, Theodore H. 1998. *Foreign Direct Investment and Development*. Washington, D.C.: Institute for International Economics.

Morris, John. 1998. *Londinium*. London: Douglas & McIntyre.

Moynihan, Daniel Patrick. 1993. *Pandaemonium: Ethnicity in International Politics*. Oxford: Oxford University Press.

Mumford, Lewis. 1961. *The City in History: Its Origins, Its Transformations, and Its Prospects*. New York: MJF Books.

Munro, Margaret. 2001. 'A Fine But Foul Spectacle.' *National Post* (31 May): A15.

Myers, Norman. 1996. *Ultimate Security: The Environmental Basis of Political Stability*. Washington, D.C.: Island Press.

Naisbitt, John, and Patricia Aburdene. 1991. *Megatrends 2000: Ten New Directions for the 1990s*. New York: Avon Books.

– 1994. *Global Paradox*. New York: Avon Books.

National Assessment Synthesis Team. 2000. *Climate Change Impacts on the United States: The Potential Consequences of Climate Variability and Change*. Public Review Draft. Washington, D.C.: NAST.

National Geographic Society. 1979. *Mysteries of the Ancient World*. Washington: National Geographic Society.

Nattrass, Brian, and Mary Altomare. 1999. *The Natural Step for Business: Wealth, Ecology and the Evolutionary Corporation*. Gabriola Island: New Society Publishers.

Noland, Marcus. 2000. 'Learning to Love the WTO.' *Foreign Affairs* (September-October): 78–92.

Noland, Marcus, et al. 1998. *Global Economic Effects of the Asian Currency Devaluations*. Washington, D.C.: Institute for International Economics.

Nordström, Håkan, and Scott Vaughan. 1999. *Trade and Environment*. Special Study for the World Trade Organization. Geneva (October).

Obudhu, R.A. 1997. 'Nairobi: National Capital and Regional Hub.' *The Urban Challenge in Africa*. Tokyo, New York, and Paris: Oxford University Press.

Odell, William. 1999. 'The Building Envelope: Ten Steps to Efficiency.' *Sustainable Business.com*. http://www.sustainablebusiness.com/insider/may99/odell.cfm.

Ohmae, Kenichi. 1990. *The Borderless World: Power and Strategy in the Interlinked Economy*. New York: HarperCollins.

Organisation for Economic Co-operation and Development. 1998. *21st Century Technologies: Promises and Perils of a Dynamic Future*. France: OECD Publications.

– 1999. *Energy: The Next Fifty Years*. France: OECD Publications.
– 1999. *OECD Science, Technology and Industry Scoreboard 1999*. France: OECD Publications.
Parkes, Christopher. 2000. 'Old Money Still Heads Los Angeles' Richest List.' *Financial Post* (30 May): C1.
Parry, Martin, and Timothy Carter. 1998. *Climate Impact and Adaptation Assessment: A Guide to the IPCC Approach*. London: Earthscan Publications.
Patterson, David A. 1995. 'Microprocessors in 2020.' *Scientific American* (September): 62–7.
Pawlowicz, Richard. 1999. 'Sea Ice Thins 40%.' *Geophysical Research Letters* (November).
Pearson, Ian D. 2000. 'The Next 20 Years in Technology: Timeline and Commentary.' *The Futurist* (January–February): 14–19.
Perry, Guillermo E., and Daniel Lederman. 1998. *Financial Vulnerability, Spillover Effects, and Contagion: Lessons from the Asian Crises for Latin America*. Washington, D.C.: The World Bank.
Pigato, Miria, et al. 1997. *South Asia's Integration into the World Economy*. Washington, D.C.: The World Bank.
Plafker, Ted. 1999. 'Home Ownership – The New Chinese Dream.' *Urban Age* (Spring): 6–9.
Polese, Mario, and Richard Stren, eds. 2000. *The Social Sustainability of Cities: Diversity and the Management of Change*. Canada: University of Toronto Press.
Postel, Sandra. 1999. 'When the World's Wells Run Dry.' *World Watch* (September–October): 30–8.
– 2000. 'Troubled Waters.' *The Sciences* (March-April): 19–24.
Postel, Sandra, Gretchen C. Daily, and Paul R. Ehrlich. 1996. 'Human Appropriation of Renewable Fresh Water.' *Science* 271 (9 February): 785–7.
Pringle, Heather. 2001. 'The First Urban Center in the Americas.' *Science* (27 April): 621–2.
– 1996. *In Search of Ancient North America*. Toronto: John Wiley & Sons Canada.
Psacharopoulos, George, and Nguyen Xuan Nguyen. 1997. World Bank Technical Paper No. 346. *The Role of Government and the Private Sector in Fighting Poverty*. Washington D.C.: The World Bank.
Rakodi, Carole. 1997. *The Urban Challenge in Africa*. New York: United Nations University Press.
Ravetz, Joe. 2000. *City Region 2020: Integrated Planning for a Sustainable Environment*. London: Earthscan Publications.
Redefining Progress. 1999. 'Genuine Progress Indicator 1998.' http://www.rprogress.org.

– 'The Footprints of Nations Study.' *Redefining Progress* (12 August). www.rprogress.org/resources/nip/ef/ef_nations.html.

Rees, William. 1992. 'Ecological Footprints and Appropriated Carrying Capacity: What Urban Economics Leaves Out.' *Environment and Urbanization* 4(2): 121–30.

– 2001. 'Ecological Footprints, Concept of.' Pp. 229–44 in *Encyclopedia of Biodiversity*, vol. 2. San Diego: Academic Press.

– 2002. 'Globalization and Sustainability: Conflict or Convergence.' *Bulletin of Science: Technology and Society* 22(4): 249–68.

Reich, Robert B. 1983. *The Next American Frontier*. New York: Times Books.

Rennie, John. 1995. 'The Uncertainties of Technological Innovation.' *Scientific American* (September): 57.

Repetto, Robert, and Duncan Austin. 1997. *The Costs of Climate Protection: A Guide for the Perplexed*. Washington, D.C.: World Resources Institute.

Rich, Norman. 1977. *The Age of Nationalism*. New York: W.W. Norton.

Rifkin, Jeremy. 1996. *The End of Work: The Decline of the Global Labor Force and the Dawn of the Post-Market Era*. New York: Putnam.

Rijsberman, Frank R. 'Daily Report: Achieving Water Security: Everybody's Business.' *Content News* (21 March). www.worldwaterforum.com/journalist/report.cfm?dagnr=4. (31 Mar. 2000).

Robb, Caroline M. 1999. *Can the Poor Influence Policy? Participatory Poverty Assessments in the Developing World*. Washington, D.C.: The World Bank.

Robert, Karl-Henrik, et al. 'Strategic Sustainable Development: Selection, Design and Synergies of Applied Tools.' www.tns.ca.

Rodrik, Dani. 1997. *Has Globalization Gone Too Far?* Washington, D.C.: Institute for International Economics.

Rogers, Richard, and Philip Gumuchdjian. 1997. *Cities for a Small Planet*. London, U.K.: Faber and Faber.

Romm, Joseph J. 1994. *Lean and Clean Management*. New York: Kodansha America.

Romm, Joseph, et al. 2000. 'A Road Map for U.S. Carbon Reductions.' *Science* (30 January): 669–70.

Rosecrance, Richard. 1999. *The Rise of the Virtual State: Wealth and Power in the Coming Century*. New York: Basic Books.

Roseland, Mark. 1992. *Toward Sustainable Communities*. Ottawa: The Alger Press.

Russel, Robert Arnold. 1986. *Winning The Future: Succeeding in an Economic Revolution*. New York: Carroll & Graf.

Sadowski, Yahya. 1998. *The Myth of Global Chaos*. Washington, D.C.: Brookings Institution Press.

Sahlins, Marshall. 1972. *Stone Age Economics*. New York: Aldine de Gruyter.

Sampat, Payal. 2000. 'Groundwater Shock: The Polluting of the World's Major Freshwater Stores.' *World Watch* (January–February): 10–22.

Satterthwaite, David, ed. 1999. *The Earthscan Reader in Sustainable Cities*. London: Earthscan Publications.

Schillhorn van Veen, Tjaart W., Douglas A. Forno, Steen Joffe, Dina L. Umali-Deininger, and Sanjive Cooke. 1996. Environmentally Sustainable Development Studies and Monographs, Series No. 13. *Integrated Pest Management: Strategies and Policies for Effective Implementation*. Washington, D.C.: The World Bank.

Schmidt Bleek, F. 1998. *The MIPS Konzept – Faktor 10*. Munich: Droemer.

Schumacher, E.F. 1976. *Small Is Beautiful*. New York: Praeger.

Schwartz, Peter, Peter Leyden, and Joel Hyatt. 1999. *The Long Boom: A Vision for the Coming Age of Prosperity*. Reading, MA: Perseus Books.

Scientific American. 1995. 'Technologies for the Next Millennium' (September): 84, 68–87, 118–167.

Sennett, Richard. 1998. *The Corrosion of Character*. New York: W.W. Norton.

Serageldin, Ismail and Andrew Steer, eds. 1994. Environmentally Sustainable Development Occasional Paper, Series No. 2. *Making Development Sustainable: From Concepts to Action*. Washington, D.C.: The World Bank.

Serageldin, Ismail, Richard Barrett, and Joan Martin-Brown, eds. 1994. *The Business of Sustainable Cities: Public-Private Partnerships for Creative Technical and Institutional Solutions*. Environmentally Sustainable Development Proceedings, Series No. 7. Washington, D.C.: The World Bank.

Servan-Schreiber, Jean-Jacques. 1967. *The American Challenge*. New York: Simon & Schuster.

Shafer, Boyd. C. 1955. *Nationalism: Myth and Reality*. New York: Harcourt, Brace.

Shaviv, Nir J., and Jan Veizer. 2003. 'Celestial Driver of Phanerozoic Climate?' *GSA Today* 13(7): 4–10.

Shaw, Steven A. 2001. 'Mad Cows and Englishmen.' *Commentary* (March): 38–41.

Simon, Joel. 1997. *Endangered Mexico: An Environment on the Edge*. San Francisco: Sierra Club Books.

Simon Moffat, Anne. 1998. 'Global Nitrogen Overload Problem Grows Critical.' *Science* (13 February): 988–99.

Smith, Anthony D. 1991. *National Identity*. Reno: University of Nevada Press.

Smith, Graham R., et al. 1997. *Getting Connected: Private Participation in Infrastructure in the Middle East and North Africa*. Washington, D.C.: The World Bank.

Smith, Merritt R., and Leo Marx, eds. 1994. *Does Technology Drive History? The Dilemmas of Technological Determinism*. London: The MIT Press.

Spears, Tom. 2000. 'Wild Salmon Face Battle for Survival.' *Ottawa Citizen* (9 January): A6.

Srivastava, Jitendra P., Nigel J.H. Smith, and Douglas A. Forno. 1996. *Biodiversity and Agricultural Intensification: Partners for Development and Conservation.* Washington, D.C.: The World Bank.

Starnes, Richard. 2001. 'Our Toxic Catch.' *Ottawa Citizen* (26 May).

Stauffer, Julie. 1999. *The Water Crisis: Finding the Right Solutions.* Montreal: Black Rose Books.

Stent, Gunther S. 1978. *Paradoxes of Progress.* San Francisco: W.H. Freeman.

Stigson, Björn. 2001. 'Maximizing Opportunities at the World Summit.' Presentation to the Business Action for Sustainable Development Meeting, Paris, 9–10 October. Geneva: World Business Council for Sustainable Development.

Stoll Design. 2000. 'Proficient Quality Standards: Aquaculture Nutrition.' www.marbro.com/quality/htm.

STRATEGICO Inc. 1993. *Canadian Fishery: Waiting for Godot?* Canada: Department of Fisheries and Oceans, Aquaculture Division.

Streeten, Paul. 1998. 'Globalization: Threat or Salvation.' In A.S. Bhalla, ed., *Globalization, Growth and Marginalization.* Ottawa: International Development Research Centre.

Strong, Maurice. 2000. *Where on Earth Are We Going?* Toronto: Knopf Canada.

Suess, Erwin, et al. 1999. 'Flammable Ice.' *Scientific American.* (7 November): 6–83.

Suzuki, David. 1999. *The Sacred Balance.* Vancouver/Toronto: Greystone Books.

Tapscott, Don, et al. 2000. *Digital Capital: Harnessing the Power of Business Webs.* Cambridge, MA: Harvard Business School Press.

Teichova, Alice, et al., eds. 1986. *Multinational Enterprises in Historical Perspectives.* Cambridge, U.K.: Cambridge University Press.

Thia-Eng, Chua, and S. Adrian Ross, eds. 1998. *Pollution Prevention and Management in the East Asian Seas: A Paradigm Shift in Concept, Approach and Methodology.* Manila: GEF/UNDP/IMO Regional Programme for the Prevention and Management of Marine Pollution in the East Asian Seas.

Thorne-Miller, Boyce, and John Catena. 1991. *The Living Ocean: Understanding and Protecting Marine Biodiversity.* Washington, D.C.: Island Press.

Thrupp, Lori Ann, ed. 1996. *New Partnerships for Sustainable Agriculture.* New York: World Resources Institute.

Thurow, Lester C. 1999. *Building Wealth: The New Rules for Individuals, Companies, and Nations in a Knowledge-Based Economy.* New York: HarperCollins.

Toynbee, Arnold. 1967. 'Cities in History.' In Arnold Toynbee, ed, *Cities of Destiny*. New York: Weathervane Books.

– 1972. *A Study of History* (abridged edition). Oxford, U.K.: Oxford University Press.

Trenberth, Kevin E. 1997. 'Global Warming: It's Happening.' *Natural Science* (1).

United Nations. 1992. *Climate Change and Transnational Corporations: Analysis and Trends*. New York: United Nations.

– 1994. *United Nations Earth Summit Agenda 21: The United Nations Programme of Action from Rio*. New York: United Nations Department of Public Information.

– 1996. *World Investment Report 1996: Investment, Trade and International Policy Arrangements*. New York: United Nations.

– 2000. *World Population Prospects: The 2000 Version, Vol. III: Analytic Report*. United Nations Doc. ST/ESA/Ser.A/200

United Nations Department of Economic and Social Affairs. 1997. *Aspects of World Employment Strategy*. New York: United Nations.

United Nations Development Programme. 1999. *UNDP: Human Development Report 1999*. New York: Oxford University Press.

– 2000. *Overcoming Human Poverty: UNDP Poverty Report 2000*. New York: United Nations Department of Public Information.

United Nations Development Programme, United Nations Environment Programme, World Bank and US Tech International LLC. 1998. *Review of Climate Change Technology in the U.S.* Washington, D.C.: U.S. Tech International LLC.

United Nations Environmental Programme. 1995. *The Oil Industry Experience: Technology Cooperation and Capacity Building: Contribution to Agenda 21*. London, U.K.: IPIECA.

– 1997. *Implementing the Urban Environment Agenda*, vol. 1. Nairobi: Majestic Printing Works.

– 1999. GEO-2000. *UNEP's Millennium Report on the Environment*. London: Earthscan Publications.

United Nations Conference on Human Settlements. 1986. *Global Report on Human Settlements*. New York: United Nations.

van Crevald, Martin. 1990. *The Transformation of War*. London: The Free Press.

Vanderschueren, Franz, Emiel Wegelin, and Kadmiel Wekwete. 1996. *Policy Programme Options for Urban Poverty Reduction*. Washington, D.C.: The World Bank.

Von Bieberstein Koch-Weser, Maritta R. 1999. 'Forests – a Century of Destruction.' *World Conservation Union – IUCN*. Message to the Media (22 December). www.iucn.org/info_and_news/press/dg2000.html.

Von Lersner, Heinrich. 1995. 'Outline for an Ecological Economy.' *Scientific American* (September): 188.

Wackernagel, Mathis, and William E. Rees. 1995. *Our Ecological Footprint: Reducing Human Impact on the Earth.* Gabriola Island, B.C.: New Society Publishers.

Waggoner, Paul. 1996. 'How Much Land Can Ten Billion People Spare for Agriculture?' *Daedalus* 25(3).

Wallace, Nancy. 1994. 'Canada's Business Leaders Outline a Voluntary Strategy to Combat Global Climate Change.' *Communiqué.* Ottawa: Business Council on National Issues (4 November).

Walter, Jonathan, ed. 1999. *World Disasters Report 1999.* Switzerland: International Federation of Red Cross and Red Crescent Societies.

Ward, Veronronica. 1998. 'Sovereignty and Ecosystem Management: Clash of Concepts and Boundaries.' *The Greening of Sovereignty in World Politics.* London and Cambridge: The MIT Press.

White, Lynn Jr. 1962. *Medieval Technology and Social Change.* London: Oxford University Press.

Wilkening, Kenneth, Leonard Barrie, and Marylyn Engle. 2000. 'Trans-Pacific Air Pollution.' *Science* (6 October): 65–7.

Williamson, John. 1993. 'Democracy and the Washington Consensus.' *World Development* 21: 1329–36.

Wilson, Edward O. 1992. *The Diversity of Life.* New York: W.W. Norton.

– 1998. *Consilience: The Unity of Knowledge.* New York: Alfred A. Knopf.

– 2002. *The Future of Life.* New York: Alfred A. Knopf.

Woodbridge, Roy. 1993. *GEF/MPMF Business Opportunities: Increasing Canadian Participation in International Projects.* Study commissioned by ISTC, Environmental Affairs Branch. Ottawa: Woodbridge & Associates.

– 1994. *Canadian Environmental Industries and Climate Change Business Opportunities.* Report for the Environmental Affairs Branch, Industry Canada. Ottawa.

– 1997. *Market Opportunities Related to Sustainable Marine Management in S.E. Asia.* Background Report for Workshop at Globe, 1998 Conference, Vancouver, B.C.: (13–17 March).

– 1997. *The Market for Water Management Technologies and Services in Turkey.* Report prepared for the Canadian Department of Foreign Affairs and International Trade.

– 1992. *Gearing Up the Technology Engine at the Community Level.* Report of the National Technology Policy Roundtable. Ottawa: Canadian Advanced Technology Association and the Economic Council of Canada.

World Bank. 1992. *World Development Report 1992.* New York: Oxford University Press.

– 1994. *Learning from the Past, Embracing the Future*. Washington, D.C.: The World Bank.

– 1995. *Argentina Managing Environmental Pollution: Issues and Options*. Technical Report. Washington, D.C.: The World Bank.

– 1995. *Private Sector Development in Low-Income Countries*. Washington, D.C.: The World Bank.

– 1996. *Directions in Development: Livable Cities for the 21st Century*. Washington, D.C.: The World Bank.

– 1996. *Mainstreaming Biodiversity in Agricultural Development toward Good Practice*. Washington, D.C.: The World Bank.

– 1997. *China 2020: Disparities in China: Sharing Rising Incomes*. Washington, D.C.: The World Bank.

– 1997. *The IDA in Action: 1993–1996: The Pursuit of Sustained Poverty Reduction*. Washington, D.C.: The World Bank.

– 1997. *Private Capital Flows to Developing Countries: The Road to Financial Integration*. Washington, D.C.: The World Bank.

– 1998. *World Development Indicators*. Washington, D.C.: The World Bank.

– 2000. *Cities in Transition: A Strategic View of Urban and Local Government Issues*. Washington, D.C.: The World Bank.

– 2001. *World Development Report 2000/2001: Attacking Poverty*. New York: Oxford University Press.

World Commission on Environment and Development. 1987. *Our Common Future*. New York: Oxford University Press.

World Commission on Water for the 21st Century. *Water Vision*. Paris: World Water Council.

World Resources Institute. 2000. *People and Ecosystems: The Fraying Web of Life*. Washington, D.C.: WRI.

– 2002. *A Guide to World Resources 2000–2001*. Washington, D.C.: WRI.

World Trade Organization. 1999. 'Seattle Press Pack, Facts and Figures.'

– 2000. Special Study No. 5: 'Trade, Income Disparity and Poverty.'

World Water Council. 2000. 'Earth's Reserves of Groundwater Threatened.' *Content News* (21 January). www.worldwaterforum.com.

– 2000. 'World Water Challenge for the Twenty-First Century.' *Content News* (19 March). www.worldwaterforum.com.

– 2000. 'Ministerial Declaration of The Hague on Water Security in the 21st Century.' *Content News* (23 March). www.worldwaterforum.com.

– 2000. *A Water Secure World: Vision for Water, Life, and the Environment*. Commission Report. Cairo: World Water Council.

World Wildlife Federation. 2002. 'Living Planet Report 2002.' Washington, D.C.: WWF.

WRI/IUCN/UNEP. 1992. *Global Biodiversity Strategy: A Policy-Makers' Guide.*
    Baltimore, MD: WRI.
Yeats, Alexander J., et al. 1997. *Did Domestic Policies Marginalize Africa in
    International Trade?* Washington, D.C.: The World Bank.
Yeung, Yue-man, and Fu-chen Lo. 1996. 'Global Restructuring and Emerging
    Urban Corridors in Pacific Asia.' *Emerging World Cities in Pacific Asia.*
    Tokyo, New York, and Paris: United Nations Press.
Zysman, George I. 1995. 'Wireless Networks.' *Scientific American* (September):
    69.

Index

Aarhus Convention 255
acid rain 231
aerospace 130
African Sahel 50
Age of Global Provisioning 22, 114;
    defining characteristics 275;
    managing the transition 275–7
Agenda 21 viii, 7
agricultural innovation: Green
    Revolution 4–5, 56, 187–8; and
    Industrial Revolution 74–5;
    integrated management 238; in
    Middle Ages 53; the present
    challenge 194–6
agricultural societies 49–58; global
    spread 50–6; impact on hunter-
    gatherers 48–9, 55; origins of 50;
    population densities 50; provision-
    ing cities 146; wealth 146
agriculture: and biodiversity issues
    190; and climate change 191–3; and
    land availability188–9; and loss of
    biodiversity 190–1; and pollution
    193–4; and production constraints
    on 188–96; and social issues 193;
    and soil quality 189–90; and water
    190

Alexander the Great 66
algae blooms 184
Alroy, John 200
American Civil War 89, 104
American Revolution 88
American rivers 236
Amsterdam 73
Anatolia 182
Andrew Carnegie 105
ants 40–1
appeasement 262
aquaculture 198–9
aquifers, pollution of 83, 183
Armageddon 262
'arrested civilizations' 47
Arrhenius, Svente 170
Asian Tigers 93
Athens 62
automobiles: and Asian growth 135;
    here to stay 245; and urban
    planning 244–6
Aztecs 84

Bangladesh 169
Bantu migrations 54
basic science 131
Basque language 52

Beijing-to-Tokyo corridor 245
Berlin 76
biological diversity viii, 3, 9; and the
  great extinctions 39; and speciation
  39–41; and survival rates of
  species 40
bio-regions. *See* integrated bio-region
  management
bipolar cities 135, 160–2, 208–9
bipolar nations 179
bipolar world 179–80, 216
Boetian Confederacy 83
Borneo 44
Bosnia 18, 212
Brazil 133
British East India Company 87
British Petroleum (BP) 280
Brundtland Commission 6
build, own transfer (BOT) 181
Byzantium 69

Caesar, Julius 148
Canada 168; income gaps 153
Canada–US Free Trade Agreement
  112
capitalism, rise of 103
carbon retention 192
Carson, Rachel 96
Chamberlain, Neville 262
Charlemagne 84
chemicals 130
Chile 133
China, 13, 41, 44, 50, 60, 77, 81, 91, 93,
  125, 134; energy options 178;
  income gaps 152–4
cities: origins of 60–1; as cause of
  environmental crisis 78–9, 233;
  city-states 14; clash of urban
  cultures 208–10; competition
  between 163; creation of mass
employment 60; growth of Third
  World cities 7, 76–7; as growth
  poles of New Economy 76; and
  hierarchical governance 63; and
  integration into nations 85; and job
  creation technologies 243–4; as
  locus of innovation 60; as loss of
  mandates 241, 246–7; poverty in
  peri areas 161; projected growth of
  78; and role in provisioning 59–73,
  83–6; and trade dependence 62–3;
  and social integration 63. *See also*
  infrastructure and informal
  economy; urban management
civic architecture 64
civilizational conflicts 210
clean energy technologies 131, 227
Clean Water Act 184
climate change viii, 167–80; competing theories of 170–5; evidence of
  168–70; international response to
  169–70, 175–7; prospects of 179–
  80; Third World's role in 177–9
climate stabilization and destabiliza-
  tion mechanisms 173–5
Cloaca Maxima 147
Clovis people 43
Club of Rome 96
Cold War viii, 14, 90
colonialism 55, 86
Commercial Revolution 71–73, 85, 86,
  102–3
communism 91–2; collapse of 95
Cornell University Center for the
  Environment 294
cultural change xiii, 20, 47, 164, 216–
  17; inevitability of 113–16, 276
cumulative effects: of inability to
  control pollution 98–99, 252
currency crisis 125

Dark Ages 52
de Soto, Hernando 32
deregulation 93, 110, 120
development decades 153
documenting pollution levels 255, 274
domestic investment 120, 125
drinking water 182
Dutch East India Company 87

eco-industrial parks 242
ecolabelling 232
ecological decline and markets 196; focus on management 203–4; market prices mislead 202–4, 228; shaping market mechanisms 243, 248
ecological decline xiii; and burden on poor 201; dispersal effects of 143, 200, 264; evidence for 4–5, 165–97
ecological footprints 10, 29, 142, 247
ecological scarcity and conflict 17; catalyst for 17, 217; ecological and social 'flips' 140–4; equity, ecology, and social violence 140, 206–17; feedback loops 140
ecological sustainability 5; actions to promote 269–70; innovation for 227; and limited market demand 227. See also sustainable development
ecosystems 40
eco-urban management 22, 233, 241–9; constraints on 244–7; mining natural capital 242; political accountability for 247–9; proposed eco-urban management programs 257; steps to implement 273

ecozones 242. See also integrated bio-region management
Egypt 65, 83; river basin management 65
employment 31; urban solutions to rural poverty 234–5
encomienda 56
energy transitions 42; in China 178; electrification 104; energy-intensive agriculture 56; Medieval innovations 53; wood to fossil fuels 74
Environmental Dispute Resolution Mechanism (ERDM) 257–60
environmental movement, rise of 96–9
Epidaerus 83
erosion of fisheries 197–8
ethical investing 231
ethnic cleansing 18
European Common Market 111

Factor Ten Institute 10
feedback loops 140–4
Fertile Crescent 50
feudalism 52
fish and land use 199–200
fisheries decline 197
fishing technologies 198–9
Florence 72
Food and Agriculture Organization (FAO) 188
food chains (ecological) 40; keystone species 40
food chains (provisioning) 30
Footprint of Nations Study 280
Ford, Gerald 93
Ford, Henry 105
foreign investment 8, 91, 95; U.S. dominance in 105–6; role of, in global economy 119–22, 124

forestry management, integrated
approaches 237–8
formal economy. *See* informal
economy
Framework Convention on Climate
Change (FCCC) 170–1, 175, 225–6,
230; integrated into proposed FCE
255
Framework Convention on Provisioning (FCP) 251–60, 268;
Declaration of War 252; international battle plans 251–60; national
battle plans 230–49; technology
battlefields 224–6. *See also* World
Summit on Global Provisioning
Freemasons 70
free trade 89–96
French Revolution 88

Group of 8 (G8) 8
galactic cosmic flux 172
Gates, Bill 152
General Agreement on Tariffs and
Trade (GATT) 90, 23
Genuine Progress Indicator (GPI) 202
GINI index 154
Glasgow 76
global economy 16, 31; benefits of 9;
cultural impacts of 206; growth
prospects for 5, 126; and interdependence of First and Third
worlds 18; organization of 118–
124; and the peace dividend 206;
and sustainable development viii–
xi; tensions within 133–5, 216;
vulnerable to ecological decline 6;
and Western growth model 114.
See also private sector networks
Global Environmental Outlook (GEO)
166

Global Reporting Initiative 231
global water crisis ix, 180–7; water
conferences ix; water wars and
equity issues 184–6
Great Depression 152
Greek city-states 66–8, 101; colonization and trade 66–7; ideal size 67
Green Revolution 4–5, 56, 187–8
green taxation 231
ground water contamination 182–4
growth poles 76
guilds 70, 102; dissolution 74

Han Dynasty 68
Hanseatic League 86
health regulations 232
Herodotus 61
Holy Roman Empire 84
Homer-Dixon, Thomas F. 207, 212
Hong Kong 133
Hudson's Bay Company 87
human allegiance, varieties of 82
human genome 226
humans: arrival of proto-humans 39;
in conflict with agriculture 45;
DNA evidence 41; egalitarianism
in 145; evolution of 41–3; genetic
variation in 44; global spread of
42–5; in hunter-gatherer societies
14, 45, 214; language and cultural
diversity in 15, 44; and loss of
diversity 50; modern challenges
for 47–8; and population densities
45
Huntington, Samuel 210
hyper-cars 177

Incas 84
income distribution: during commercial era 150; effects of Renaissance

on 149; after fall of Roman Empire 148; and gaps between countries 152–3; and gaps within countries 153–8; history of 144–52; impact of colonialism on 152; and Industrial Revolution 151–2; under manorial system 148–9; in New Economy 152

incorporation 70

India 153, 183

Indonesia 212

industrial ecology 225, 227, 229: application to cities 242–3; and market incentives 230–3; proposed programs for 256

Industrial Revolution 71–6, 87, 100, 103, 222; and energy transitions 74; impact on cities of 75–6; and social transformations 74

informal economy 31–6; employment in 32–3; implications for provisioning 31, 34–5, 64–79, 234; role of infrastructure in 30–2; and transition to formal sector 33–4, 215

Information Age 76, 94–5, 109

infrastructure 31, 107; employment impacts on 31–5; hard and soft 31; and investment imbalance 226–7; meeting needs of the poor 225–6; outreach to natural capital 145; urban infrastructure for mass employment 235, 270, 243–8; and policy needs 232; proposed programs for 257, 273. *See also* cities; informal economy

innovation divide 227; options to redress 228. *See also* technological innovation; 'War to Provision the World'

integrated bio-region management 22, 233, 235–41; ancient efforts 65; global bio-region programs 256; knowledge needs 241; organizational constraints 238–9; political accountability 239–41; steps to implement 272–3

intellectual property laws 120

Intergovernmental Panel on Climate Change (IPCC) 169

International Earth Science Information Network 188

International Finance Commission (IFC) 90

International Financial Institutions (IFIs) 123–4

International Institute for Sustainable Development (IISD) 280

International Monetary Fund 122; conditionality clauses 123

International Society for Ecological Economics 292

International Standards Organization (ISO) 231

Internet 113, 167, 193

irrigation 64–5, 178, 181, 183, 185, 189–90, 192–5, 235

Israel 182

Japan 134, 152, 210

Khoisan 45

Kyoto Accord and Protocol 175–6

Lake Chapala 235

land claims 46

latifundia 56

Law of the Sea 295

League of Swabian Cities 85, 86

leagues of cities 102

life-cycle costing 232
Limits to Growth 96
Lombardy League 86
Lyonnaise Des Eaux 294

McDonald's 155
maintaining ecological viability
    253–25
Malaysia 133
Malthus 4, 139, 142
Manchester 76
Manila 183
Marxism 14
mass transit 151
Mathare Valley 208
Medici 72
medieval cities 69–71, 85; intercity
    trade 70
melting pot societies 88
mergers and acquisitions 109
methane hydrate deposits 175
Mexico City 182, 236
Middle Ages 69–72, 84–5
migrants, economic 17, 224
migration of crops and animals 51–5
migration of industries 118
monastic orders 69, 102
Mongols 63, 84
monitoring and preparedness 224;
    proposed programs 253–55
monopolies 110, 121
Monte Verde 43
Montreal Protocol 171
MOPITT satellite 166
Moscovy Trading Company 87
multilateral environmental agree-
    ments (MEAs) 252, 253
Multinational enterprise (MNEs) 100;
    first MNEs 72; and investment in
    Third World 110; and ownership

of technology 119; reasons for
    scale 106–13; rise of 104–6; role of,
    in global economy 115, 118–19, 226
Muslim fundamentalism 210

nation-states: integration of cities
    85–6; origins 80; rise and spread of
    83–7; role in provisioning 83, 86–8;
    transfer of provisioning to private
    sector 87–99
national industrial ecology programs
    233
national values 120
nationalism 82, 88
NATO 263
natural capital xii; absorptive
    capacities of xii; in-bound flows
    xii; organizing to access 10–12, 17,
    35–6; role of, in wealth creation
    28–9, 34–6, 144
natural capitalism 11
Natural Step movement 10
neoclassical economics 82, 97, 222
New Agriculture programs 256
New Economy 16, 29, 127, 261: basis
    for national competitiveness 226;
    natural capital needs of 29; sources
    of wealth 152; technologies 270
New International Economic Order
    (NIEO) 111
new materials 130
newly industrialized nations (NICs)
    92
nomadic herdsmen 51
North American Free Trade Agree-
    ment (NAFTA) 112
'not me first syndrome' 250–1, 258

ocean currents 40, 174
OECD 125, 250

Ogallala aquifer 183
old-style wars 267, 275
Oracle at Delphi 83
origins of life on earth 39–9
Ottawa 23
ozone layer viii, 39

Pakistan 183
Pentagon 263
pesticide treadmill 193–4
Petrella, Ricardo 160
Phoenicians 63
photosynthesis 42
Plato's rant 68, 114
pollution havens 97
pollution: of aquifers 183; and
    ecological flips 140; of fish 184; in
    Greek city-states 147; inability to
    control cumulative impacts of 99;
    arising from Industrial Revolution
    150–1; long-range transport of 166;
    in Roman times 147–8, 150; and
    spread effects 143, 145, 167
pollution of poverty 96–7; wealth
    and avoidance of 144–52
pollution registers: proposed
    programs for 254
poor laws 77
population controls 274
population growth: AD 1000–1200 53;
    hunter-gatherers vs global
    economy 14; impact of Industrial
    Revolution on 75; projections 5,
    158
'population, growth, resources and
    environment' paradigm vii
portioned responses 265; Principle 7
    of the Rio Declaration 296
poverty: effects of growth 155–6;
    informal economy sectors 32; mea-
surements of 157; persistence of
    155–8; poverty and pollution 147–
    52; prospects 158; relation to
    provisioning 35, 144, 162–4; urban
    challenges 159; World Bank and 124
poverty and culture 16, 161, 215–16
poverty reduction as UN goal 5
precautionary principle 97–8
private-sector networks 14; as agents
    of economic integration 115;
    rationale for 100, 114; and rise of
    international business 104–11; and
    role in provisioning 99, 118–24;
    and trade blocks 111–12; See also
    global economy
privatization 93
protectionism 89–96
protein conversion: fish vs chicken,
    pork and beef 200
provisioning societies: conflict
    between rounds 15, 18–19;
    definition of xiii; detailed descrip-
    tion of 23–36; differs from sustain-
    able development xv; document
    needs 269; limited means of
    outreach 12; options to address
    224–5; population growth and
    outreach 12; provisioning and
    equity 162–4, 273–4; provisioning
    Ottawa 30; provisioning require-
    ments by 2025 4–6, 223–4; relation-
    ship to social violence 20, 114–16,
    213–16, 266; rounds in the organi-
    zation of xiii, 12–14, 39–136, 275–7;
    See also Rounds; World Summit on
    Global Provisioning
public works 64

R&D; basis for growth 105
Reagan, Ronald 93

Rees, William E. 142
regional trading blocks 111–12
Renaissance 71, 102
Rhenish League 86
Rio Conference on Environment and
  Development viii, 7
Rockefeller, John 105, 151
Roman Empire 25, 52, 65, 101;
  collapse of 148; provisioning
  arrangements in 68–9
Romania, income gaps 155
Rotterdam / Amsterdam corridor
  245
Round One 13, 39–48
Round Two 13, 49–58. See also
  agricultural societies
Round Three 13, 59–79. See also cities
Round Four 13, 80–99. See also
  nation-states
Round Five 14–15, 100–36. See also
  private sector networks; global
  economy
Round Six 20, 22, 114, 261–77. See also
  Age of Global Provisioning
Royal Africa Company 87
rural development 58; agreement on
  role of 272
rural violence 207
rural/urban relationships 61;
  provisioning cities 64–79, 234
Russia 176
rust belts 93
Rwanda 18, 212

Sadowski, Yahya 212
sanitary laws, first: Rome 147–8;
  Europe 150–2
savings rates 125
science and technology infrastructure
  226

Second Industrial Revolution 104
September 11 263
service industries 27
Shanghai 77, 161
Sherman Anti-Trust Act 109
Silent Spring 96
Silk Road 68
Singapore 133
small business era 70–1, 102
Smith, Adam 61, 89
soil degradation 189
squatter settlements 207
Sri Lanka 183
standards and regulations: employment effects of 26; ISO 1400 231
start-up firms 109
Stockholm Conference on the
  Environment 8, 96
strategic industries 112
structural adjustments 117
Sumer and Akad 65
Sumeria 61–2
sustainable development xv;
  popularized 6; refocus on ecological decline 9–10; shortcomings of
  10, 98. See also War to Provision
  the World
sustainable development programs:
  proposed rationalization of 274–5
Suzuki, David 42
Syria 182

Taiwan 133
Tarim Basin oil reserves 178
tax shifting 231
technological innovation 26; document employment impacts 270–2;
  for ecological sustainability 224–6;
  employment impacts 26–7; key to
  global economy 118–19; proposed

programs 253–7. *See also* innovation divide; War to Provision the World
technology futures 127–32
technology ladder 118; competing for space on 132–5
technology transfer 118; during Industrial Revolution 89–94; monastic orders 67; and ownership of technology 119; postwar 92–5; role of MNEs 119
terms of trade 91
terrorism, war on 3, 263
Thatcher, Margaret 93
Third World 16, 90, 91–2; growth prospects 126; integration with First Worlds 108
Third World energy demands 178–9
Three Gorges 178
Tobin Tax 113
Toynbee, Arnold 47, 83
trade liberalization 93
trade policy 232
tradeable permits 231
transborder data flow (TBDF) 112–13
tribalism, rise of 206
trickledownism 160–1; weaknesses 244–6
triple bottom line 231
Turkey: price of a coffee in 24–9; water management 180–2

UN Economic Commission for Europe (UNECE) 255
UNDP 165
United Nations Environment Program (UNEP) 96, 165
United Nations vii, 8, 90; call to host WSGP 268; poverty goals 5

United States: as beneficiary of Industrial Revolution 105–6; biomass potential of 195–6; and climate change 175–6; income gaps in 153, 156; pollution in 183; postwar leadership of 90; response to terrorism 263
urban age viii, 46, 60
urban management 16; impact of population growth 77. *See also* cities, provisioning societies
urban peri-areas 16
urban violence 207–8

van Creveld, Martin 207
Venice 71
venture capital 226
virtuous circle of growth 8; flaws in 9
voluntary measures 321

Walkerton, Ontario 184
war between rich and poor 17, 20, 213–16, 224, 265–8. *See also* War to Provision the World
War to Provision the World 19; battlefields of technological innovation 255–7; choosing our wars 265–8; declaring war 252–3; decline as enemy xiii; global battle plans for 253; waging war against xiv. *See also* Framework Convention on Provisioning
Washington Consensus 8, 96
water management: early water wars, 180; equity issues 184–5; global water crisis 180–7; holistic approaches 235–7; irrigation issues 183; policy needs 186–7; pricing issues 186; transborder issues 186

Wealth of Nations 89
weaving 51
WEHAB papers ix
Western growth model 16
Wildlife Conservation Society 188
William of Warenne 149
wired world 226
World Bank 8, 90, 92, 155, 165
World Business Council on Sustainable Development (WBCSD) 227
World Economic Outlook 122
World Meteorological Organization
  169
World Resources Institute 165
World Summit on Global Provisioning (WSGP) 268–75; and bio-region
  and eco-urban management 272;
  and city actions 273; design ERDM
  275; to document pollution 274;
  and employment benefits 270; and
  innovation 269; and population
  controls 274; preparations for 269;

provisioning needs 269; and
  rationalization of sustainable
  development programs and MEAs
  274–5; social issues and provisioning 273; strengthen ecological
  monitoring 275; urban and rural
  roles in 272
World Summit on Sustainable
  Development viii; failure of 8
World Trade Centre 263
World Trade Organization (WTO) 8,
  90, 122, 155, 257–9
World Water Forum 187
World Wildlife Federation 279
writing, origins of 62

Yanomamo 29

Zambia 18
zero-emission technologies 11
zero-emission vehicles 177
zones of peace 211